DESCENT
INTO
DARKNESS

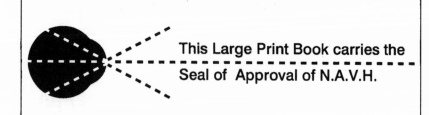

This Large Print Book carries the
Seal of Approval of N.A.V.H.

DESCENT
INTO
DARKNESS

Pearl Harbor, 1941:
A Navy Diver's Memoir

Edward C. Raymer

G.K. Hall & Co. • Thorndike, Maine

Published in 1999 by arrangement with Presidio Press.

G.K. Hall Large Print American History Series.

The text of this Large Print edition is unabridged.
Other aspects of the book may vary from the original edition.

Set in 16 pt. Plantin by Rick Gundberg.

Printed in the United States on permanent paper.

Library of Congress Cataloging in Publication Data

Raymer, Edward C.
   Descent into darkness : Pearl Harbor, 1941 : a Navy diver's
memoir / Edward C. Raymer.
    p. cm.
   Originally published: Novato, CA : Presidio, c1996.
   ISBN 0-7838-8503-2 (lg. print : hc. : alk. paper)
   1. Raymer, Edward C. 2. Pearl Harbor (Hawaii), Attack on, 1941
— Personal narratives, American. 3. Unites States. Navy —
Biography. 4. Sailors — United States — Biography. 5. Divers —
United States — Biography. I. Title.
  D767.92.R37 1999
   940.54′26—dc21   98-50737

To Marilyn:
A woman of lasting beauty, a confidant
and supporter,
a wise counselor and critic, a loving mother,
a perfect wife

ACKNOWLEDGMENTS

Looking back over the last five years, I realize that the writing of this book was a collective effort.

Grateful acknowledgment is tendered to historian Eric M. Hammel for "strongly encouraging" me to pursue this book; to author Hank Searls for his many helpful suggestions to improve my writing skills; to Sara Trotta for her encouragement and help in editing; to my sons: Christopher for his many valuable suggestions; to Marshall and Terry for pushing me to finishing my memoir; and last but not least, to my wife for her understanding and encouragement during the dark days when I wanted to chuck it all.

Without all these people this book probably would never have been written.

CONTENTS

PREFACE

Descent into Darkness is a salvage diver's memoir of the raising of the sunken battleships after the attack on Pearl Harbor in 1941. The book is also a history of the salvage work performed by the USS *Seminole* in the South Pacific theater of war.

Navy divers and Pacific Bridge civilian divers formed one leg of a salvage triad, salvage engineers and the Pearl Harbor Naval Shipyard comprised the other two. One leg needed the assistance and support of the other two to be effective.

Once divers entered the interiors of sunken battleships, they experienced a world of total blackness, unable to see the faceplates in their helmets, a scant two inches from their noses. The abundance of sediment, oil, and other pollutants inside the ships rendered diving lamps useless, since the beams of light reflected into the divers' eyes, blinding them.

Navy divers using only a sense of feel groped their way hundreds of feet inside the ships to their work assignments. They developed a superior sense of touch, much as blind persons do. They also experienced an eerie phenomenon in the underwater wrecks. They could sense the presence of floating human bodies long before they felt them.

Divers also learned to cope with unseen dangers in the blackness, such as falling machinery, sharp, torn metal, jagged holes in the deck, and other hazards. Upon reaching their underwater work sites they used all types of tools to perform a multitude of tasks.

Because of the nature of these underwater conditions, the divers worked by themselves, unattended and unsupervised. Much of their work went unappreciated until months later when the ships were dry-docked, and their efforts could be seen in the light of day.

By reading this book you will see what it was like exploring and working inside the USS *Arizona* and the other sunken ships. You will learn how repairs were made to the ships and how these versatile divers modified and adapted tools and equipment to enable them to perform a host of difficult salvage jobs.

I have tried to recapture the flavor of wartime Honolulu and Pearl Harbor by giving the reader a glimpse of how the divers lived and played in our off-duty hours.

The base at Pearl Harbor and the city of Honolulu in 1942 bear no resemblance to the present-day sites. Enlisted men disgustedly called Oahu "the Rock," after its namesake, Alcatraz prison, in San Francisco Bay. Pearl Harbor offered no rest and recreation areas. The few baseball diamonds built on the base before the war became storage areas for war materials, or were converted to encampments for armed troops. Swimming pools belonged to the officers. Most beaches were ringed with barbed wire. Nightly movies at the outdoor theaters were closed because of the blackout conditions in effect. Not even Bob Hope and his USO troupe had started their Pacific tours. After we worked a fourteen hour day we were usually too tired to do anything except shower and climb into the sack. Most of us were at the height of our virility, so girls were always foremost on our minds. But the type of girls we had grown up with and dated in our hometowns was not available on the Rock. We could close our eyes and dream about them, but that was the extent of our relationship. Most enlisted men satisfied their desires by visiting one of the many houses of ill repute in downtown Honolulu. Others of us hoped to establish a more lasting liaison if somehow fate would intercede on our behalf. There were precious few available women on the island at the time but fate did in fact intervene for a favored few of us. I have changed the names of a few of the participants in order to save them possible embarrassment. But all of the anecdotes and the divers' exploits while at work and at play are true accounts. The stories of casualties to salvage personnel are also factual, despite their omission by the writers of history.

Many of the divers' conversations in the book

are paraphrasic in nature because I had to rely on my memory and the personal reminiscences of a few surviving members of our old diving crew. I believe the dialogue reflects the language the actual characters would have used under the circumstances. But most importantly, the dialogue portrays their personalities accurately.

Unfortunately, during those early days of the war, no pictures were taken of the divers, to my knowledge. The salvage of the battleships was a classified subject, so no personal cameras were permitted in or around Pearl Harbor. There were some official navy photographs taken of the condition of the raised ships, but none showing the divers at work. Much later there were pictures taken of divers, but it was after our original crew departed Pearl Harbor.

Some divers marched to different drummers, but all of us were united by two common bonds: love of country and a desire to serve our nation.

Edward C. Raymer
Commander, U.S. Navy (Ret.)

PROLOGUE

Pearl Harbor, Territory of Hawaii
In solemn stillness, the USS *Arizona* lay at peace. Jarred by massive explosions and gutted by fire, the battleship had slipped beneath the waves of Pearl Harbor on 7 December 1941. Only the mast and part of her superstructure remained visible. But she was not abandoned, for she served as an underwater tomb for more than one thousand American sailors and marines.

On 12 January 1942, the once great battleship was boarded again, this time by me, a navy salvage diver.

Our diving barge tied up to the starboard side of the *Arizona*. I looked at the pitiful wreckage and wondered if we could ever raise her. As senior petty officer and leader of our diving crew, I decided to make the first dive.

My dive that day would be the first salvage dive inside the sunken hull. An external survey revealed what appeared to be a hole below the mud line on the after port side, presumably made by an unexploded torpedo or bomb. My mission: find the missile and attach a lock on the propeller to prevent it from arming itself

13

and exploding. The submarine base assigned a chief torpedoman to provide technical assistance if we needed help to disarm the torpedo.

No salvage work could begin until the missile was rendered safe. This is a simple task for a trained diver. But as it turned out, there was nothing simple about it.

It was standard procedure before each dive for the diver and the telephone talker to lay out the route the diver expected to follow within the ship. The ship's plan was used as a road map to direct the diver from the entry point in the ship to his ultimate destination. The plan was never memorized by the diver, since he had too many other things to occupy his mind as he moved through the ship. Rather, the diver familiarized himself with the general layout of the route, while the telephone talker used the details of the plan to direct the diver on his path.

The ship's plan showed the frame numbers and the location of doors, fire hydrants, blower motors, and so on for each deck. Explosions and fires had destroyed many of these signposts, which forced us to take numerous detours, so the plans were invaluable for us to use as a starting point.

We determined that the external hole below the mud line placed the missile in the vicinity of the general workshop located on the third-deck level. There was no visible damage to the main deck above that area, so we were confident the missile had not exploded.

Now that I had my route fixed in my mind, I was ready to start my dive.

I pulled on my rubberized diving suit and shoved my feet into the thirty-six-pound lead-soled shoes. Then my tenders bolted the metal breastplate to my suit. I stood and thrust my arms through the shoulder straps of the eighty-four-pound lead-weighted belt. Then, with some difficulty, I straightened to my full height of six feet. The diving suit was cumbersome above water.

I gestured toward the heavy copper helmet. My tenders placed it on my shoulders and secured it to the breastplate with a twisting motion. Now my vision was limited to what I could see through the small glass ports in the helmet.

With exaggerated deliberation, I climbed down the wooden ladder and entered the oil-covered water. My helmet was barely awash as I walked aft on the battleship's main deck, skirting wreckage. The dense floating mass of oil blotted out all daylight. I was submerged in total blackness. Only a line of air bubbles that popped to the surface marked my path for topside observers as I traveled the thirty-five feet to the *Arizona*'s entrance.

Grunting with exertion, I tried to open the large hatch. "Topside, this damn hatch is stuck," I said into my helmet phone. "The gasket probably melted from the heat of the fires.

I'm going forward to the access trunk hatch and use that opening."

I slowly groped my way across the littered deck to the hatch. I forced the trunk hatch open and descended into the darkness below.

This trunk on the *Arizona* was a square shaft that extended uninterrupted from the main deck to the third deck. I extended my right hand to guide myself down through the trunk. By following the shaft straight down, my hand was pointed in the direction necessary to follow the working plan. As I landed on the third-deck level I knew by the position of my extended arm that I was headed for the starboard side of the ship.

"Topside, I'm on the third deck. Give me three hundred feet of slack."

"Slack comin' down. Take it in," came the response.

I pulled down my coupled lifeline and air hose, coiling them at my feet. My lifeline contained a quarter-inch-diameter wire built to withstand a strain of three thousand pounds. Telephone wires were wrapped around it and encased in rubber. There was a watertight telephone connection attached to the rear of the diving helmet. Telephone wires ran inside the helmet to the transmitter-receiver located in the top of the helmet. The other end of the telephone wires and lifeline connection were attached to the telephonic transmitter-receiver box on the diving barge. The diver could transmit and receive messages. The telephone talker could receive the diver's messages continuously. When the talker wanted to communicate with the diver he depressed a transmitter key and sent his message. The diver could not transmit until the key was released.

At three-foot intervals, the air hose was tied to the lifeline with waterproof twine, creating small loops in the air hose so that any strain in lifting and lowering the diver remained on the lifeline. When I received the slack in my lines, I straightened up to get my bearings.

I moved cautiously, feeling my way with ungloved hands toward the starboard bulkhead in the compartment, which was my starting point. What I would find I had no inkling. Eventually, it would severely draw on every ounce of courage I possessed. As I looked up, I saw a light that glowed dimly, flickered, and disappeared. It must have been phosphorescence in the water, I thought as the blackness enveloped me once again. I shrugged as I thought: I would settle for just enough light to be able to see the end of my nose.

Suddenly, I felt that something was wrong. I tried to suppress the strange feeling that I was not alone. I reached out to feel my way and touched what seemed to be a large inflated bag floating on the overhead. As I pushed it away, my bare hand plunged through what felt like a mass of rotted sponge. I realized with horror that the "bag" was a body without a head.

Gritting my teeth, I shoved the corpse as hard as I could. As it drifted away, its fleshless fingers raked across my rubberized suit, almost as if the dead sailor were reaching out to me in a silent cry for help.

I fought to choke down the bile that rose in my throat. That bloated torso had once contained viscera, muscle, and firm tissue. It had been a man. I could hear the quickening thump of my pulse.

For the first time I felt confined in the suffocating darkness and had to suppress the desire to escape. "Breathe slowly, breathe deeply," I commanded myself. I must stay calm, professional, detached. The dangers from falling wreckage, holes in the deck, and knife-sharp jagged edges were real, formidable hazards. I must not succumb to terror over something that could not harm me.

I concentrated on finding the first road sign before starting toward the shop.

"Topside, I'm facing the bulkhead and my left hand is on the fire hydrant."

Moon's voice answered. "Move to your left about ten feet and reach your hand up to the overhead and you should feel a large blower motor. Continue six feet beyond and you will feel a watertight door in the after bulkhead of the workshop."

I did as instructed and felt my way through the darkness toward the door to the machine shop, accompanied only by the sound of the air hissing into my helmet from the air hose trailing behind me.

At the shop doorway I hesitated and drew my lifeline toward me. "I'm inside the shop doorway." There was that feeling again.

"Turn and face the after bulkhead and move to your right about twenty feet. There should be a fire hydrant on the bulkhead waist high."

"Got it."

"Good. Now turn around, and with your back to the bulkhead, slowly walk forward through the shop."

Then I got the eerie feeling again that I wasn't alone. Something was near. I felt the body floating above me. Soon the overhead was filled with floating forms.

Obviously, my movement through the water created a suction effect that drew the floating masses to me. Their skeletal fingers brushed across my copper helmet. The sound reminded me of the tinkle of oriental wind chimes.

This time I did not panic. Instead, I gently pushed the bodies clear and moved through the compartment. I shuffled through the workshop area, threading my way around lathes, milling machines, and drill presses. I stopped and again found myself surrounded by ghostly bloated forms floating on the overhead, all without heads. This shop had been the damage control battle station for one hundred of the crew. The violent explosions from bombs and torpedoes, plus the forceful impact of water, must have thrown the sailors like rag dolls against bulkheads, breaking their necks and severing skulls from spines. Voracious scavenger crabs had finished the job.

It was not something I wanted to think about, and I pushed it from my mind as I moved forward again. That is when I stumbled over what felt like a torpedo, the object I had come down here to find.

"Topside, I found it. I'm at the nose cone."

"Careful," warned the voice from topside. "That's where the detonator is located."

"I know. I'm still at the nose cone. It's wedged under a lathe. As soon as I circle this machine, I'll feel my way down the torpedo body and attach the propeller lock."

"Keep us posted on your progress."

Once in position, I reached out for the torpedo, but there was nothing there. "I'm on the other side of the lathe, but I can't feel the body of the torpedo," I reported.

Silence. Then a voice said, "The chief torpedoman thinks that the nose cone may have separated from the body of the torpedo after impact."

I slowly worked my way to the hole in the side of the ship where the torpedo would have entered. Strangely, I still could not find the torpedo body, and I reported this to topside.

No one topside seemed to have any ideas regarding the missing torpedo, so I returned to the detonator. I felt around the cone and soon determined that I had found a large-caliber shell instead of a torpedo. It had metal fins welded to its base and the nose cone was shaped much like a shell. I reported this information.

"The chief torpedoman thinks it's a shell, too. He thinks the Japanese welded fins on it so it would spiral like a bomb when it was dropped from a plane. The chief says it doesn't pose any danger under the lathe. Are you ready to come up?" topside asked.

"Take up the slack in my lines and see if they are clear." I gave the lines a hard yank. "Did you feel that?" I asked.

"Negative."

Then, as if someone had thrown a switch, my air supply stopped. "What's wrong with my air supply?" I yelled.

No answer. The topside phone key was depressed, but all I could hear was panic-stricken shouting.

I quickly closed the exhaust valve in my helmet before all the air escaped from my helmet and suit. "Take in my slack, I'm coming up," I yelled, fear rising in my voice.

Back came a rapid reply, "Your lifeline is hung up. Retrace your steps and clear it as quickly as you can." I knew the oxygen remaining in my helmet could not sustain life for more than two minutes. By now the air had escaped from my suit, causing the dress to press tightly against my torso, the pressure from the surrounding water flattening it. As the pressure increased, I felt the

21

huge roiling mass of panic surge into my throat. I tried desperately to hold back the growing anxiety within me. I had seen what terror could do to a man. It could take possession of mind and body and prevent him from helping himself, even cause him to give up completely. I told myself to concentrate on surviving.

I grabbed the lifeline and started back, pulling hand over hand toward the access trunk. The 196 pounds of diving equipment on my shoulders became an incredible weight. Without buoyancy in my suit, it became a heavy burden dragging me down.

Stumbling, wildly now, I bumped into milling machines and fell into drill presses, my breath quick and shallow from fear and exertion. Blind terror could destroy me. I fought it as best as I could. I finally felt where a loop in my air hose was caught on the handwheel of a lathe. I cleared my lines and yelled, "Take up my slack!"

Almost immediately, I felt the answering strain on the lines as my diving tenders heaved them in.

"It's free," someone shouted over the phone. "Stay calm. We'll have you up in a minute."

I did not have breath enough to answer.

Without air pressure in my suit, foul fetid water poured in through my suit cuffs and the exhaust valve in my helmet. I could feel the coolness of it around my neck. I felt the constant frantic pull on my lines as my tenders heaved me in. I stumbled and fell as they pulled me over and around a milling machine. Filthy water gushed into my mouth. Somehow I was able to regain my feet, only to be slammed against a lathe and then pulled over the top of it in a mad, tumbling journey to the surface and fresh air.

But time had run out for me. I fell again, and putrid liquid rushed into my face. I stood up again, coughing and gagging. My breathing was labored and the panic was like a rat behind my forehead, twisting and gnawing. I was not aware that my instinct to survive had vanished. Bursts of stars and brilliant white shards of light exploded before my eyes. A loud ringing filled my ears. Even in my dire state, I recognized the symptoms of carbon dioxide toxicity and oxygen deficiency. A hundred ugly visions flashed through my mind, grim reminders that I was going to die down here among these headless corpses.

The strain on my lifeline was from above my head now, holding me upright. A red haze passed before my eyes, grew fainter and fainter and finally disappeared into blackness. I was dying and the part of me that still cared, knew it. But for now I would just close my eyes and go to sleep.

I
San Diego, California

Training for War

"Hey, Ed, let's volunteer for diving school." This suggestion came from my best buddy in the navy, Robert "Moon" Mullen. He was reading a Repair Unit directive when an announcement caught his eye. It requested volunteers for a one-month, second-class diving course commencing 1 May 1941 aboard the USS *Ortolan*, tied up at the foot of Broadway pier in San Diego Harbor.

Mullen was a Boston shanty Irishman, fun loving and full of blarney. Six feet tall, he weighed in at 185 pounds. Moon had straight black hair parted in the middle and ears that stuck out of his head like two open car doors. His nickname, Moon, came from a vintage cartoon character.

"Sure, Moon, why not?" I said. "It doesn't look as if I'm ever going to be a pilot. Might as well learn to work under the water instead of flying over the top of it." I smiled ruefully as I thought about the disappointments I had experienced trying to become an aviator.

Despite that, I liked navy life. It had trained me in welding and shipfitting and had given me rapid advancement to metalsmith first class. Best of all, it had given me a chance to apply my leadership abilities. But, despite all the benefits, I would have given it up in a second for a chance to become a flier.

I never thought of myself as a "twenty-year man." I planned to stay in the navy for my four-year enlistment and then see if the economy had improved enough to get out and find a decent job. College did not appeal to me, because far too many college graduates from my hometown of Riverside, California, were pumping gas in service stations.

It was the navy's recruitment pitch that caught my attention and fired my imagination. In May 1939 visions of adventure and travel appealed to my young, restless spirit. I enlisted, toughed out three months of boot training, then was assigned to the repair ship USS *Vestal* swinging around her buoy in San Pedro. To my dismay, she got under way only once every quarter for an overnight cruise. Some of the old hands aboard her swore the purpose of the trip was to prevent the ship from going aground on the mountain of coffee grounds beneath her.

In 1940 the *Vestal* sailed with the fleet to Hawaii, where it remained to provide repair services to the battleships. During two years on the *Vestal*, I learned shipfitting, welding, and burning skills. In May 1941 I was transferred to the Destroyer Repair Unit I, which was formed at the destroyer base in San Diego.

Mullen handed me the directive regarding the diving course as we hurried over to the administrative office. We requested diving school, and we both were accepted.

Diving school on the *Ortolan*, a submarine rescue vessel, proved to be exciting and challenging to me and the other eight men in the class. We learned how to handle ourselves underwater, to ascend, descend, and move through thick mud. We learned to use an underwater gas cutting torch, a stud driver to fasten steel plates together, and how to dig trenches in the mud using a washout nozzle.

After we returned to the Destroyer Repair Unit, we resumed our regular duties repairing the ships assigned for overhaul work. Mullen and I had previously discussed building a small diver's training tank on the pier to practice our underwater cutting and welding skills. We approached our division officer with the idea and he gave us the okay, provided we built the tank with scrap metal and did the work on our own time. We built the tank and it was in service within thirty days.

None of us second-class divers could be considered experienced, since our training had been minimal, and we had little or no practical experience. Our biggest achievements were our new-found abilities to burn and weld underwater.

War

On the morning of 7 December 1941 Moon and I

and some of our buddies won our division softball tournament. We joined the losing team for soft drinks at the base gedunk stand (or soda fountain) after the game. The radio in the corner was blaring out swing tunes when suddenly an announcer interrupted the program with a special bulletin: "Pearl Harbor was bombed by the Japanese at 8 A.M. today, Hawaiian time."

Everyone was incredulous over the news. We shook our heads and muttered doubts that this could happen to our navy.

My disbelief turned to white-hot anger as the reality of the attack registered in my mind.

America is at war! A feeling of excitement welled up in me. By God, we'll kick their butts, I thought. I couldn't wait to get at the enemy. I had no idea of the horror I was so eager to encounter.

The repair department sent word to all of the divers to report to the office at 1200 hours. I hurried over to the barracks to clean up and then report for duty. After showering, I stepped out of the stall and wrapped a towel around my waist. I glanced approvingly in the mirror at the well-developed muscles in my arms and shoulders that tightened and relaxed as I vigorously lathered my even-featured face. I had always been strong and in good shape. Football and baseball helped in school and the navy strengthened and filled out my muscular body even more. I finished shaving, patted on some lotion, straightened to my height of six feet, and ran a comb through my dark brown hair.

I changed into my working uniform and reported to my division officer, Lt. George Dawnes, in the repair office. After all the divers were assembled, Dawnes told us that something big was in the wind for us, and that he would have more information on the matter after the all-officers meeting scheduled for 1300. At 1400, Lieutenant Dawnes again herded us into his office and closed the door.

"Men," he began, "you have two hours to get packed and be in front of your barracks. A bus will pick you up at 1630 and transport you to Naval Air Station, Coronado. You will be making a long flight tonight. I am not at liberty to tell you where you are going or how long you will be gone, or even if you will return to San Diego. You are directed not to make any telephone calls to your families or to girlfriends before you leave. You can send them a postcard when you arrive at your final destination. As the senior petty officer, Raymer will be carrying your service records, sealed orders, and pay records with him. Good luck to you. Get moving; you don't have much time!"

We filed out of his office and hurried over to the barracks. Moon occupied the bunk and locker next to mine. As we packed our seabags and ditty bags, we speculated on the secret mission. We both agreed, from all the evidence, that our destination must be Pearl Harbor.

We were naively unaware of the number of

ships sunk or damaged. The president had described only minimal damage in his brief statement regarding the attack, except for the sunken battleship *Arizona*.

The navy bus picked us up promptly and made the short trip across San Diego Bay by ferry. The bus dropped us off at the seaplane ramp in the air station at 1700.

We trooped aboard the waiting PB2Y aircraft with our personal belongings. Already onboard were four army colonels, three navy captains, and several civilians. We nine divers were the only enlisted men aboard.

The plane taxied out into the bay and took off immediately as we settled down on the floor, using our seabags for headrests. The pilot informed us that our cruising speed would be 150 knots, and we should arrive at our destination in approximately fourteen hours.

The noise and vibration from the plane's engines were deafening. It was impossible to speak above them or to be heard. We divers had to be content to sleep, read, or be silent with our thoughts.

I looked across at the men with whom I had spent the last few months learning the intricacies of underwater diving techniques. These were the men I would depend on for my life in the days to come.

There was Moon snoozing on his back, his long arms folded neatly on his chest.

Next to him, Tony Salvatore, a tall, very dark,

good-looking Italian. A mystery to us all. He had never revealed much about himself, past or present.

Sitting up, with pencil and paper perched on his bent knees, was Andy Davis, the unsophisticated boy from Iowa, writing yet another letter to his Enid, the only girl he had ever loved.

Bill Rush was next in line. Bill was from Oklahoma and bragged incessantly about his two big accomplishments: breaking horses and breaking the hearts of "babes." None of us believed the stories of his latter accomplishments, so we settled on the nickname Bronco Bill for him. Despite all his bluster, Bronco turned out to be an excellent diver and an asset to our diving crew.

Sleeping noisily next to him was Ben Apple, an inappropriate name for this burly, 250-pound horse of a man. Coarse and foulmouthed, but a tireless worker, Ben had the strength of a giant. By contrast, Jimmy Willson, with his dark curly hair and innocent face, looked almost childlike as he lay sleeping on his side.

Martin Palmer sat next to him, quiet, bookish, squinting over a copy of *Time* magazine.

And lastly, Cameron Walker, the wiry, talkative Texan, nervous and twitching even in sleep.

Their ages ranged from twenty-one to twenty-six, and all were intelligent and able. These men wanted that greater degree of adventure associated with diving and now they were headed for an unknown, dangerous mission.

Good men, I thought, every one of them.

Hours later, I was able to sleep fitfully as the plane's engines droned on, carrying us ever closer to the islands. All at once the plane encountered rough weather, and its shuddering and bouncing awakened me. I glanced at my watch, 2300. I tried to sleep again but too many thoughts crowded my mind. I closed my eyes and thought of my hometown. What a great place to grow up. What good times to remember at old Poly High, and Laurie. Oh yes, Laurie Hampton, I could see her in my mind's eye. Her face framed with her honey-blonde hair.

Laurie was my high school sweetheart, my unforgettable first love. I hadn't seen her since before my enlistment and by this time she was probably married with two kids.

I wondered what she thought about my enlisting in the navy. Did she hold me in the same low regard that so much of society held for the American sailor? Perhaps she had heard the comment President Roosevelt's wife, Eleanor, had made about sailors: "The cleanest bodies and the dirtiest minds in the world."

The hell with Eleanor, I thought. How many sailors does she know? How can she judge the whole navy?

Eleanor was not the only one who held sailors in low esteem. I had heard that the city of Norfolk, Virginia, erected signs in their parks that read "Sailors and dogs keep off the grass."

I recognized that the navy had a few bad apples, but the vast majority of sailors were dedicated fighting men.

I recalled a favorite poem of mine by Rudyard Kipling that compared the public's attitude toward the British soldier serving in peace time and war time roles. I smiled ruefully as I thought things have changed little since Kipling's time.

Maybe the country has not appreciated sailors in the past, but as Kipling predicted, the public will exalt us as heroes now that the United States is at war.

A wave of homesickness and loneliness engulfed me, and I tried unsuccessfully to shake it off. I had just attained the ripe old age of twenty-one. All the people and places I loved were far away, and I didn't know if I would ever see them again.

Aftermath of the Attack

We were awakened by the pilot's voice. He reported that he had just made contact with two U.S. Navy fighter aircraft that would be escorting the plane into Oahu. Our estimated time of arrival was thirty minutes away.

Spotting the two airplanes out the porthole, flying gracefully alongside, caused me to mourn once more the missed opportunities and disappointments that had prevented me from becoming a pilot. I had missed joining the Army Air Corps cadet program by just one year.

I almost made it on the next try, just six

months ago. I had heard rumors the RAF and RCAF had stationed a recruiter, Captain Wright-Melville, in a room at the Hollywood Roosevelt Hotel. He was signing up U.S. active duty military personnel as pilots if they passed the written and physical examinations for the British Air Force. In addition, the British recognized that the American military volunteers were mature, seasoned fighting men, so they were being commissioned with ranks equivalent to U.S. Army Air Corps first lieutenants and captains. I rushed to Hollywood for an interview, then completed all the examinations and passed them easily. I was due to be discharged from the navy on 1 July and sworn in as an officer in the RAF, but to my distress, the entire program was canceled by the federal government in late June. A very powerful group known as the America First Party, headed by Charles Lindbergh, put pressure on Congress and the president, so the program was discontinued.

Rightly or wrongly, the America Firsters felt the United States was becoming too involved in the European war. Ironically, I thought bitterly, my boyhood hero, the famous Charles Lindbergh, played a large part in denying me a chance to become an aviator.

The seaplane captain was again on the speaker, reporting that the landing site had been changed from Ford Island in Pearl Harbor to Kaneohe NAS on the windward side of the island. He said there were a lot of nervous gunners in and around Pearl Harbor and four or five carrier aircraft from the USS *Enterprise* had been shot down the previous evening. He also noted that armed sentries were shooting first and asking questions later during the night patrols.

The pilot advised us that dawn would be breaking soon and we would make a flyby of Pearl Harbor, keeping out of gunnery range on our way around the island to Kaneohe Bay.

The sun was just coming up out of the ocean when Oahu came into view. I was numbed by shock and disbelief at the panorama of wholesale destruction below. The airfields of Wheeler, Hickam, and Ford Island had been burned out. Damaged planes were tossed about like abandoned toys on their runways. Pearl Harbor was a disaster. Although the ships could not be identified, it looked as if there were at least twenty, either damaged or sunk, and most of these appeared to be the pride of the navy, the battleships.

A hundred questions raced through my mind as I stared at the scene below: How could this have happened? How could our huge armorplated battleships be sunk by foreign airplanes? With so much of the fleet out of commission, how would the navy protect America? Why didn't Japan land its troops and capture Hawaii after such a successful raid? Why did President Roosevelt report only minor damage sustained from the attack?

Huge, billowing clouds of black smoke

engulfed three of the battleships; orange tongues of flame leapt up through the black vortex. Wrecked ships were strewn about within the dry docks. Other ships showed signs of great damage, with weird outcroppings of twisted metal that changed their silhouettes beyond recognition.

But it was the sea of heavy bunker oil in which all the ships were floating that brought down a curtain of finality to the scene. The viscous oil thickly layered everything in the harbor. The hulls of ships and the pilings on docks were coated with it, and the entire shoreline was blackened. Nothing escaped the oil's ravages. Early rays of the morning sun created an unreal reflection on the surface of the oil that mirrored the grotesque shapes of the broken ships.

I stared in horror at America's terrible loss. There was no longer any doubt in my mind about our final destination or what our job would be.

Arrival in Pearl Harbor

After our plane landed in Kaneohe NAS, we were picked up by a navy bus and transported across the island to the receiving station at Pearl Harbor. We were issued lockers and bunks in the last barrack in the row of buildings. We were the only occupants. The Officer of the Deck directed us to report to the Salvage Unit, which was newly formed at the Pearl Harbor Naval Shipyard. Warrant Officer Albert Calhoun was the designated officer in charge. He looked tired and harassed. He informed us that he had not closed his eyes in twenty-four hours.

I delivered our records to Calhoun and inquired about our diving assignments. The bosun ordered us to take a truck and pick up four sets of deep-sea diving gear from the submarine base. When we returned with the diving outfits he sent us to Ten-Ten Dock, where we selected a suitable sampan from the dozen that were tied up. The sampans had been owned by alien Japanese fishermen and were confiscated months before by the U.S. government, because aliens were not permitted to own boats in Hawaii.

We selected a seventy-foot craft, installed a diving air compressor, and outfitted it with two complete sets of deep-sea diving gear. After spending three hours equipping the boat, we reported back to Mr. Calhoun.

We took seats in the room adjoining Calhoun's office. I gazed out the large windows lining the room, aghast at the morbid scene of destruction in the harbor.

I looked toward the northern end of Ten-Ten Dock and the first thing that caught my eye were the masts of the capsized minelayer, *Oglala*, draped over the dock.

Farther down the dock were two of our newer light cruisers, *Honolulu* and *Helena*, their crews fighting to save them from sinking.

Turning to the unbelievable scene in the harbor was gut-wrenching in its sadness. Huge oil fires burned out of control on the surface of the waters, fed from ruptured fuel tanks on the *Arizona*. Fires were still being fought aboard the battleships *West Virginia*, *Tennessee*, and *California*.

It appeared that the fires that had burned so fiercely on Ford Island had been extinguished. The huge pall of black smoke that hung over the battleships obscured parts of the island, but clearly visible were the tangled remains of the dozens of wrecked and burned-out airplanes scattered about.

My gaze shifted to the southern area of the harbor, where the naval shipyard was located. The first casualty that met my eyes was the destroyer *Shaw*. She was in Floating Dry Dock Number Two, which had been sunk by bombs. The *Shaw* lay crazily on her side and most of her bow was blown away by the force of heavy explosions. She appeared to be a total loss.

From my vantage point I could look down on one of the most sickening sights of all in this devastating scene. The number one dry dock was at the head of Ten-Ten Dock. The battleship *Pennsylvania* and destroyers *Cassin* and *Downes* were dry docked at the time of the attack.

The battleship had been hit with a small bomb. The two destroyers were bombed and caught fire, and all hell broke loose when the fires ignited shells, depth charges, and torpedoes, which then ripped the destroyers apart.

The dry dock was purposely flooded to help

extinguish the flames. The flooding caused the *Cassin* to topple over on the *Downes*, which helped create visually an even worse disaster than really existed. I was sure that the *Pennsylvania* must also be heavily damaged.

We later learned that both destroyers were total losses, but the battleship suffered only light damage. It was repaired and fully operational by 20 December 1941.

"Before I start on the list of damaged and sunken ships, I need to find out a little more about each of you," said Calhoun. "Right now all I have is a list of names and a pile of service records. My boss, Lieutenant Haynes, whom you will meet later, will want to know about your navy background, what your specialties are, qualifications, et cetera. So just hit the high points and keep it brief." He glanced down at the sheaf of papers. "Raymer, let's start with you and work clockwise around the room."

"Raymer, metalsmith first class. Much of my experience has been welding, and I am a qualified pressure hull welder. I served aboard the *Vestal*. I have practiced underwater arc welding and cutting with a gas torch."

Following my remarks, the rest of the divers indicated their repair specialties and work experiences.

"Welcome aboard the Salvage Unit," Calhoun said. "You will be attached to this command on temporary additional duty, which may not be so temporary judging from the amount of diving work you see before you."

The bosun read us a directive from the commander in chief, Pacific, that ordered all repair facilities to get the least damaged ships back in fighting condition first. He also told us that our primary work would involve raising the sunken battleships, since few of the ships afloat suffered underwater damage.

To the best of my knowledge no one had ever raised a battle-damaged battleship before. No salvage histories or guidelines were available to educate us. Our perceptions of what was involved in raising such a ship were very restricted. From a practical and logical viewpoint, I opined, the exterior holes in the hulls must be made watertight first. Then the interior of the ship would be emptied of water by pumping or being blown dry with compressed air. But I had no idea how all this would be accomplished or how long it would take.

Bosun Calhoun then launched into an account of the attack the day before and reviewed the damage suffered by the sunken battleships. He said the USS *Nevada* was berthed astern of the *Arizona* when she was struck by a torpedo in her bow. She managed to get under way with her guns blazing, the only battleship able to do so. As she rounded the southern tip of Ford Island, she was smashed with an avalanche of bombs, which started intense fires.

When the thick, pungent smoke from the fires poured into the machinery spaces, the black gang, or engineers, headed for topside and fresh air. This forced abandonment left the pumping machinery inoperative.

The forward ammunition magazines were purposely flooded to prevent explosions from the fires, but the after magazines were also flooded by mistake, which caused the ship to sink lower and lower in the water. In addition, ballast tanks were flooded on the starboard side to correct a port list. As more water entered the ship, many fittings that passed through watertight bulkheads began to leak, flooding all machinery spaces and causing loss of all electrical and mechanical power.

Nevada was sinking in the ship channel. Admiral William R. Furlong, senior officer afloat, ordered tugs to take her in tow and beach her before she sank and bottled up the only entrance and exit to Pearl Harbor. She was grounded with her stern near the shore and her bow in deep water. The *Nevada*'s wounds alone were not serious enough to sink her; rather it was the loss of her watertight integrity, combined with progressive flooding, that doomed her.

The bosun yawned, rubbed his bloodshot eyes, and continued as we all listened in silent fascination and disbelief.

He told us the former battleship *Utah* had been converted to a practice bombing target. Her antiaircraft guns and decks were covered with shields to protect them from nonexplosive practice bombs. He guessed that enemy planes probably mistook her for an aircraft carrier, since one was often berthed in that space. Two torpedo hits sent the unprotected ship to the harbor floor, bottom side up. The bosun said he doubted the navy would raise the *Utah* because it had little military value.

In addition, he indicated, a similar fate awaited the USS *Arizona*, since most of the eyewitness accounts of her sinking reported that her entire bow leapt out of the water from the force of a tremendous explosion in the forward section. These accounts indicated that she was broken in two pieces and probably was not worth salvaging. The *Arizona* sank, right side up, within nine minutes. He said it was feared that more than one thousand men died aboard her. Fires fueled by her ruptured tanks were still raging out of control and were threatening to destroy other ships in the path of the flames.

One of the threatened ships was the USS *California*. She was hit by two torpedoes and one bomb. Numerous other bombs exploded alongside. One near-miss at the bow tore a fifteen-foot hole in the hull and opened leaks in the gasoline storage tank and lines. After she was torpedoed, the ship listed sixteen degrees to port. To compensate for the list, two fire rooms and the starboard torpedo blister were purposely flooded. As she settled lower in the water, progressive floating started throughout the ship from open manholes, ventilation systems, pipelines, and the inadequate setting of battle-ready closure conditions.

A combination of water and oil flooded the machinery spaces, rendering pumps and other machinery inoperative. These vital pumps were needed to fight fires and dewater compartments.

The bosun's voice took on an almost defeated tone as he told us that at 1000 hours yesterday, raging fires swept down on *California*, engulfing her in flames. The order was given to abandon ship, because the crew had no means of fighting the fires. This abandon permitted uncontrolled flooding to continue throughout the ship. He said it was very unlikely that the crew could prevent her from sinking, since they lacked the pumps to dewater the compartments.

Next on his list of casualties was the USS *West Virginia*. She was hit by three aerial torpedoes on her port side. She keeled over, listing twenty-five degrees. Four more torpedoes struck her. Fearful that she would capsize, the senior officer aboard ordered the starboard torpedo blister counterflooded. At this point *West Virginia* became impaled on USS *Tennessee*'s bilge keel, preventing her from capsizing.

Electric power was dead, pumps were inoperable, and a huge oil fire burned belowdecks. A wall of burning fuel oil from the stricken *Arizona* surrounded the ships. Without the means to fight the fires, the order was given to abandon ship.

The last ship on the boson's list was the *Oklahoma*. He said she was struck amidships on her port side by seven torpedoes. A gash two hundred feet long was opened in her hull and she took a thirty-degree list to port. Bursting her mooring lines to the USS *Maryland*, inboard of her, she rolled over upside down. Four hundred men were trapped inside and maximum efforts were currently under way to rescue them.

I looked out the window and saw two hundred feet of *Oklahoma*'s starboard bottom above water.

Diving Assignments

The bosun gave us our assignments for the afternoon. We were to proceed to the upside-down *Oklahoma* and report to Commander Kenworthy. If he had no diving work for us, we would then proceed to the *Nevada* and report to Lieutenant Commander Thomas.

We climbed into the sampan and headed out through the dead sea of bunker oil strewn with flotsam and wreckage. Bill Rush inched the sampan through the debris until we reached the *Oklahoma*. As we pulled alongside, I wondered out loud if it was possible that anyone was still alive in the hulk.

There was tremendous activity around the *Oklahoma*. Floodlights were set up and the bottom hull was crawling with sailors and shipyard workmen. The sound of pneumatic hammers reverberated against the steel bottom plates, beating out a cadence that could be heard around the harbor. It sent a message of hope to the men trapped below, assuring them that help was on the way.

Mullen asked one of the workers why they were chiseling out holes in the bottom when a cutting torch would be so much faster. The worker replied that they had tried that yesterday and the toxic fumes from the burning paint and cork had killed two trapped men. Now the only safe way to rescue the men was to chisel holes in the bottom hull. We also learned that eight men were rescued just thirty minutes before we arrived and had been sent to the hospital for observation after their terrifying experience. All told, thirty-one sailors were released from their underwater tomb before rescue efforts were abandoned.

I later read a statement from Machinist Mate Second Class W. F. Staff, a survivor of the cap-sized USS *Oklahoma*. Staff was one of the last men rescued at 2 A.M. Tuesday, 9 December 1941. His statement testifies to the mounting terror the survivors experienced.

Sunday morning at 0750 on 7 December 1941, I was in the Carpenter Shop when the general alarm was sounded. I immediately went along the starboard side of the third deck to my battle station. I felt several explosions on the way to Repair II. When I got to Repair II I took my phones and went to get a flashlight but they were locked up so I went on down to A-28, the forward air compressor room, and started to set Zed. There was an electrician's mate and fireman also, Centers, J.P. MM2c and myself in the compartment. When the lights went out the fireman and electrician's mate started to go out the zed hatch which had been set by repair II; they were yelling and screaming. Water and fuel oil were coming down the hatch. I tried to stop them from opening the hatch, but couldn't.

The next thing we knew we were all under water and oil. Centers and myself were the only ones that came up.

It took us some time in the dark to find out that we were back in A-28 and the ship had capsized.

We then tried to get into the linen storeroom. It was on the starboard side and was out of the water. A-28 was about half full of oil and water. The storeroom was locked and it took several hours to beat the lock off with a wrench that we found on the air compressor. We could not get into the storeroom as gear must have wedged against the door.

We tried to get into a small storeroom which was on the overhead, but it was also locked and we could not get into position to beat the lock off.

About Monday noon we heard tapping and we answered them. After so long they were right overhead and we could hear them

45

talking. When they started to cut into us it let out air and we were under air pressure, the water came up as our air escaped.

The water came up and ran out the hole they were cutting, and they left. But we still had about six inches of air space.

We tried the linen room again and it gave a little. Apparently the water had cleared the gear from the door, we went in and started tapping again.

The rescuers soon got out to us again, and we left the ship at 0200 Tuesday morning.

I wish to thank these men for their hard work in rescuing us: Keenum CBM, Thomas SF1c and Harris CM2c.

Commander Kenworthy did not need us on the *Oklahoma*, so we proceeded to the *Nevada*. The senior officer aboard, Lieutenant Commander Thomas, directed us to sound the sunken hull at thirty-foot intervals.

To accomplish this, we lowered a diver from the sampan to a depth of twenty feet. Swinging a five-pound hammer, he rapped on the hull three times, then stopped and listened for an answering signal. We took turns for five hours. No answering signal was ever heard.

We learned later that all the men killed or injured on the *Nevada* were either blown overboard or were carried from belowdecks by crew members on the day of the attack.

46

Tired and filthy after our disappointing mission, we piled into the sampan and headed for Ten-Ten Dock.

Rescue Attempts

Early on 9 December we assembled on the sampan, eager to start salvage work on the *Nevada*. Before we could cast off the lines I spotted Bosun Calhoun hurrying down the dock, waving to us. With him was a stranger wearing the insignia of a lieutenant. This must be the diving officer, I thought to myself.

The bosun arrived slightly out of breath from his sprint down the dock. "Men, this is Lieutenant H. E. Haynes."

Haynes was a small, wiry man, fiftyish, balding, with a florid complexion that escalated to bright red whenever he became angry or flustered. He was a mustang, meaning an officer who had come up through the enlisted ranks and attained officer status.

"Thank you, Mr. Calhoun. I want to talk to the divers alone," he said brusquely, dismissing his assistant.

I eyed our new boss with some apprehension as he climbed down the Jacob's ladder to the float and stepped aboard the sampan.

"Good morning, sir. Raymer, Metalsmith First Class." I saluted briskly.

"Ah yes, Raymer," he said, returning my salute. "I've seen your service record as well as the records of the other divers. I am pleased to have you all aboard as members of my diving team."

We shuffled about and mumbled acknowledgments in unison, unaccustomed to such a personalized greeting from an officer.

The crusty old diving officer cautioned us about some of the hazards we could expect to encounter on the ships. But he was careful to point out that no one could identify all the dangers because few, if any, divers had experienced diving inside a battle-damaged ship strewn with wreckage. He emphasized that because of the floating oil, sediment, and debris in the water, underwater lights would be useless. Diving inside the ships would be done in complete and utter darkness. This would require us to develop a keen sense of feel, great manual dexterity with tools, and a high degree of hand-to-brain coordination. Since the navy had no safety precautions for such a situation, we would be required to devise our own.

Lieutenant Haynes motioned for me to step out on the float, so we could speak privately. He explained that the diving crew would rarely have a diving officer attached, and even then, he would not be experienced in salvage work.

He lit his pipe and puffed a few times until the tobacco glowed. He told me that, over his objections, the senior salvage officer had assigned the exterior hull work to the Pacific Bridge and Shipyard's civilian divers. Interior work on the ships was to be the responsibility of the navy divers because they were familiar with the insides of battleships.

I told him that to my knowledge none of us had served aboard a battleship, but that this fact should not create too many problems salvaging the ships. I was expressing more confidence than I felt.

While it was true that none of us served aboard battleships, Mullen and I were attached to repair ships before the war and we had performed repair work aboard some battleships. While serving aboard the *Vestal* as a welder, I spent some time aboard battleships, increasing their battle condition. We cut out portholes in their hulls at the second and third deck levels, and welded in metal blanks to replace them. This experience was no substitute for the knowledge of the ships I would have gained as a member of the crew.

Lieutenant Haynes then gave us our diving assignments: dynamite the concrete quays that pinned the *Tennessee* against the *West Virginia*, and sound the hulls of the sunken ships to insure that no one was trapped within them. He indicated that the rescue of any possible survivors took precedence over every other operation.

Haynes also pointed out that since we would not be diving deeper than forty-five feet within the ships, we could stay down all day and not concern ourselves about suffering from the bends or other diving illnesses. He neglected to discuss the possibility of performing our necessary bodily functions after hours underwater, but we soon learned how to cope with that.

Our diving team did not attend morning quarters, because our new bosses in the Salvage Unit didn't operate under a structured type of organization. Most of the time we received our orders directly from the diving officer. At other times, when an officer was assigned to a special project, we were directed by the diving officer to take orders from him.

I assigned Mullen, Rush, Willson, Palmer, and Salvatore to the job of sounding the hulls, while the rest of the men and I worked on freeing the *Tennessee*. Mullen and his team started sounding the hull of the *Utah*, since it was possible there were some crew members who might have escaped into the double bottoms, as some men did on the *Oklahoma*. But before Moon and his divers could start sounding the hull, the last man to survive the upside-down battleship *Utah* was rescued by crew members from the *Utah* and the *Raleigh*.

His name was John Vaessan, fireman second class. He courageously remained at his post on the electrical distribution board until it was too late to get off the overturning ship. His act of courage kept the lights burning and allowed many of his shipmates to find their way off the ship, which they may not have been able to do in the dark. He hammered incessantly on the inside of the hull with a wrench for two terrifying days. Trapped in the black interior of the ship, he was weakened by lack of water, food, and sleep, and sick with the heat, which reached 150 degrees. Desperate with thoughts of death, his waning tapping was finally heard by shipmates on Ford Island. A volunteer crew returned with a cutting torch, burned a hole in the bottom, and finally released Vaessan. Tragically, Vaessan died soon after from unknown causes.

Mullen used a careful and thorough search technique designed to locate any survivors on the remaining sunken ships. Beginning at the bow of the ship, the diver was lowered twenty feet under the water. At that point he hammered on the hull three times with a five-pound hammer. He then listened for a response. If there was none, he was moved in intervals of twenty-five feet and the procedure repeated until he finally reached the stern.

Upon reaching the stern, the diver was lowered an additional twenty-five feet to the mud line, at which time he repeated the same sounding procedure until he reached the bow. Then the opposite side of the ship was covered in the same fashion.

Generally, the starboard sides of the ships were sounded first, since they suffered the least damage from bombs and torpedoes. We reasoned that if there were any survivors they would most likely be alive on the undamaged side. We also felt that the underwater sounds of our hammering would penetrate the ship's hulls more effectively through an intact starboard hull.

Moon and his team were able to sound one battleship during each fourteen-hour day. When they returned at night they were exhausted from the grueling schedule. Moon said it was the only time that the tenders had to work harder than the diver. Holding a diver suspended at twenty feet for three hours at a time strained the muscles of even the strongest among us. We all worked together on the last two ships to give them some relief.

The last ship sounded was the *West Virginia*. We worked the portside first, because the starboard side was partially blocked. The portside hull suffered a gaping torpedo wound three hundred feet long.

When Moon moved to the starboard side they were unable to sound two hundred feet of her hull amidships because the *West Virginia* was pressed tightly against the side of the *Tennessee*. This unfortunate situation would later return to haunt us.

Meanwhile, my crew finished drilling holes in the concrete quay, set the dynamite, covered the blast area with sandbags, and detonated the charges. The *Tennessee* was freed and tugs moved her over to the shipyard. She incurred only minor damage to her hull from the dynamite charges.

We were disappointed that we had not been able to find any survivors on the sunken ships, but after six days of sounding, we were sure no one was alive within them.

While our diving crews were occupied sounding the ships and freeing the USS *Tennessee*, the shipyard constructed two diving barges, each one twenty feet wide and thirty feet long. Buoyancy was provided by three cylindrical pontoons. Wooden planks formed the deck, while corrugated sheet metal on the roof provided protection from the elements. A long pipe spanned the upright stanchions along the side of one barge, which provided an area to hang the divers' rubberized canvas dresses. Along the opposite side were hangers for the four sets of lifelines and air hoses. A large workbench was situated in the middle of the barge. Installed at one end was a wooden diving ladder that led down to the water four feet below. Next to the ladder was a table that held the diving telephone equipment. Four dressing stools were neatly stacked near the table.

The second barge held the air compressor, a salvage dewatering pump, and a workbench used to repair equipment. Two large barrels of diesel oil were maintained on the barge in order to clean bunker oil from the diving equipment and our bodies.

Our next diving assignment was on the *Nevada*, so we got under way from Ten-Ten Dock with the two barges in tow, and headed for the sunken ship a half mile away.

We were to begin our diving careers without knowing the basic rudiments of diving safely inside damaged ships. In our ignorance we hoped we could just muddle through and escape any danger by using our common sense. Fortunately, this approach worked pretty well for us.

Our first safety measures began after my near brush with death when the yard maintenance people came out to the *Arizona* and removed my air compressor. We placed metal plates on the diving compressor after that which forbade anyone from touching it unless they checked with us first. As an added safety feature, we acquired a large high-pressure air flask that held enough air to allow a diver an extra twenty minutes of bottom time if the compressor failed.

We also required that a standby diver be fully dressed so he could tend the working diver at the entrance to the ship. This precaution was used whenever a dive was more than one hundred feet inside the ship.

II

USS Nevada

Salvage Begins

Diving operations on the *Nevada* began in mid-December as a joint effort with units in Pearl Harbor who had divers attached. Divers from submarine rescue vessels *Widgeon* and *Ortolan* excavated mud from under the stern and dynamited and removed sections of her bilge keel in an effort to attach a large patch over the forty-eight-foot-long, twenty-five-foot-high torpedo hole. The patch was made by the shipyard, and the bottom of the *Oklahoma* was used as a pattern because she was a sister ship of the *Nevada*. The divers from the *Widgeon* and *Ortolan* tried to secure the patch for more than a month before a halt was called to the work. After the *Nevada* was dry-docked, it was discovered that the torpedo blister on the side had blown outboard about two feet, which explained why the patch would not fit. Eventually, the patch was aborted and diving efforts were concentrated on isolating and making watertight all interior bulkheads contiguous to the hole. This required closing watertight doors and fittings, welding or caulking split seams, and driving wooden plugs in small holes. Our crew from the Salvage Unit was assigned this work. At the same time, Pacific Bridge civilian divers fitted and secured wood patches over bomb holes in the *Nevada*'s outside hull.

The *Nevada* had two divers who were familiar with the location of valves and other fittings in the engine room, which facilitated the transfer of bunker fuel and other liquids from the ship's tanks to barges alongside. This transfer was accomplished using pumps run by compressed air.

The inside areas of the *Nevada* were littered with tons of debris. While lighter items floated, heavier items blocked our access to the workplaces. We pushed and shoved mattresses, loose fire hose, chairs, tables, desks, ammunition containers, and other untold items we could not identify to clear a path to our destinations.

The *Nevada* suffered less damage than the other battleships, so there were fewer underwater hazards to worry about — hazards we would soon encounter on the other ships.

The *Nevada* was beached and not completely submerged, so much of her topside was above water, which facilitated her repair work.

All of the dead and wounded crew members had been removed or taken care of so there were no bodies below decks.

On 20 December, members of our permanent command, Destroyer Repair Unit I, arrived from San Diego aboard the Matson liner, *Lurline*. Various enlisted ratings were assigned to the vital salvage work on the *Nevada*. As she was dewatered they disconnected electrical motors and machinery, washed them with a caustic solution to remove the oil, water, and sludge, and delivered them to the shipyard. The shipyard overhauled and reconditioned the units so that they could be reinstalled when the ship went into dry dock. Patching of holes and damaged areas proceeded, but it became clear that additional steps were needed to lighten her. Hundreds of tons of ammunition were off-loaded at this time.

The first major salvage problem surfaced when one of the civilian contract divers attempted to burn holes through the hull with an underwater oxygen-hydrogen cutting torch. Holes were needed so that J bolts could be inserted and used to fasten the wooden patches over the bomb cavities. After the diver burned four holes, a shaking explosion occurred. No one was hurt, but it terrified everyone within range. The civilian diver came bobbing to the surface, visibly shaken.

"Holy Moses, what the hell caused that explosion?" he asked.

No one could explain it.

"Well, I ain't about to cut anymore till we find out. I just smashed my lip on my breastplate."

It was determined that the cause of the explosion was a collection of the unburned torch gases, which had escaped inside the ship and formed a gas pocket on the overhead. A speck of burning slag or other flaming debris had floated upward in an air bubble, and when it reached the large gas pocket, it exploded. No further burning was attempted for the time being.

Our divers were alarmed over the incident. None of us realized the gas torch was dangerous. We had used it only out in the open where the unburned gases could escape.

Underwater cutting was certain to play a major part in the salvage of the battleships, but it was obvious that the gas torch could not safely be used in the interior of ships.

I assembled our crew that evening in the diving locker located on Ten-Ten Dock. It was a fifteen-minute walk from our barrack in the receiving-station complex. The locker — or shack, as it was sometimes called — was forty feet wide and fifty feet long. Corrugated sheet metal covered its walls and roof. The floor was concrete, and the walls were unburdened by windows.

In one corner was a large expanded metal enclosure that housed new tools, hose, diving dresses, and spare parts for diving equipment. A long workbench extended along one wall, which provided a working area to repair diving outfits.

The opposite corner contained a long picnic table and two benches. In the middle of the table sat a dilapidated old Crosley table-model radio, its sides and top warped from exposure to humidity, the varnished finish mottled and peeling. It was a cranky music box, capricious and erratic in its reception of stateside programs and music. One night it dispensed beautiful music clear as a bell, the following evening it spewed out nothing but static. Nevertheless, the divers treasured the old radio and its link with the mainland and home.

The only other furniture in the shack was an old discarded wicker chair that Jimmy Willson rescued from the yard dump. Illumination was supplied by four large incandescent lightbulbs screwed into ceiling fixtures.

I had gotten permission from Lieutenant Haynes to use the diving shack as an afterhours hangout for the divers, with the understanding that we would keep it in shipshape condition.

Our conversation that night started off on a positive note, as we wrestled with the idea that something must be done to reduce the danger from gas explosions when using the gas torch. But no one could suggest a satisfactory way to accomplish it. No one, that is, except Ben Apple.

Benjamin Franklin Apple was of middle height but weighed 250 pounds. This was not flabby fat but solid, rock-hard muscle. He was balding, and at age twenty-six he had only a fringe of curly hair circling his round head. He was a man who chose to hide his intelligence and warmth behind a facade of profanity and coarseness. He often told sea stories about his exploits. He would ramble on and on until someone changed the subject or told him to shut up.

We all groaned with boredom as Ben began his

story about his days welding on a pipeline down in Texas. All too often we had heard tales about his welding experiences. But we soon realized that this time Ben had a point to make. He was saying that one of the pipeline welders wanted to cut some metal, but was too lazy to walk over and use a gas cutting torch. Instead, he jacked up the amps on his welding machine, held a long arc with the electrode, and cut the plate.

That was how the idea of using an arc-oxygen underwater cutting torch was born. All of us were sure it would help solve most of our dangerous cutting problems on the battleships.

Diver's Ingenuity

The torch was constructed using a one-inch globe valve with standard pipe threads. One end of the valve was fitted with a quarter-inch male oxygen fitting that was connected to an oxygen hose. The female end of the valve was reduced to a quarter-inch pipe. The electrode was a fourteen-inch length of quarter-inch seamless steel pipe, which was threaded on one end and screwed directly into the female end of the globe valve. A standard connecting lug for an electric welding cable was fastened to the side of the valve with silver braze, and the entire assembly was made watertight by wrapping with rubber tape.

To use the cutting torch, the diver opened the valve, allowing oxygen to flow through the electrode. He then gave the order "Juice on." A topside tender threw a knife switch, sending six

hundred amps of electricity flowing to the electrode. When the operator struck an arc, the
torch cut through metal as though it were butter.
Armor plate fourteen inches thick could be penetrated with the contraption.

Ben was anxious to try out the new torch and
was the first to use it on the *Nevada* the next day.

"Juice on, topside." After a few minutes: "Hot
damn, it's workin' like a charm. I've already
hacked out four holes. It would have taken me
four times as long with the gas torch."

We were all as pleased with the torch as Ben
was, but then a new problem surfaced. Every
time Ben touched a metal part of his helmet with
his bare chin, a tingling stream of electricity
coursed through his body and caused the metal
fillings in his teeth to ache. We finally reduced
the flow of electricity by wrapping the pipe electrode with rubber tape, further insulating the
torch.

As soon as one problem was solved, another
cropped up to bedevil us. Regardless of the
blackness of the water, the electric arc rays, especially the ultraviolet ones, penetrated the water
and burned our eyes. We solved this by attaching
a darkened welder's lens to the helmet faceplate.
It worked well to protect our eyes from the damaging rays.

We finished cutting the holes used to hold the
hull patches in place. Our new torch reduced the
chances of gas-related explosions, and it was
used exclusively in all successive interior cutting

jobs on the sunken battleships.

A second major problem appeared early in the work on the *Nevada*. It was the discovery of a deadly gas, generated within the ship. This poisonous gas was hydrogen sulfide. It was formed from a mixture of salt water, paper products, and other organic materials. In low concentrations it produced an odor much like rotten eggs, but in high concentrations it was odorless and highly toxic.

One morning two of the surviving crew members on the *Nevada*, Lt. Lawrence Gray and CPO Daniel Folsom, came aboard and opened a compartment test cap which allowed the poisonous gas to escape into an unventilated access trunk space. They were overcome by the gas and died almost immediately. Four other crew members came to their aid. They, too, were poisoned but managed to survive the dose of toxic gas.

Although the Japanese planes were long since gone, the aftermath of their vicious attack was still killing American sailors.

A Still Is Born
On 7 December martial law was declared for all of Hawaii. The U.S. Army imposed a blackout, a 9 P.M. curfew, and saddest of all, prohibition. Hawaii was dry! There was no hard liquor, no wine, no beer. Some paradise this turned out to be!

Two weeks after we started work on the *Nevada*, we got together one night at the diving shack to discuss how the day's work had progressed and to consider any problem areas.

I began by pinpointing the most vexing dilemma facing us. How the devil were we going to circumvent the institution of prohibition? I stated that if we could find our way through a maze of wreckage in complete darkness, seal off the interiors of ships and use tools to repair damage, surely we could find a simple solution to the problem of prohibition.

All the guys nodded in agreement. True to our reputation for resourcefulness, when confronted with a new and difficult challenge our solution was ingenious, decisive, and unanimous. We would construct a still.

Drawing upon every ounce of knowledge within the group, most of which was based on rumor, we assembled the ingredients: pineapple juice, raisins, sugar, and yeast. These were packed without regard to measurement into a wooden water breaker, or small barrel, obtained surreptitiously from an abandoned lifeboat. Somebody referred to the fermenting liquid as whiskey, or maybe it was rum or possibly wine. More accurately, it should have been called moonshine.

We capped the barrel tightly and carefully placed it out of reach and out of sight in the rafters of the diving shack.

One week later, anxious to see how our still was working, we reassembled. The yeast had worked its miracle, feeding on sugar and eliminating its waste in the form of alcohol. The 150-degree heat generated from the tin roof of the shack made the yeast extremely hungry, and it consumed sugar eagerly, producing much alcohol and gas in the process. The moonshine fizzed and bubbled inside its wooden confines at an alarming rate. The expanding gases built up tremendous pressure, anxious to be released.

All of us gazed longingly at the concoction in the ceiling, while the happy yeast continued to eat and belch.

My thoughts, and those expressed by my comrades, strayed to the culmination of the fermentation process. Booze meant more than a chemical escape from the daily toil below the harbor waters. If it was offered to the local women, it would enable us to break into their cliques. I had seen some of the local Portuguese people on the beaches and in the parks during my last tour in the islands. Their parties were loud and raucous and were made more so by the presence of liquor. Now prohibition had silenced those parties, and I was sure the local girls would pay a premium for liquor and that premium would definitely boost our morale.

Since the war began, the influx of servicemen had increased the ratio of men to available women to a staggering number. Some estimates ran as high as ten thousand to one. If alcohol would gain entry to the cloistered parties of the locals, then we were certainly willing to brave the perils of prohibition.

We continued discussing the fermenting liquor. It had been the only topic of conversation during the past week.

First Bronco Bill Rush and Jimmy Willson expressed their thoughts regarding the length of time the mixture should ferment. We looked at each other in turn, but no one seemed quite sure how long the fermentation process should continue. From each man's remarks, no one was prepared to admit he was not worldly, and we searched frantically for some wisdom to impart.

"You know, you let the juice stay up there too long, it could go bad," Cameron offered. Cameron had the irritating habit of always starting his sentences with "you know." Most often "you" did not know, but neither did Cameron. "Also, if you open it up too soon it won't ferment again."

"You mean we'd have to start over if it's not fermented enough?" Bronco asked.

"Yep." Cameron nodded. "Might as well throw the whole batch away. You know, bacteria or yeast or whatever all dies when you open it."

"You mean it's got germs in it?" asked Andy Davis incredulously.

Cameron nodded knowingly.

Several of the divers mumbled among themselves at this new revelation. But, as Bill might say, if anyone asked him, liquor meant babes. The possibility of a health hazard required some consideration, but babes always posed some risks. Ultimately, the choice was simple.

"But what about the germs?" Jimmy asked.

65

"You want booze and babes, you gotta take a chance," Rush replied.

I turned as I heard the shack door open. Lieutenant Haynes entered hesitatingly, peering inside while his eyes became accustomed to the dimly lit diving shack. Those of us who were seated rose grudgingly to our feet.

Lieutenant Haynes was a good officer. He had always been fair and up-front with us. But he was an officer and that fact created an uneasy relationship between us. As he walked toward us, we shuffled around and straightened slightly but did not actually come to attention. He wore freshly pressed khaki pants and a long-sleeve shirt. His long, black uniform tie was held in place with a gold-colored clip. His shoes were polished to a high sheen and he wore his cap as he entered the shack.

Haynes came by quite often to check on the appearance of the diving shack used by us as an after-hours hangout. His usual routine was to come in, wander around peering into the work area and corners of the shack, then rejoin us to ask how the day's work was progressing. He did not really fraternize with us, but it was obvious that we divers were his fair-haired boys. We enjoyed minor privileges that were not available to others, such as the after-hours use of the shack. He seemed to relish talking shop with us and telling us tales about his early days as a diver. His behavior reminded me of a doting father who relives his life through the achievements of his sons. It was through this appraisal that we nicknamed him "Pappy," but we never used that name within his hearing, of course.

"At ease," Haynes said.

Most of us were already standing casually about and we shifted our feet back and forth almost as if we had been released from bondage. Those of us in the front row smiled thinly and painted on our most attentive expressions. My thoughts focused on the hope that his visit tonight would be a short one because I wanted to question Cameron about our moonshine.

He greeted some of us by name. To others, whose names he had forgotten, he nodded his acknowledgments. Finally he settled himself comfortably in the dilapidated old wicker chair. I groaned inwardly, since he always stayed longer when he was seated. His performance was progressing as it had been played out in the past.

"Well, men," he began, "I'm proud of the job you're doing on the *Nevada*. That's dangerous work out there, diving without any visibility." He removed his cap and ran his hand through his few remaining strands of hair. "You're working as a team now. You're well oiled and running smoothly." He chuckled here as if on cue. I knew he was making a joke about us diving through the thick layer of bunker oil floating on the water, so I smiled faintly.

He finished speaking his lines by asking us if we had experienced any diving problems he was not aware of.

Now it was time for audience participation.

Cameron, the brownnoser of the crew, in a vain effort to be noticed, always offered some nauseating drivel. I did not object to Cameron's quest for recognition, because I knew where he was coming from and no one paid any heed to his remarks anyway.

Cameron had just opened his mouth to speak when suddenly the ceiling exploded with a loud whooshing noise. The room was alive with flying bits of wood and brown mist. It was as if a bomb had landed directly on the small shack. Debris rattled against the walls. The shack was a site of wreckage and mayhem.

I was stunned by the explosion. I stood frozen for a second. The room was a mess, but my senses received conflicting signals. I could not recall any noise I would have associated with a bomb blast. I thought I might be in shock.

Remembering my Boy Scout training, I flexed my muscles slowly to detect any injury. Everything felt okay, but I felt wetness on my shoulder. I reached cautiously upward while I averted my eyes. Yes, I noted, my shoulder was damp. This could mean only one thing: I was bleeding, probably from a shrapnel wound. My finger groped for the expected point of entry. I summoned all of my courage to turn my head and look at my injury. What I saw perplexed me. On my left shoulder was a glop of brown foam. I rolled the foam between finger and thumb. It was sticky. It didn't look like blood. I sniffed it, and pulled my head back in revulsion. The foam smelled sickeningly sweet, putrid, and foul.

I blinked my eyes in recognition and looked to the ceiling for confirmation. The barrel of moonshine was gone, replaced by the remnants of its wooden confines and the slow drip of oozing brown foam.

The others in the shack were coming to their senses as well. No one appeared hurt, which was miraculous considering the dispersion of flying shards. As yet, no one had spoken. Everyone was looking around at the devastation and at each other. I finally gestured at the ceiling and one by one the guys gazed up at the empty rafters.

Through all of this, Pappy remained planted in his chair. A quick inspection revealed that he received the brunt of the explosion. He was covered with the foamy liquor, his khaki work clothes made a darker brown by the putrid liquid. He sat stock-still. Foam dribbled on and around him from the rafters. I began to wonder if he was injured.

With deliberate purpose, Pappy raised his head.

"What happened?" he growled in a tone reflecting total restraint. He raised his eyebrows to clear his vision. He blinked in pain as the liquid trickled down his forehead into his eyes and down the bridge of his nose.

"Uh, let me get that for you, sir," said Cameron. He pulled a handkerchief from his back pocket and approached the seated figure and began dabbing at the globs that still clung to his face and neck.

"I said, what happened?" Haynes shouted.

"Someone must be playing a joke on us or trying to get even, or . . ." I was trying to manufacture a credible lie. I lowered my eyes, waiting for an inspiration. As the lieutenant stood, the brown foam slid slowly from him to the floor. Numerous wood chips stuck stubbornly to his thinning hair. He looked quickly at his billed cap and placed it on his head. He rolled his shoulder, his shirt sticking to his back. He held his arms out from his body, like a scarecrow. The brown liquid dripped from his outstretched arms.

He began to pick his way through the slivers of wood strewn randomly across the floor. "Get this place cleaned up," he barked, turning and shaking some residue from his uniform. "I'm getting out of here before some dumb knucklehead gives me another shower of suds."

He kicked at a large piece of wood as he made his way out. He slammed the door in a final show of displeasure.

At his exit, we looked at each other, then broke into gales of laughter. Everyone, that is, except Bill. He stood there in the middle of his shattered dreams and looked forlornly in the direction of Honolulu.

"Now how the hell can we get any babes?" he asked plaintively as he left.

Someone asked how we thought "the scarecrow" was going to get back to his quarters a mile away without being seen. The recollection of Pappy as a scarecrow sent all of us howling with laughter again.

Wiping the tears from my eyes, I managed to gasp, "What shall we do about Bronco and no babes?"

A waggish Moon had the answer. "We'll all chip in a quarter and send him over to a cathouse."

Christmas 1941

Christmas day came and went. We divers hardly realized that it was an American holiday. We worked our normal thirteen-hour day; 6 A.M. to 7 P.M. The navy did serve a special turkey dinner in the mess hall at Ford Island, which we all appreciated.

We had all sent postcards to families and girl-friends when we first arrived. The cards gave the minimum information such as:

— I have arrived at my destination.
— I am safe.
— Please write to me.

Then you listed your name, rank, serial number, unit, and Fleet Post Office number. Postage was paid by the U.S. government.

The loved ones who wrote letters or sent packages could not know that it would be many weeks before mail arrived in Hawaii. Air mail was transported by clipper flying boats, the lumbering seaplanes that crossed the ocean to the islands once a week. Packages came by slow boat, and it was a lucky man who got a Christmas gift before the New Year.

One day a bundle arrived in brown wrapping paper, addressed to Andy. Ben had picked up the mail and came shambling into the barrack, yelling to Andy that he got a package from Enid that probably contained corncobs.

Andy's smile lit up his sunburned face as he removed the white string and tore off the paper. Martin and I stood by, interested to see what Enid had sent him.

First he pulled out a long blue-and-white striped wool muffler, hand-knitted by his love. He gazed at it happily.

"I guess Raggedy Ann doesn't know we're working in temperatures around eighty-five degrees summer and winter," Ben scoffed. "That's gonna look real good on you when you're standing in line at a cathouse. It'll keep your neck warm while you got your pants down."

Andy ignored him and dug deeper into the packing box. He pulled out an inner box, which contained his favorite chocolate cookies. But rough handling during shipping had reduced them to a layer of brown crumbs that scattered over the floor when he lifted the lid.

An edible fruitcake and a batch of fudge were still in recognizable condition. Andy shared them with us, and his face glowed with pride when we declared that Enid's candy was the best we'd ever tasted. He laughed at Ben, who was also enjoying his share of the cake.

Successful Underwater Repairs

The following day our diving crew started working in the after section of the *Nevada*, patching holes and closing off compartments. A split seam in one bulkhead was allowing more water to flood into the compartment than the pumps could handle. We proposed to repair the leak by welding the seam underwater, amid much skepticism from the salvage officer in charge.

These doubts were expressed mainly because underwater welding was in its infancy, and while it had been experimented with under the best of controlled situations, usually in a tank with good visibility, it had never been tried on an actual salvage job. But other methods of plugging the leaking seam had failed, so we got the go-ahead to try our luck.

A standard welding electrode holder was used, and the electrical connections were taped with rubber to make them watertight. Three-sixteenth-inch diameter coated steel electrodes were dipped in a solution of acetone and celluloid (acetone dissolved the celluloid), which when dried coated the electrode with a watertight covering. The diver struck an arc, much the same as he would if he were welding above water. Then he positioned the electrode at a thirty-degree angle to it, and slowly fed the electrode into it as the weld metal was melted and deposited. The welded seam proved to be a success, and later we used underwater welding successfully on other sunken ships.

Bait for Babes

Two weeks after Christmas, Bill Rush's dream of meeting "one of those babes" became a possibility.

Rush was twenty-six years old. He had served a four-year hitch in the navy, then stayed out four years and was settled in his beloved Oklahoma, where he worked the rodeo circuit part of the year and raised white-faced heifers on a section of his father's ranch. He was recalled to active duty in early 1941 after the national emergency was declared. He had never met a "babe" he didn't like, and he was always on the lookout for new ones.

It was on the twenty-fifth day of diving on the *Nevada* that Bill found the key to social acceptance by the island women. It was fitting and proper that it should have been he. Bill seemed to be the most disappointed at our failure to produce potable moonshine.

"Hey, topside, I just stumbled over a box down here, and it feels like it has a bunch of bottles inside. What do you figure they are?" Bill asked on the diver's telephone.

Jimmy was manning the phones. He traced Bronco's direction of travel on the ship's blueprints and determined that he must be in the vicinity of the after battle dressing station. He duly reported this news to Bill.

Ben uttered a string of expletives and rushed over to the diver's phone. He pushed the transmitting key and spoke in a hushed voice to Bronco. He told him that what he found were most probably bottles of pure alcohol and to keep quiet. He told Bill to bring up one bottle and he would take it from him when the coast was clear.

We all glanced around furtively and waited expectantly for the bottle to surface.

Rush finished his dive and finally emerged, obeying his instructions. He handed the bottle to Ben, who concealed it in a piece of toweling. When we left the diving barge for the night, we brought the bottle onboard the sampan. Cameron uncorked the bottle while we looked on eagerly, impatient for a self-described "expert" to identify the contents. Cameron was obviously enjoying his moment of undivided attention. He sniffed the clear liquid and rolled his eyes.

Then he took a small sip and swilled it around in his mouth. "Hot damn, this stuff is just like white lightnin'."

A great shout went up. We danced around pounding each other on the back and roaring with laughter at our good fortune. Moon asked Rush how many bottles there were, and he guessed between twenty and thirty.

After learning of the discovery, Andy and Martin waived claim to their shares. Andy said he did not like the taste of hard liquor, and he imagined this would be harder than most. Martin came from a Mormon background, and though he never preached against smoking and drinking, he never indulged in either one. Tony wanted his share of the alcohol, but he said he would find his own women to share it with.

We decided that the first diver down in the morning would move the box of bottles out of the way so nobody would step on it.

We were faced with a number of dilemmas regarding the disposition and transportation of the alcohol. After many worthwhile suggestions, it was decided to store the cache in a seabag and suspend the bag ten feet under the surface of the water. The end of the rope holding the bag would be tied to the center pontoon, out of the way and out of sight.

How we were going to conceal the contraband from the prying eyes of the marine sentries on the main gate was a more difficult problem to solve. Someone remembered the base directive, issued a few days before, requiring all hands to carry gas masks and helmets ashore on liberty. We had not paid too much attention to the order, since we had not been granted liberty as yet, but I thought of a possible way to sneak the bottles past the sentries. I explained that if we removed the canister, hose, and mask from the carrying bag and substituted a pint bottle of alcohol, no marine would think of inspecting a gas mask.

Everybody agreed the plan should work. The fact that we would be unprotected in the event of a gas attack bothered none of us in the least.

Moon's final words on the subject said it all. "Who the hell cares if we get gassed, if we can get us some broads."

The following morning Ben carried a seabag down with him and took custody of thirty-four pint bottles of 190-proof straight ethyl alcohol. He tied the bag safely out of the way under the diving barge.

One week later we finished our work on the *Nevada* and headed back to the diving locker, planning to do maintenance work on our equipment the next day. But this was not to be.

Arizona Accident

Lieutenant Haynes met us as we tied up to Ten-Ten Dock that evening. He told us that a new decision had been reached regarding the *Arizona*, and to stand by in the morning for further orders.

After weeks of indecision by the Navy Department, a salvage plan was approved to cut off the badly damaged bow section of the *Arizona* and raise the stern portion of the ship. Our orders were to seal off the interior and make it watertight.

Before we could start salvage efforts, we had to investigate a reported hole in the after port side of the hull below the mud line, presumably made by a torpedo or bomb. Since no other damage had been discovered in the area, the consensus was that it had not exploded and was armed and dangerous inside the general workshop located on the third deck.

The submarine base sent out a chief torpedoman to give us advice on how to handle the torpedo when we found it.

We moved the barges out to the *Arizona* and tied up to the after starboard side.

I decided to make the first dive, so I was dressed and descended into the interior of the *Arizona*. I had been down a little over an hour when my air supply was cut off.

Moon told me later that everybody topside was discussing how to get the alcohol past the sentries and it wasn't until they heard me yell "What's wrong with my air supply?" that they realized I was in trouble. He also said he spotted the *Maryann*, a crane barge, coming alongside, but he hadn't attached much significance to its appearance at the time.

Moon told me that everybody panicked when they heard my distressed voice, but they soon calmed down and set about rescuing me. Martin had jumped up on the superstructure deck to see what had happened to the air compressor. When he returned he uttered the first swear word any of the divers had heard him use. "Those damn fools disconnected the diving compressor and already had it aboard when I got there. The yard workmen finally started it, so there should be air back on the line soon."

Andy and Bill jumped into the water and swam over to the mushroom ventilator near the open hatch where I emerged, and they opened my faceplate. After losing consciousness, my first recollection was the sight of the two anxious faces of Andy and Bill peering through my open faceplate.

"Damn." Rush whistled softly. "We thought you were a goner."

"What happened to my air?" I asked wearily. But I hardly listened to the explanation as I stood up on the *Arizona*'s main deck with my two buddies on either side, and sucked in the life-giving fresh air.

"As soon as you're able, we'll walk you over to the barge," Andy said.

The air had cleared my brain, and I was able to think clearly. My first inclination was to follow Andy's suggestion and walk back, climb aboard the diving barge, and seek the safety of a dry deck. But I had the definite feeling that if I did I might never have the courage to go back down into the blackness of another ship. "You'd better do it right now," an inner voice nagged me. "If you wait, you'll lose your confidence."

"Close my faceplate," I said to a bewildered Bill. Then I spoke through the phone. "Topside, I'm going to open my control valve and blow the water in my dress out through the cuffs. That should get the water level down to my chest. Then I'm going to the access trunk and drop down to the third deck again. I'll stand there for

79

a little while and then come up."

Moon later said he knew what prompted me to go back down again. I walked over to the trunk and lowered myself and reported to topside when I reached the third deck. I rested there in the darkness, feeling grateful to whatever forces allowed me to live through this experience. A shudder chilled me as I realized how close I had come to death. Then the sound of wind chimes announced the arrival of my floating companion hovering overhead. No longer did I fear his presence. This time he seemed to bring with him a strange aura of comfort and protection. Reaching out almost tenderly, I pushed him back behind a locker, where the whorls and eddy currents generated by the living would not disturb his peaceful repose.

"Topside, take in my slack. I'm coming up," I said calmly.

As I climbed the ladder I felt a new sense of strength and pride, precipitated by my decision to return to the depths of the ship. I knew I had gained the courage to dive again.

III

USS Utah

Deceptive Behavior on *Utah*

After my dive on the *Arizona*, no additional diving on her was scheduled. The Pearl Harbor salvage engineers argued convincingly to Washington that the salvage efforts should be directed to raising less damaged ships first, such as *California* and *West Virginia*. Otherwise the available salvage equipment and manpower would be diluted on *Arizona*, *Utah*, and *Oklahoma*. Admiral Nimitz concurred with this argument.

This tug-of-war over salvage priorities between the Navy Department and the engineers on the scene delayed plans to salvage the remaining ships. It was during this period of indecision that Lt. Clifford Arnold received permission to use the divers to recover a safe from the *Utah*. While this was his stated purpose, we soon found out that Arnold had a hidden agenda designed to benefit only himself.

Lieutenant Arnold was a small, slightly over-weight man with a florid complexion. Even when he was clean-shaven and in a freshly pressed uniform, he appeared untidy. Perspiration stains under his arms contributed to this impression. His eyes darted nervously from side to side, never meeting the eyes of the person he was addressing. When he smiled, the effect was to give a pinched look to his face, resembling an oversize rat.

Arnold brought Warrant Bosun Dudley McClung with him and introduced him as the diving officer in charge of removing the safe.

The Bosun stood respectfully by as Arnold explained our diving mission. He said the ship's store safe contained at least two thousand dollars that had been generated from the sale of store items. These funds belonged to surviving members of the crew, and he was honor bound to see that they received their rightful shares of the two thousand dollars he was allocating to them.

"But I am sure there is more than two thousand in the safe," Arnold said, "and any excess over that amount can be split among you nine divers."

Then the bosun chimed in. "I spoke to the ship's store officer last night, and he's pretty sure there was about three thousand dollars in the safe."

We looked at each other in amazement, hardly believing our ears. As strange and lucrative as this plan seemed to us, we did not doubt its legitimacy or the veracity of its architects. The rigid caste system in the prewar navy taught one that enlisted men did not question an officer's words or motives.

Greed and avarice dulled our minds, and we were happy to carry out orders, and in the process fill our pockets with sunken treasure.

"One last reminder," Arnold said. "The safe must be brought out intact, because I don't want any of the money in it to float away underwater."

Bosun McClung then explained his diving plan to recover the safe. A diver would cut a hole in the side of the ship at frame number 60, a location identified as an officer's stateroom on the ship's plan. He would enter the stateroom, then proceed along the wardroom passageway until he located the ship's store safe. He would unbolt the safe and remove it through the designated stateroom.

The safe weighed four hundred pounds and had been bolted to the deck, but with the ship upside down, it was now on the overhead.

The bosun marked the area on the ship's plan where we would cut the hole. He announced he would make the first dive and attach a line to the stateroom porthole.

"Your porthole is open, isn't it?" McClung asked Arnold.

"I'm sure it is. I never had time to close it before we abandoned ship."

After this exchange, Arnold stepped into his boat and departed for the shipyard.

The bosun returned with us to pick up our diving barges. We towed them to the *Utah* and moored them to her side. The *Utah* was located

on the west side of Ford Island opposite battleship row.

Moon and Jimmy lowered the descending line
and weight about fifteen feet away from the side
of the ship. Bill and I dressed the bosun and
Rush led him to the diving ladder. He staggered
slightly, huffing and puffing under the bulk and
weight of his diving outfit. He climbed down the
ladder until his helmet was underwater. Then he
grabbed the descending line and started down.

Warrant Bosun McClung was of medium
height and build. His personal appearance was
immaculate and military. His hands were devoid
of calluses; soft and white; and his fingernails
were polished. This was not the rough-and-
tough guy image we expected from a warrant
bosun, who had previously been an enlisted
boatswain mate. So we were wickedly unsympa-
thetic when nothing went well for him on his
diving debut.

His first image problem began when he could
not equalize the air pressure in his ears. It took
him a full half hour to get to the bottom, only
forty feet below. Once there, he could not seem
to stretch his circling line out and locate the side
of the *Utah*, fifteen feet away. His lifeline and air
hose kept getting tangled and he spent most of
his dive freeing them. Finally, after two hours,
trying to find the hull of the *Utah*, he gave up and
signaled he wanted to come up.

Since the bosun was a recent graduate of the
Deep Sea Diving School in Washington, D.C.,

his poor performance must have embarrassed him greatly. Fortunately for him, we were the only witnesses, so Arnold never learned about the incident.

McClung climbed out of his diving suit, a haggard, weary, and defeated man, bathed in sweat and utterly exhausted.

That was the first and last time any of us ever saw the bosun in a diving dress.

Later in the afternoon, Andy located Arnold's stateroom and secured a line to the porthole closing bolt, or dog. Then he and Martin burned a six-foot-square hole in the side of the ship.

That evening, Moon reported a conversation he had had with Lieutenant Arnold's room steward. The steward had been given orders by Arnold to prepare a bedroom in his government quarters for Bosun McClung. This was difficult for me to believe, because the rigid caste system in the navy seldom mixed naval academy graduates, like Arnold, with lower rank officers, and especially not a "lowly" warrant officer.

The next day it became clear why the entrance to Arnold's stateroom was to be used to bring out the safe. Arnold and McClung came out to the ship and Arnold ordered our crew to bring up every stick of furniture and personal apparel we could find in his room. He had served several tours of duty in the Far East and had collected a number of carved wooden tables, chairs, and fancy screens made in China.

It was my turn to dive. My assignment was to

locate the safe and determine what type of rigging gear was needed to retrieve it.

My first problem became apparent even before I hit the water. The *Utah* was upside down, so I would be walking on the overhead instead of the deck. The raised deck beams in the darkness would be a problem, because they could cause me to stumble and lose my balance. Machinery that was secured to the deck was now hanging precariously from the overhead, and if bumped could crash down. Also, directions from the telephone talker to the diver became confusing: right turns became left turns and identifiable signposts on deck were now on the overhead.

With these thoughts in mind, I readied myself for the dive. I planned to take one hundred feet of Manila line with me to stretch between the door to Arnold's stateroom and the area where the ship's store safe was located. The line could be followed easily by subsequent divers, thereby saving much time.

My tenders dressed me, and I descended the line leading to the entrance hole in the hull that had been cut the day before. I entered Arnold's stateroom and cautiously felt my way through a maze of tables, chairs, mattresses, clothing, and other furnishings. A large motor, probably belonging to a blower, blocked my way. It was too heavy to move out of the way, but we would have to deal with it later when we brought down chainfalls to move the safe.

I skirted the motor and debris and exited the stateroom to the passageway.

"Face the door and extend your left hand about two feet off the deck and you will find a fire hydrant," said Ben.

I reached my left hand out and felt nothing. "Are you sure you are in the right place?" I asked.

"Hell, no, I'm not," said Ben. "Wait a minute until I turn this damn plan upside down and get under it so I can read it."

There were a few moments of silence.

"Okay, I've got it now. Stick your right hand out and feel up near the overhead and you should find it."

I located the hydrant and began inching my way down the passageway, paying out the Manila line as I went. Other than a lot of clutter my pathway was relatively clear.

Ben directed me through two watertight doors without further misdirection, and I arrived at the safe, which had broken away from its deck mounting and was lying on its side.

The position of the safe made our retrieving job much easier, since we didn't need to concern ourselves with unbolting it and lowering its four hundred pounds to the deck.

We used chainfalls to lift the safe over the raised doorways and other impediments. We rigged blocks and tackles to move the safe down the passageway and out through the hole in the hull.

It took us a week to recover the safe, and luckily no one was injured during its recovery. Although there were fifty-eight men who died on the *Utah*, none were found within our work areas.

The Divers Learn a Lesson

Because the ship was upside down, confusion reigned above and below the water. Adding to our frustration was Arnold's order to clear his room of all articles.

Each time we finished a four-hour dive, we were reminded to bring up an article of furniture or clothing from Arnold's stateroom. We came to hate that last direction, coming always at the end of our dive when we were drained and ready for a rest. But we always complied and soon had collected a huge pile of oil-stained uniforms and waterlogged furniture.

Arnold's closet and wardrobe furniture were bolted to the deck, so they were now on the overhead. When we opened drawers all the articles and clothing fell out and either floated away or were trampled underfoot.

At first Arnold bugged us about losing one of his blue uniforms, two pairs of white uniform pants, and one of his half-Wellington boots.

Eventually we found his uniforms floating in a corner, but we never found one of his boots. We also recovered all of his carved tables, chairs, and screens. These were made of teak wood; since teak doesn't float, these items didn't drift away.

Arnold sent his steward, Ed Field, out to the barge with orders to wash out the uniforms with fresh water and clean the oil off the furniture. Clothing was hung from ropes that had been stretched across the length of the barge.

One of the divers remarked that the barge looked like a junkyard, with bargain items blowing in the breeze. None of us could figure out why the lieutenant wanted all of his belongings removed from his stateroom when water and oil had stained them so badly.

One day, Ed Field came out to the barge and gave us the explanation. It seemed Arnold had a brother in Long Beach, California, who owned a tailoring and dry cleaning business. Arnold's clothing would be cleaned and resewn, and made good as new. In the meantime, Field said, Arnold had submitted a claim and would be reimbursed by the government for his loss.

Ben expressed his sentiments bluntly. "They ought to hang the little bastard by his heels. If you wanna know what I think, we'll never see a dime of that ship's store money. If he'd cheat Uncle Sam, he sure as hell wouldn't think twice about screwing us enlisted men."

After we had wrestled the safe out of the *Utah* and hoisted it up on the diving barge, Arnold and McClung came hurrying out on the *Maryann* to relieve us of it and return it to Ten-Ten Dock. The safe was heaved onto a truck and away it went, never to be seen again. True to Ben's prediction, the charade was played out when Bosun McClung appeared with a saddened face to tell us the bad news. It seemed there was only a little over nineteen hundred dollars in the safe. "Somebody's estimate was way off," he stated. "I'm sorry, men, but, by George, you did a damn fine job getting the safe out, and I know the crew of the *Utah* will be eternally grateful to you."

Our disappointment was minimal because we were not surprised at the outcome. We all felt a little better when Ed Field reported that Arnold was kicking the bosun out of his quarters to make room for an incoming navy lieutenant.

As faithful as we had been in clearing Arnold's stateroom of his possessions, we could not find one of the Wellington boots he insisted was there. He nagged us so incessantly about it, it became a favorite joke with us. No one ever admitted finding it, but Bill always suspected Ben of stomping it in the mud when he overheard Ben on the diver's phone, muttering to himself on his last dive on the *Utah*, "Stick that up your old tokay, you cheap bastard."

But whatever happened, the boot was never recovered and no one but Arnold and Ben gave it another thought. Periodically Ben would ask Arnold, with as straight a face as he could muster, if he had ever found his missing boot.

I made the last dive on the *Utah*. My job was to disconnect the blocks and tackle and send them topside. I dressed myself in heavy woolen diving underwear, and pulled on my thick woolen socks. I jammed my feet into the suit and slipped my arms into place.

"Hey, this isn't my regular dress," I said to Martin.

"Yeah, I know. It's one we got from the locker. Your regular one needed a knee patch."

My tenders pulled up my suit bib, then I sat down on the dressing stool waiting as they attached my breastplate.

"Are you ready for your belt?" asked Cameron.

I grunted and stood to receive it. My tenders finished dressing me, and I climbed down the ladder and entered the water. I asked for a light. I thought it might be helpful for this particular situation. I carried the light with me and when I entered the stateroom, and I asked for slack in the cord.

"Turn on the power," I said. The 250-watt light flashed on, blinding me. I could not see much of anything because of the sediment in the water, but I decided to hang on to the light a while longer to see if the sediment cleared.

I waited fifteen minutes, but to no avail. I left the light burning in the stateroom and headed down the passageway and asked for more slack in my lifeline and air hose.

I was busy pulling the slack down in my lines, so I did not feel the creeping along my bare neck. Soon I felt a movement, but dismissed it as a loose thread in my bib. I twisted my head around hoping to push the irritant away. Up to this point

I did not realize there was something alive in my suit. It was not until it crawled up on my chin and wiggled its way across my mouth that my sixth sense flashed me the hideous realization that it was a spider. Rising bile erupted and spewed bitter liquid and spider against my faceplate. I groaned as panic and dread paralyzed my movements and speech.

My terror and hatred of spiders was formed when I was four years old. I had crawled into an unused dumbwaiter shaft in our house, to hide from my sister. The shaft was home to dozens of spiders. They tangled themselves in my hair and crawled on my face and inside my shirt. I screamed and cried until my mother came to my rescue. I had terrible nightmares for years afterward.

There are situations when a person can withstand excruciating pain and agony, but everyone has a breaking point when something is so horrible or unbearable that the mind is deadened and refuses to control the body. Bravery and cowardice are not involved, because these are instinctive actions. For me, spiders were unbearable. The sight or thought of them induced terror and panic. I was a child again, trapped within the family dumbwaiter shaft, crawling with spiders.

The faint illumination from the light I left burning showed the outline of the spider as it cleared itself from the wetness of my faceplate.

I clawed at my faceplate trying to grab the

damn thing, forgetting, in my panic, that I could not reach it. I also thought of flooding the inside of my helmet with water to drown it, but quickly realized that it would rush to my face again to escape the water. The thought that it could be poisonous made me shudder. I had seen black widows on the island. Oh God, help me, I prayed. But before I could think further the demon crawled to the top of my helmet.

"Ed, why are you groaning? What's the matter with you?"

I could not answer.

"Goddammit. Answer me!" Ben's booming voice jarred me back to reality.

"I'm . . . Oh God, Ben, there's a spider in my helmet. Get me the hell out of here."

I turned and started through the stateroom. I tripped over an exposed beam, stumbled and fell spread-eagle, dislodging the spider into my hair. My scalp prickled with fear.

The spider traveled down to my forehead. Tracing its movements, I fought furiously against the panic. Slowly the devil moved between my eyes and down the bridge of my nose. Its path of unseen terror left a gauzy trail of gossamer as it crawled across my cheek.

I finally reached my breaking point. I heard a scream coming from above my head. I vaguely realized it came from me. I struggled to remain conscious. For a brief moment I was a gibbering idiot.

When I surfaced, my tenders frantically

hauled me up the ladder, and I stumbled over to the dressing stool.

"Hurry up and get his helmet off," said Ben. "Give him some air."

Crouching in one of the top window ports was a nonpoisonous Cane spider. Moon grabbed a glove, reached into the helmet, and squashed it.

I was still in shock, but when my senses returned, I turned to Moon. "That goddamn spider really spoiled my day." I tried to make light of my experience, but from that day forward I never pulled on another diving dress before turning it inside out to make sure it was free of any varmints.

Naval Aviation

It was about the time we finished work on the *Utah* that word came that the navy was soliciting applications from enlisted personnel for pilot training.

As soon as the sampan reached the dock, I headed for the diving officer's office. I knocked on the door, and Haynes invited me in. I related my long-held desire to become an aviator and also described my many disappointments in trying to attain that goal.

"Sir, I don't know if you have seen the notice requesting volunteers for the Naval Aviation Cadet Program, but I want to volunteer for it. This may be my last chance —"

Haynes released a puff of cigarette smoke and interrupted. "Maybe you were never meant to be a flier. Maybe somebody is trying to tell you something. Think about it."

I did not tell him I had been thinking about it for years. I just said I still wanted to try for it.

Haynes laid his cigarette in the ashtray and looked me in the eye. "Go ahead and see my yeoman — make out a request, and I'll recommend approval of it. I don't like losing you, Raymer, you are a valuable member of the diving crew."

My request was subsequently approved by the commanding officer of the Salvage Unit. In a few days I was ordered to report to Lt. John Crowe at the Naval Air Station, Ford Island, for my physical and mental examinations. I fretted over being rusty in mathematics, but that worry proved to be groundless, as I passed all the tests with flying colors. Lieutenant Crowe informed me that I should be receiving orders for flight training within a few weeks.

Meanwhile, diving continued. The diving officer called me into his office the following morning, and informed me that the crew would be diving on the *Arizona* after all.

"It sounds like the powers that be are confused, sir. First we're going to raise the *Arizona*, then we aren't. What's next?"

"I know, I know, Raymer, but this time around, the salvage work makes some sense despite the fact that political considerations helped bring it about."

Haynes explained that the officials of Honolulu requested that the U.S. Army provide them with additional antiaircraft protection. Since neither the army nor the navy had any spare AA rifles available, the Navy Department offered to loan the *Arizona*'s guns to the army. The guns were scheduled for installation around Pearl Harbor and Honolulu.

IV
USS Arizona

Removing the 5-Inch AA Guns
Despite the widespread damage to the first two hundred feet of the bow section, the starboard side aft of number two turret was largely undamaged in the area where four 5-inch antiaircraft guns were located. These rifles were accessible for salvage.

We moved our two barges, with the seabag full of bottles dangling below, over to the *Arizona* and made preparations to remove the 5-inchers.

The guns were in carriages, and each was secured to the deck of the *Arizona* by thirty-two threaded studs and nuts. Each stud was two inches in diameter. At high tide the nuts and studs were covered by six feet of water.

Cameron was dressed and made the first dive in order to ascertain if the nuts could be removed by using an impact wrench. He reported that the starboard side deck was in good condition and that an impact wrench could be used. We borrowed a heavy-duty pneumatic impact wrench from the shipyard and started work to remove the guns. As each gun carriage was unbolted, the *Maryann*, a crane barge, came alongside. We rigged wire straps to the carriages, and they were hoisted aboard the barge and delivered to the yard ordnance shop for reconditioning.

The guns were later distributed around Oahu for antiaircraft protection. Lieutenant Haynes had promised us liberty as soon as we finished removing the four guns. He said recovery of the shells could wait until later, since they could be reconditioned much faster than the guns.

After the last AA rifle was delivered on 27 February, we headed for the barracks that evening full of anticipation and plans for our first liberty the next day. Sleep did not come easily for most of us that night.

First Liberty

Since our arrival in Pearl Harbor on 8 December we had worked fourteen-hour days, seven days a week. The stress and strain of the job was beginning to tell on us. Pearl Harbor offered no rest and recreation facilities. There was nowhere we could go and nothing we could do to recuperate from nerves rubbed raw from the strain of facing the hidden dangers within the ships. Being surrounded by filthy conditions was a debilitating experience to endure without respite. Divers and tenders were covered with oil and slime, while the stench of decaying bodies and the putrid smell of hydrogen sulfide gas permeated the water and air. Stories filtering back from sailors who had been granted leave much earlier did nothing to boost our morale. We needed the companionship of women and rest and relaxation badly. In addition, we still had an untouched seabag full of bottles of 190-proof straight alcohol dangling under the diving barge, which we were sure would open the gates of the island and the arms of the girls of Honolulu.

By popular demand, Mullen and I were selected to be the point men to ferret out the most promising companions, notify them of our alcohol cache, and arrange a party to celebrate the end of prohibition, at least for a favored few of us.

When I had been stationed in Pearl Harbor the previous year, I had consumed a delicious twenty-four-ounce porterhouse steak at Ernie's Bar and Grill on Hotel Street. I remembered that not only was the food excellent, but that Ernie employed Portuguese girls as waitresses and bartenders, all of them buxom and fun loving. I was sure they were the party girls we were looking for.

All of us were in a happy mood as we pulled on our immaculate white uniforms. The garments looked even whiter against our deep island tans.

Andrew and Martin headed for Waikiki. They said they wanted to spend time on the famous beach and visit a zoo they had heard about. Andy also planned to shop for a present for Enid.

"Jesus, Andy," Ben teased. "You're planning one hell of an exciting and strenuous day. Are you sure you'll be able to work tomorrow? What you really need is a good lay. You come along with me, and I'll show you how it's done." He chuckled wickedly.

"You go your way, and I'll go mine, Ben," Andy said as he slammed the barracks door.

Ben, Bill, Cameron, and Jimmy crowded into a cab outside the main gate of the receiving station. Ben had informed anyone who would listen that he knew the best cathouse in all of Honolulu.

The four divers headed for the nearest cathouse on Hotel Street, only to find out they had a two-hour wait in a line of white and khaki uniforms that stretched for three city blocks.

Tony, always the loner, decided to lose himself in one of the many all-day movie theaters in Honolulu, then try to find a good Italian restaurant, and maybe finish the day with a visit to one of the electric massage parlors that dotted Hotel Street. He heard they had been started by the Japanese, but had been taken over by enterprising Chinese and made even more exhilarating. He was not inclined to stand in line for any prostitute. "If you had to pay for it, forget it," he declared.

Later in the day, Moon and I carried the required helmets and gas masks over our shoulders and passed through the main gate of Pearl Harbor. The gate guards made no move to inspect the masks, so I felt confident that when the time came to transport the alcohol out of the base, we would have no trouble.

We lined up to wait for a nine-passenger

taxicab into town. It was driven by an enormous brown Hawaiian, who spoke fractured Kanaka pidgin.

"Where fo' you go?" he asked when we crowded into the cab. A hollow question, when everyone knew the Pearl Harbor taxis had only one route, directly to the Army-Navy YMCA in Honolulu and back to the station. They never picked up passengers or dropped them off at any other location.

As the ancient taxi chugged past Aala Park and passed over the narrow Nuuanu Stream Bridge, the stench of River and Hotel Streets assailed our nostrils. "Time to hold your noses, guys," I said, grimacing.

The stink permeated the area and was unlike any other I had ever smelled. Old China hands claimed it reminded them of the odors around the waterfronts of Shanghai and Hong Kong.

The best theory was that it came from the carcasses of animals and fish entrails hanging in the open-air butcher shops along the streets.

The cab moved slowly past the many dilapidated, ancient two-story buildings jammed together, each carrying a different name: New Senator Hotel, Ritz, Anchor, Service Rooms, and so on. They all had one thing in common. They were part of Honolulu's red-light district. By 10 A.M. the lines of patrons stretched four blocks down the street and disappeared around the corner.

The cab inched its way up the narrow, bustling

North Hotel Street to the Army-Navy YMCA. The Y was set back from the street, and its best feature was a beautiful courtyard in the front that was planted with majestic palm trees. It was an inviting sanctuary, but it was avoided by the divers, who disdained to enter its doors even to make a phone call. They claimed it was only for the use of guys who were lonely or homesick or teetotalers with nothing better to do on liberty. He-man divers looked for booze and women, not books, playing cards, or letter-writing material.

Across the street was the notorious Black Cat Café. It was housed in an old wooden frame building that had been painted at one time. Hawaiian weather had taken its toll, and the paint was checked and peeling. As with most other businesses along North Hotel Street, the Black Cat's front was open to the street. Sailors often used it as a meeting place, because everyone knew its location. However, only the unwary stopped for a drink. It was well-known as a clip joint to be avoided like the plague.

When we arrived at the Y my mouth was watering in anticipation of the succulent steak I planned to eat at Ernie's. Apparently Moon's appetite was focused on things other than food.

"I'll walk down to Ernie's with you, buddy, but then I think I'll mosey down to the Service Rooms and see if any of the old prewar hookers are still around. It's been a year since I was there, but maybe I'll see a familiar face. Sure you don't want to join me?"

"No, thanks."

Moon Visits Honolulu's Fairest

As Mullen walked away down the street he yelled back, "I'll meet you at Ernie's in a couple of hours. By that time I'll be counting on you to have the gals all lined up for a luau on the beach next week."

"Sure, sure," I replied, thinking that standing in a long line in the hot Hawaiian sun to visit a whorehouse was not my idea of a fun liberty. I didn't blame the other guys for doing it, but it wasn't for me.

My reverie was cut short as a cacophony of honking horns and other street noises blasted my ears.

I looked down narrow Hotel Street, made narrower by cars parked on both sides of the street, leaving one lane of traffic down the middle. Hundreds of pedestrians crowded the narrow sidewalks, pushing and shoving in their haste to reach their destinations. Traffic was stopped as soldiers and sailors crossed the street to reach the trashy attractions lining the sidewalks: souvenir shops selling junk; shooting galleries whose pretty attendants egged on the gullible to prove their marksmanship; photo studios with girls in hula skirts, eager to pose for a picture to send home; sleazy bars; mom-and-pop saimin (pork and noodle) shops (one of the few worthwhile businesses on the street); barber shops featuring Oriental girl barbers; electric massage parlors with signs depicting lightning bolts; and finally Ernie's, the only bar and grill in the area that employed Portuguese women and served delicious twenty-four-ounce steaks at a reasonable price.

I saw a long line of servicemen waiting to enter Ernie's, so I decided to get a haircut at one of the shops that employed lady barbers, to kill some time before Moon returned.

Afterward, I returned to the bar and grill and was happy to see the line was much shorter. I was finally motioned to a booth, after gorging myself on steak and french fries, I looked up and saw Moon frantically waving his arms at me.

I wormed my way out of the booth and approached Ernie, who was perched in his usual position atop a high-backed stool.

"Hey, Ernie, see the sailor with the black hair about tenth in line? He's with me. How about letting him in? He'll be sharing my booth."

Ernie motioned Moon to the head of the line amidst much grumbling and booing from the men ahead of him.

The waitress took his order, and we settled in to wait for it.

"Well, did you get your ashes hauled?" I said.

"Yeah, I think so. It's kinda hard to tell, when you're in and out as fast as I was. Let me tell you, friend, things are sure different from the way they were last year."

"I can imagine."

"No, you can't. Not till you've been there and seen it with your own eyes."

"I'd have to be pretty hard up to take on a prostitute under the present circumstances."

"Believe me, buddy, I was hard up."

Moon began by saying that war breeds many ironies, and perhaps one of the biggest was that while the general population of Honolulu was losing many of their civil liberties, the prostitutes of Honolulu were being liberated. For the general public, under U.S. Army martial law, full prohibition was in effect; most bathing beaches were closed to swimming, with barbed wire strung across the sand; stringent blackout rules were mandated; and a rigid nine o'clock curfew was enforced.

Before the attack on Pearl Harbor, prostitutes in the brothels off River and Hotel Streets had few, if any, rights. They were enslaved by the system, which decreed what they could do and when and where they could do it. There were many unwritten laws designed to keep them segregated from society. Not even the Negro slaves before the Emancipation Proclamation suffered greater deprivation of their freedom. The Honolulu prostitutes enjoyed only the rights the vice squad chose to allow them. They were nothing more than chattels to be bought and sold, their duties set forth by each individual madam until their contracts expired.

There was no running away or escaping from the system. Escape routes from Oahu were carefully monitored by the island vice squad. The only transportation was the weekly sailing of the commercial steamships or the clipper flying boats.

The girls were not allowed to leave one house to work in another unless both madams approved. The girls were subservient to the madams, completely at their mercy. More than one girl who tried to rebel against the system found herself at the business end of a rubber truncheon, swung by a vice squad officer. She was never hit or jabbed in the face, arms, or legs, because that would leave bruises and damage the appearance of the merchandise. Instead, she was beaten across the buttocks or stomach; painful but undetectable.

Moon continued to reminisce about his days in prewar Honolulu when he and a buddy went ashore and discovered the Service Rooms. He soon learned that cathouses around the world were pretty much the same.

The customer entered the main "bull pen" where the girls were assembled. There was always a jukebox blaring out the current hits of the day. Sometimes the girls danced with a pro-spective customer if the music was slow and dreamy. The girls paraded by the customer, and by word and deed apprised him of their wares. He was allowed to pat the merchandise, even pinch it gently to test for authenticity. Then the customer usually bought one or two drinks for himself, and a look-alike drink for the girl of his choice. Madams did not want the girls drinking alcohol during working hours, since this could impair their work and deprive the madam of her revenue.

After a few drinks to bolster his courage, the customer and his girl retired to a private room. After a reasonable period of time, not too long to seem unrealistic or too short to be embarrassing, the customer came out with a smile on his face and exited unhurriedly.

Moon said he soon found out the war and two million soldiers, sailors, and marines who passed through the islands had changed the procedures.

Under the U.S. Army's control, Honolulu prostitutes were emancipated to a degree never thought possible. Under martial law they were largely protected from the Honolulu Vice Squad. They could live away from the houses if they desired, and they were free to visit any place they could afford.

This change was mandated because of the huge influx of military men who needed to be serviced. Honolulu whorehouses were modernized to serve the largest number of customers in the shortest space of time, so that the fighting men would be taken care of promptly and efficiently.

Along with this degree of freedom, the prostitutes had to agree to sacrifice more for the war effort by increasing their production from a prewar output of ten to fifteen tricks per day to a new quota of more than one hundred tricks per day. The prospect of this new plan had most of the girls clutching their crotches in disbelief and dismay. But rising to the occasion, and displaying all the zeal and trappings that made Hawaii great, the girls set a schedule of work that had never been attained before.

By allowing an average of three minutes per trick, an enterprising prostitute could rack up her quota in five or six hours. This would net her about three hundred dollars a day after paying the madam her cut. By assuming a twenty-two-day work month, a hard-working girl could earn seventy or eighty thousand dollars a year, tax free. Also, every whore in Honolulu was guaranteed a full day's work for as long as her stamina held up. The long lines of fighting men patiently waiting their turns was assurance of this. The lines started forming shortly after 7 A.M. when liberty began, and as the day wore on, the lines grew longer and longer and tempers grew shorter and shorter. The men at the end of the lines became edgy and concerned that they would not gain entrance to the house before their liberty expired at 5 P.M. This would mean five long days before they could come ashore again, if in fact they were not shipped out in the meantime. Only the vigilance of the military police kept fights from erupting.

Moon's order arrived, and he began devouring great chunks of rare beef.

"So . . . tell me about your day with the ladies

of the night, or morning, as it happens to be."

In between bites of steak, Moon continued on with his favorite subject. He said it had taken him two hours to move up to the front entrance of the Service Rooms. When he reached the security door, an enormous Kanaka man opened it and grunted, "Ten mo'." Moon was one of the ten admitted.

He said the aroma inside reminded him of a men's locker room. The smell was a combination of disinfectants, sweat, bath powder, and tobacco smoke.

He said he could recognize the area as the old bull pen, but it had undergone some big changes. What had once been a relaxed, comfortable, uncrowded reception room now resembled Grand Central Station. The bull pen had been converted into a long passageway lined with doors covered with half-opened curtains. Inside the doors were small cubicles not more than ten feet square. Each room contained a rattan chair, a bed, and on the floor a lahala mat. In one corner, behind a screen, was a shelf with the tools of the trade: douche bag, towels, soap, and bath powder.

A huge Kanaka woman told him to point out the girl of his choice as the hurrying forms darted in and out of the curtained rooms. He said he had no idea who to select because none of the prewar girls were around anymore. Neither could he describe the type and color of the wearing apparel of his choice because the girls were wearing none. He finally told the woman he would take the blonde with big boobs in Number 4.

Once he made his selection, an Oriental mamasan herded him into the tiny room and told him he had three minutes to complete the sex act. She urged him to undress "chop-chop" and get ready for the arrival of "Missie F — F —"

Moon paused. "Can you believe the nerve of those broads, givin' a guy three measly minutes?"

"Well, how is Missie going to perform her one hundred tricks a day if she has to wait around for a bunch of slowpokes like you?" I laughed.

"If this keeps up, 'Wham, bam, thank you, ma'am', will become a more popular battle cry than 'Praise the Lord and pass the ammunition'," said Moon.

We Meet the Babes

Moon changed the subject as he gazed about the room, picking out the feminine figures tending bar and waiting on the many tables. "Ooeee. Those are some fine-looking ladies. Old Ernie is a lucky guy to have 'em."

I glanced over at the door where Ernie still sat on his stool regulating the number of military who could enter his establishment. Ernie was a brawny, overweight Portuguese, nearing fifty, who rarely smiled but occasionally pulled his heavy lips into a grimace that served as a substitute. His expression was one of constant concern

110

for the potentially explosive situation that was present at his restaurant. Far too many hungry, love-starved men were lusting after the few available girls.

I agreed that Ernie was a lucky fellow. There wasn't another café on the street that had a line waiting to get in. And I was sure it wasn't just the good food.

We watched as one of the girls paused to take a rest. She stood with an elbow hooked over the bar behind her, her rich body indolently curved. The men at the tables whistled, cheered, and stomped as she laughed, tossed her head, and headed for the kitchen.

"Wait till you've been in here a while and listened to these gals. They're a pretty independent bunch. They will tell a customer off in no uncertain terms if he gives them any kind of guff, and that goes for Ernie too. Just before you came in I heard the redhead yell over to him, 'Up yours with a broomstick, Ern'."

We lit up cigarettes as we watched the girls strut their stuff. The women working the bar were more attractive than the waitresses. I had my eye on the redheaded bartender, Hattie. She was well-built with eyes that flashed darkly in her olive-skinned face. She smiled seductively as she wiggled her hips and flirted outrageously with the customers, obviously enjoying her work. I'm sure she was not worried about the consequences of her actions, because liberty expired for her admirers at 5 P.M., well before she and her friends cleaned the restaurant and went home.

Mullen expressed some doubts about our chances of talking these Portuguese "dollies" into going out with us, even if we supplied the booze. While I had my doubts too, I was not about to admit it, at least not until we had given it the old college try.

I jabbed a finger at the tall bartender whose curly black hair was piled high on top of her head. As she leaned forward the blue cloth of her blouse was strained tight against her ample chest. We heard her repeat an order in a rather coarse, husky voice using the island pidgin English. "I think that gal is leader of the girls. She seems to have the most to say. Her name is Margaret. I think if we can convince her, the others will go along."

The island Portuguese community were direct descendants of sailors, fishermen, and explorers who had come early to Hawaii and made it their home. Many of them still spoke the language, though it had been many years since they thought of Portugal as their mother country. They tended to live and congregate among their own, finding it more comfortable, as many of the island minorities did, to mingle with the people who looked and behaved most like themselves.

I knew these girls had heard every line in the book. Their contact with servicemen and their own raucous people had helped them develop a vocabulary that matched Ben Apple's. I knew we had to come up with a good story, or they would laugh us out of Ernie's and shower us with a string of obscenities that would make a madam blush.

Our waitress came by and cleared the table. She was short with sturdy brown legs, a big rear end, and grapefruit-size breasts. She asked us if we wanted anything else.

"Yeah," Moon said. "What's your name?"

"Katie," she snapped. "If it's any of your business."

Moon asked her to tell Margaret we had some very important information that would be of great interest to her and her girlfriends. Katie walked away and then turned and gave us a long questioning look. Then she walked to the bar and whispered in Margaret's ear, jerking her thumb in our direction.

A few minutes later, Margaret left the bar and slammed through the swinging doors to the kitchen. We finished our coffee as Margaret entered the room again and headed for our booth.

"What do you two bubbleheads want with Katie?" she asked, noting the diving insignias on our arms.

"We have a proposition we know you'll be interested in —" I began.

Margaret raised a plump hand in a gesture of rejection. "Stop right there. I know what you're interested in, what every guy who comes in here is interested in."

113

"Look, Margaret, we want to invite you to a special party. Moon and I and four more of our buddies are planning a luau, Portuguese style." I emphasized the "Portuguese."

Her eyes widened, and she raised her black eyebrows. "Where did you hear the expression, 'luau, Portuguese style'?"

"I was here last year when I came in with the fleet and I overheard you and your friends talking about one of your outings."

"Then you must know that you need one special ingredient for that kind of party, and martial law has snatched it off the market. No booze, no luau!"

We could hardly believe our ears. This was exactly what we wanted to hear.

"That's where we come in," Moon chirped, a wide, happy grin crossing his face. "We wouldn't think of inviting you ladies to a party without providing the liquor. We've got enough for a luau every night of the week."

Margaret narrowed her eyes with a look of suspicion. "You wouldn't snow old Margaret, would you?"

"Hell, no. It's true. We've got it, and we want to share it with you and your girlfriends. If you could round up some canned pineapple juice, Ed can make some of his famous 'Sneaky Pete' punch, and we can plan a party Sunday after next. What do you say?"

Suddenly the woman's skepticism turned to interest.

"Well . . . maybe we could work something out," she said slowly. "I could sure use some fun. Let me kick it around with some of the girls. I'll be back."

We could hardly contain ourselves. We congratulated each other profusely, agreeing we were a couple of irresistible gobs, when we noticed Ernie glowering at us.

We had occupied the booth an overly long time. We had also commanded special attention from his head bartender, and he looked like he was ready to show us the door. But nothing short of dynamite could have budged us from that spot until Margaret returned and gave us definite word that the girls would cooperate. When she returned she said that Hattie, the redheaded bartender, was willing and Katie, our waitress, would go, and she was sure she could find enough party girls to satisfy all six divers.

We made plans to meet in two weeks. I figured we could remove the 5-inch shells from the *Arizona* within that time frame and wangle another liberty.

"Hey, kiddo, you never said where you were getting the booze." Then she put her hands over her ears and shook her head. "Never mind, don't tell me, I don't care as long as you get it. . . . and listen, you two, this better not be some kind of joke. Margaret's going to be awfully mad if you show up empty-handed." She turned and marched back to the bar, her ample hips swaying and stretching her blue skirt to its limits.

115

The news of the upcoming party and our success in persuading the feminine guests was told
in exaggerated detail as we gathered the divers
around my bunk that evening.

Everyone was excited by the prospect and
demanded that Moon and I repeat over and over
the description of each of the girls. Even Andy
and Martin hung around and listened and were
pleased that we'd had such luck.

"Shee-it, I want the one with the biggest, fat-
test butt," Ben shouted to no one in particular as
we disbanded and finally fell into bed after the
first liberty in two months ended happily.

Removing Five-Inch Projectiles

Our crew returned to the *Arizona* Monday
morning, anxious to tackle the job of removing
the five-inch antiaircraft shells from the after magazine, unaware of the problems awaiting us.

The removal of the five-inch projectiles from
the magazines proved to be a taxing and difficult
job. It was decided that the fastest and safest way
to gain entrance to the magazines was to cut
holes directly through the decks into the top of
the magazine spaces. A cargo net could then be
lowered straight down into the magazine, and
divers could load the shells into it. The net
would be hoisted by a crane to topside. We
began cutting the hole between numbers three
and four turrets.

Cutting the ten-foot-square holes through the
first few decks went along fairly smoothly,

although some difficulty was experienced burning through the heavy steel deck beams with the arc-oxygen cutting torch.

Bronco Bill was the first diver to try his hand.

"Juice on," came the command from Rush. We heard popping sounds and then some mumbled profanity.

"Juice off, topside. There's something wrong with this damn cutting torch. It won't cut through the deck."

"There's probably nothing wrong with the torch," I said. "It's probably the cork insulation on the overhead of the magazine that won't allow the molten slag to fall through. We'll jack up the oxygen pressure to about 150 pounds and see if that will blow the slag through."

After a few moments, we heard from Bill. "It's working fine now. I'm getting through okay."

Suddenly there was the muffled sound of an explosion and the water rippled and bubbled over the hole that had been cut in the deck.

Moon shouted down on the telephone. "Bill, are you all right? What's happened?"

No answer was forthcoming, and Bill's diving lines seemed to be hung up, preventing us from pulling him up.

"Get me dressed," I shouted. "I'm going down."

The tenders were just fastening my helmet when Rush's dazed voice came over the phone. "Where am I? The deck came up in my face and coldcocked me."

In a calm voice, Moon told him his lines were fouled — to clear them, and we would bring him aboard.

We brought Rush aboard and undressed him. The moment his helmet was removed, he looked around with a stupefied gaze.

He had suffered an angry cut on his chin that was bleeding profusely.

Martin said, "We'd better get some pressure against that cut. Use this handkerchief. I don't want you to bleed to death."

Bill held the balled handkerchief against his chin as we questioned him about the explosion.

"I don't know what caused it," he exclaimed. "But no bucking bull ever kicked me that hard."

The explosion halted diving operations for the next few days. After consulting the salvage experts it was decided that the most probable cause of the explosion was a mixture of fuel oil fumes and unburned oxygen from the torch, which formed a gas pocket on the overhead and then exploded when it was touched off by the molten slag or spark from the torch.

There seemed to be no solution to the problem except to reduce the severity of the explosions by cutting a few feet at a time, then wait for the gas pocket to bleed off through the cut made by the torch. This procedure worked fairly successfully in preventing another major explosion, but minor explosions continued to plague us.

Ultimately, we decided to continue cutting

into the magazine. A foam rubber strip was fitted over the lip of the metal breastplate to partially protect the diver's lip and chin from being cut when an explosion occurred. Andy was the man up for the first dive after Bill's experience.

"Hey, Andy," Ben laughed. "Let's see if our farmboy can take it on the chin."

Andy managed a nervous smile. "Don't worry about me, Ben. I don't mind making the first dive, unless you insist on doing it."

"No, thanks, sonny, I'll wait my turn. You can be the guinea pig."

I told Andy to remember to pull his suit bib up with his teeth and rest his chin against the foam rubber padding before he started cutting. Then he slowly descended into the total blackness of the interior of the *Arizona*, recovered the torch Rush had left behind, and began the job.

Everybody waited and watched. This dive would tell us what we would have to contend with while this job was in operation.

After a few minutes, small rumblings could be heard over the topside phone. I called down to Andy to stop cutting for a while and let the gas bubble bleed off. But before I could finish the message a loud *wahrummppph* reached our ears, and Andy came popping to the surface spread-eagle.

"Take in his slack, Tony," I shouted. "Let's get him over to the ladder and see how he is."

We all gathered at the ladder, and Moon opened his faceplate. "How you doin', pardner?" Moon asked worriedly.

"I th-think I'm okay. Kinda shaken up, I guess. This is not exactly the way I like to surface, though." He told us the bib and foam pad seemed to work. The breastplate had not cut him as it had Bill.

Then he asked to be taken over to the hole. "I'll drop back down, and see if I can finish the job. There's only about eight more feet to cut."

Bill and Ben looked at each other, raising their eyebrows in surprise.

Moon closed the faceplate, and Andy lowered himself once more into the access hole.

"By God, Raggedy Andy's got more guts than I gave him credit for," Ben said, in uncharacteristic admiration. "Bein' down there not knowing when the blowup is coming has got to scare the hell out of a guy."

Andy's obvious courage came as a surprise to us. He was a reserved man, and we had no idea he possessed such inner strength and resolve.

He stood five feet ten inches, with a lean frame and muscled arms that had forked many a bale of hay. He had bright orange hair that was so unruly he kept it sheared almost to the scalp. He didn't smoke or drink, and he saved every cent of his pay so that he and his girlfriend, Enid, could be married some day.

All of the divers except Cameron managed to exhibit the kind of physical courage necessary to overcome the terror of the frequent underwater blasts. The nerves in our bodies readied themselves for the inevitable explosion, and just as the tension was relaxed another shattering blast would occur. By the end of a four-hour dive, we were physically and mentally spent.

When it was Cameron's turn to dive, he developed various ailments: an ear problem, a stomachache, or a strained back muscle.

His acting was convincing enough to satisfy the doctors, as they placed him on light duty. But after all the holes had been cut through the tops of the magazines, all the mysterious aches and pains disappeared, and he became the healthy, chattering Cameron of old.

Cameron was a medium-size man, wiry, but stronger than he appeared. He moved in quick, nervous motions and seemed almost uncomfortable in his lean body.

Coarse blond hair framed his long, sun-browned face, sharp pointed chin, and hawkish nose. His mouth was a narrow line, the lips tight and thin. He was a Texan through and through and though he had been a runt as a kid, he told us he had taken up wrestling in high school to add muscle to his frame.

Once the opening was cut in the top of the five-inch magazine, we began loading hundreds of rounds of shells into the lowered cargo nets, then the shells were delivered to West Lock ammunition depot. Later they were reconditioned and delivered to the army for reissue.

After lights out that night I lay in my bunk, eyes open, thinking about the day's events.

Andy's courage made an indelible impression on me. I tried to remember the definition of courage my father had given me many years ago when I was a teenager. They were meaningless words at the time, a time when I thought I knew everything, but knew little.

My father's words finally came flashing back: "Moral courage compels truthfulness, makes a dependable quality, and gives a man the courage of his convictions. Whereas, physical courage is an unnatural thing and exists only when a person's character is strong enough to overcome the fear instinct sufficiently to prevent its taking charge."

Ben Finds a Bomb

The following Monday we finished removing the shells from the magazine.

Our next assignment was to explore and survey the damaged areas between frames 78 and 90 on the second deck of the *Arizona*.

Ben was the designated diver. He was dressed and waiting to don his helmet when suddenly Bill yelled to all of us to come and look at something on the port side.

We watched while tugs pushed and shoved the *Nevada* into dry dock.

"What a great sight," I remarked. "One down and five more to go."

The successful raising of the *Nevada* was made even sweeter when I recalled the skepticism voiced by Adm. Chester W. Nimitz and others who had thought her salvage impossible.

Apple's rough voice brought us all back to the present. "Damn it, guys. Either get me in the water or undress me. I'm hot as hell."

Tony led him over to the ladder, and he lowered himself to the main deck.

Soon after he had reported that he was at the hatch and was "undogging" it, his tone of voice changed to a roar. "Ouch! Goddammit, I fell into a hole in the deck, and my leg's caught. I can't get up."

Apple managed to extricate himself and discovered that the hole must have been made by a bomb. Because there was no apparent damage in the vicinity we assumed it had not exploded. He traced the path of the bomb through two more decks and found it in the walk-in meat freezer under hanging sides of beef.

He reported that the shell/bomb felt similar to the one I found earlier in the *Arizona* general workshop. I told him to bring the shell to the surface.

Ben rolled the two-thousand-pound shell out of the freezer, and we used a chainfall to lift it aboard the diving barge.

It was a fifteen-inch shell that at one time had been used by old U.S. coastal guns, long since obsolete. The U.S. imprint was clearly visible stamped into the base of the shell. Stabilizing fins had been welded to its base in order to give it the characteristics of a spiraling bomb.

The old shell had been sold to Japan years

123

before as scrap iron, and it had been returned to the U.S.A. with a vengeance. Ordnance experts came out, retrieved the shell, and sent it back to the Bureau of Ordnance in Washington, D.C., for analysis.

As we watched them haul the bomb away, Martin remarked, "One thing's pretty clear. Japan must have been planning their attack on the U.S. for years, or they wouldn't have retained old fifteen-inch shells instead of melting them down for scrap."

Portuguese Luau

Sunday finally arrived, the day we had looked forward to for so long, the day we were going to meet Hattie, Margaret, and her friends and have a real party.

Expectations were intense as Bill, Ben, Jimmy, Moon, and I got dressed in our immaculate white uniforms.

"Poor ol' Cameron. What a time to come down with 'cat fever'," Moon said as he adjusted his black neckerchief.

"Yeah, I guess he'll be in sick bay for at least two days. He's spent plenty of time goofin' off over there, but this time he was really suffering. I didn't think anything would keep him from going ashore today," Jimmy said.

"Damn," Ben yelled as he labored over the shine on his black shoes. "I'm nervous as a friggin' whore in a cathedral."

"The only thing I'm nervous about is getting

past those jarheads at the gate. If they catch us with that alcohol, we'll be in bad trouble," said Jimmy.

"Just pull the guts out of your gas mask and put the bottle inside like I'm doing," I said to him as I worked busily with the mask. "Hide the guts inside your locker so nobody finds 'em while we're gone."

"The marine guards won't catch us. We watched them for a long time the other day, and they didn't check a single mask," Moon said. "Raymer and I each have one bottle. Who wants to carry the other two?"

"Gimme one." Bill grabbed a pint.

"I got the other one," Ben said. "If these broads decide to stand us up, I'll have a party all by myself!"

We passed through the gate with no trouble from the marine sentries. We managed to find space in a cab headed for the Army-Navy YMCA, and I settled back, relieved at passing the first hurdle of the day.

"Geez, Moon, look at my hands. I scrubbed the skin off and still couldn't get the crap out from under my fingernails. The bunker oil gets into every pore, and nothing takes it off." I examined my stained hands. "I look like a damn auto mechanic."

"Ass why hard?" the cabdriver piped up, using the strange pidgin wordage.

"What say? I don't understand," Moon said.

"Tha's island talk for, life is tough for you folks, yeah?" the cabbie replied.

"Yeah, it's tough sometimes, when you're eating fuel oil all day."

The cab wound its way through North Hotel Street. The perpetual lines of uniformed men waiting to get into the whorehouses were blocking some of the side streets and causing traffic to inch cautiously along.

"Ovah deah, get plenny grinds fo' the money," recommended the driver, nodding toward Ernie's.

"Yeah," said Moon. "Whatever. This island pidgin is weird as hell. We'll have to get Margaret to teach us."

The taxi arrived at the Y, and we climbed out. I looked toward the Black Cat Café, hoping the girls had not changed their minds and backed out of the date. It had been two weeks since we had set things up with Margaret, and I had no way to reach her and confirm the party date. So I was relieved to see five of the girls grouped together, busily chattering among themselves, ignoring the whistles and wisecracks of the service men roaming the area. They were a bright spot on the street, their colorful sundresses and skirts contrasting with the white and khaki worn by the uniformed men.

"I see what I want," Ben said. "The little chubby one with the big boobs and the round butt."

"Well, for Chrissakes, let's don't stand here

like a bunch of high school jerks. Let's get over there and meet these island queens," Bronco said impatiently.

Margaret and Moon made the introductions. Margaret told us that one girl couldn't come, but things worked out well because Cameron couldn't make it either. I had already seen the red-haired Hattie and the short, stocky little Katie that Ben favored. Ben thought Katie looked like a series of circles: round little head covered with dark curls, round enormous eyes, the O of her little mouth, and balloonlike breasts and buttocks.

Josie was almost as tall as Margaret, with a finer bone structure but the same black eyes and hair. Her younger sister, Mary, completed the fivesome. All seemed to possess a hearty, indomitable vitality. "Okay, handsome." Margaret turned to Moon. "Where the hell's the booze you promised Margaret?"

"We couldn't carry it in the open," he answered, sidling up to her. "We've got it tucked away in our gas masks. Don't you worry about it, darlin'."

Margaret made it clear by her remark that the girls' basic motivation for being there was the booze and not the company. Our looks and personalities were bound to charm the girls later on, I told myself, but at the moment, Cary Grant could not have scored with them without a bottle of hootch.

"We'll catch the bus that goes past the Kahala

area," Margaret said. "There's a beach called Hanauma Bay. There's no barbed wire blocking it. We've been there for parties before the war, but nobody goes there anymore."

Our little group of hardy revelers climbed aboard the bus marked Kokohead and headed out toward Waikiki. Moon and Margaret paired off naturally. I found a seat next to Hattie. I thought her short bobbed hair showed a little individuality. Ben stuck with his original choice. Katie giggled incessantly at his colorful vocabulary. The other two men seemed perfectly content with Josie and Mary.

The bus found its way up King Street. Margaret became the self-appointed tour guide as she proudly displayed her knowledge of the sights of historic Honolulu.

"See that big tower on your right, down on the waterfront? That's the Aloha Tower. Back of you on the left is the Iolani Palace, built by King David Kalakaua in 1882." Her husky voice grew louder, presumably to capture the waning attention of her audience.

"Across the street is the statue of our famous King Kamehameha," she shouted.

The bus reached Ala Moana Boulevard and headed past Ala Moana Beach Park.

Margaret was not getting the desired attention and apparently decided to use other tactics.

"Hey, Hattie, remember when we had that big luau over on that beach and you and your boyfriend, David Nuuanu, got so drunk? You put on a hell of a show for us in the water. Remember? He took so long diddlin' you, I thought he'd fainted or somethin'." She laughed raucously.

Her statements brought the attention she desired, especially from the girls. Hattie's black eyes flashed with anger, and I was sure Margaret realized she might have gone too far.

The bus continued its journey to Kalakaua Avenue and turned right, taking us through the Waikiki district.

"That pink hotel is the Royal Hawaiian and next to it the Moana Hotel. They have the biggest banyan tree in the world right in their courtyard. That's Waikiki Beach." She pointed to the beautiful aqua water splashing vividly white as it sent breakers onto the sand. "It don't look very exciting right now, but before the war the surfers and war canoes were thick out there, riding the waves."

Margaret finished her role as tour guide and settled down in her seat next to Moon, teasing him about his long legs that were crowded awkwardly in the small bus space. For the rest of the bus ride around Diamond Head, the giggling and chattering continued unabated as girls and sailors became better acquainted.

We traveled past the lovely beaches of Kahala, which were strung with barbed wire and patrolled by soldiers, and on to Kealaolu Road and the intersection of Kalanianaole Highway. We finally swung right toward Kokohead and the end of the line. Margaret asked the bus driver to let us out on the bluffs above the bay, which was a few hundred yards below.

The bus driver released his happy passengers and turned the bus around for its return trip to Honolulu.

"What time does the last bus run?" Moon yelled to the driver.

"Four-thirty da last one, bruddah," he shouted back.

We walked down the steep pathway to the ocean below. No barbed wire ringed the sandy beach, and there was no sign of an army encampment.

I was delighted. "Look at those breakers out beyond the reef. They're perfect for body surfing. Wish I'd brought my trunks."

"Maybe we'll all go skinny-dippin' if we get drunk enough." Bill looked hopefully at Josie.

"Yeah, and maybe you'll s— if you eat regular," she shot back.

Ben threw his head back and howled with laughter. "I couldn't have said it better if I tried."

"Well, let's get with it," Hattie said. "Each of us brought a can of fruit juice, and I've got paper cups."

"And here's the good stuff." I smiled triumphantly, pulling the pint bottle proudly out of its hiding place and raising it high above my head for everyone to admire.

Everyone gave approving shouts except

Hattie, who cried, "Uh-oh! What are we going to mix the punch in?"

Moon stuck out his helmet. "We all had to carry one ashore along with the gas mask. We'll use a couple of these. We'll take out the lining, which leaves a nice little metal pot, ideal for mixing 'Sneaky Petes'." He laughed.

"Yessir, the good old U.S. Navy thinks of everything. They want us boys in blue to be happy," Jimmy said.

"Well, I won't be happy till one of you boys in blue takes those helmets down and rinses them out. I don't want hair oil floatin' around in the first good drink I've had in months," declared Margaret.

The punch was put together with one can of grape juice, one of orange juice, another of pineapple juice, and one pint of 190-proof ethyl alcohol. The purplish, sweet, innocuous taste belied the devastating strength and potency of the drink. The combination of the hot Hawaiian sun and high alcohol content soon turned the party into a raucous, lively affair.

The Portuguese luau was a smashing success even though nobody went skinny-dipping or got laid. But there were a few who staggered into the surf barefoot, with pant legs rolled or skirts held high; and there were some sloppy, alcoholic kisses exchanged as the party broke up, and we boarded the last bus into Honolulu. We thanked each other for one hell of a great time, and tearfully expressed regrets that it had to end so soon.

We vowed to meet again in two weeks for a repeat performance.

We caught a taxi to Pearl Harbor, arriving an hour over leave, and were placed on report.

Lieutenant Haynes was able to get our report slips for overleave canceled. He also issued a stern warning to us to get our tails back on time in the future.

We poured ourselves into the barracks, seeking the comfort of our bunks. However, sleep came fitfully, interrupted by twitching seizures as the effects of the harsh alcohol wore off.

"That hootch was pretty strong stuff," I said.

"Sure was," Moon replied. "It did something to our voices. I'm so hoarse I sound like I've got a mouthful of gravel."

"Yeah, for a minute I thought you were Tallulah Bankhead!" I laughed.

"Well, go to sleep, Tallulah. We gotta work tomorrow," hissed a raspy voice down the row of bunks.

Recovery of Bodies

Within a few months after the attack, the navy was pressured by Congress and the White House to bring up the bodies of the men who died on the *Arizona*. They felt it was imperative that they be given a proper burial. The navy argued long and hard behind the scenes against this proposal. Their primary objection was that none of the bodies, up to that point, had ever been recovered with heads or even finger flesh intact. Individual dog tags that had been worn around the neck for identification had fallen off in the murky water and been lost. Based on this, it seemed impossible to positively identify any of the bodies.

It also would have been heartless and cruel to describe the condition of the bodies to their families. There was no kind way to explain that scavenger crabs had devoured the exposed body parts.

The fact that bones placed in a hero's grave could be those of any one of the 1,177 killed on the *Arizona* seemed not to be a consideration. Rational arguments were ignored, and as Congress became more and more pressed by grieving constituents to bury their boys in an honorable fashion, nothing could deter them. They were determined to comply with their wishes. The army, responsible for burying the dead heroes, sided with Congress.

Early Monday morning, a flotilla of small boats arrived at the *Arizona*, commanded by an Army Medical Corps colonel from the army hospital. A large group of navy and army hospital corpsmen made ready to receive the bodies, put them in canvas bags, and transport them to Red Hill Cemetery for burial. The diving crew had not been notified of this plan, and we were not prepared for its execution. Ben was on his dive and was already inside the ship closing off doors and hatches when the medics arrived. We all agreed that Ben would not be the shining example of decorum to represent the team in such a delicate and emotionally charged atmosphere. So I called down to him and said we were bringing him up and that we had visitors.

"Whatta ya mean? Hell, I just got down here," he grumbled. "Who the f— are these visitors?"

By this time the last boat, carrying the colonel, was within earshot of the barge. "Never mind who they are, just get your tail clear and come up . . . and keep your mouth shut on the way," I answered in a hushed voice.

An army captain explained to us what the procedure would be. He asked if bodies were concentrated in any specific area of the ship.

I told him there were at least a hundred or more floating in the shop area. I said the divers could pull them over to the access trunk, and they would pop up to the surface.

We got Andy dressed and lowered him into the ship. Two of the small motor whaleboats stationed themselves on either side of the access trunk, and medics made ready to receive their cargo.

"Okay, topside, I'm sending the first one up," came the nervous voice of Andy. Then, "Oh God, my hand just went through him. Geez, I think I lost part of him through the shirt opening."

He finally got the corpse to the third deck trunk, and unfettered by bulkheads or wreckage, the body shot up to the surface. The collar of the shirt was buttoned, as were the cuffs of the long sleeves. Where the head had been, only a stub of an arctic white vertebrae remained, surrounded by rotted flesh. No identifying dog tags were visible around what had once been his neck. The flesh of both hands had long since been picked clean by the crabs, and only the finger bones remained.

The body floated in a spread-eagle position; the filthy cloth covered arms extended straight out from the torso. The areas of the body protected by clothing were bloated four or five times their normal size. The buttons strained at the buttonholes and seams were barely able to hold the expanded flesh intact.

One at a time, Andy sent up more of the nightmarish parcels. The medics in the boats had their hands full trying to keep up with the traffic. They tried to pick up the cadavers and stuff them into the canvas bags, but as they pulled them clear of the water and tried to haul them into the boats buttons popped off, seams split, and the putrid, malodorous flesh oozed out onto their clean white uniforms, and on the boats' decks.

It was the sickish, sweet, gut-wrenching odor of rotting flesh that made the recovery operation the most difficult. It flooded not only the air, but it seemed to cling to every article of clothing and enter every pore of the body. It was an odor like no other. Having once been exposed to it, it could never be forgotten. Months after handling and working with the corpses, I maintained I could still detect the odor on myself.

Many of the medics got sick and spent their time retching over the side. It became necessary to supply them with gas masks. But they soon discovered that working in the tropical sun, faces covered by gas masks, was hot, uncomfortable, and downright hazardous. The areas of visibility were considerably reduced by the masks, and the perspiration produced by the heat was blinding as it collected in their eyes. It was easy to make a misstep on the wet, slimy decks while performing the heavy lifting. We counted at least four of the medics who slipped, lost their balance, and fell heavily into the oily water.

Frustrated, exhausted, angry, the hospital personnel, their uniforms oil-soaked and ruined, finally set sail for the safe harbor of the hospital grounds with their grisly cargo of forty-five body bags.

Waving them off, Cameron remarked to Ben, "To think we were worried about insulting their ears with your foul mouth. I never thought them nice, clean 'Dicksmiths' knew that kind of language. They sounded like a whole boatload of Ben Apples!"

"Who could blame 'em," Ben sympathized. "But don't kid yourself, you friggin' deck ape. None of 'em can hold a candle to me when it comes to expressing the good old English language."

Cameron's attention turned from Ben, and he shouted at us to look at the weird sight coming down the harbor.

We gathered on the barge to watch the strange-looking ship sail by on her way around Ford Island, making a triumphant sweep through the anchorages to show the fleet she was proudly sailing for home. All hands were manning the rail in their white uniforms. The sharp-looking white-clad sailors stood at attention as they passed the *Arizona,* and we divers returned the honors.

The strange ship was the destroyer USS *Shaw.* It had been outfitted with a temporary bow fifty feet long. Instead of the long, graceful look of the "greyhound of the sea," as destroyers were affectionately known, the stubby bow made her look more like a bulldog. Regardless of how she appeared, all the assembled divers expressed a sense of pride in our country as we watched the first heavily damaged ship sail back to America under her own power, knowing she would be able to fight once more.

When the medics did not return the following day, we were informed that their experience with the recovery of the bodies had proved to the army that further efforts in this endeavor would be useless. Later the army and the navy convinced Congress of the futility of continuing the removal of the bodies from the USS *Arizona.*

Hot Money

Early in our investigative dives on the *Arizona,* it was proposed by one of the supply officers that we attempt to open the disbursing office safe, located on the second deck between frames 81 and 84. The officer allegedly had the safe combination. The safe contained tens of thousands of dollars, but more importantly, it contained the ship's financial records. Any money we recovered would be turned in to a federal bank for destruction.

Bill was the next scheduled diver. He was dressed and descended through the hatch leading to the second deck. I directed him down the ladder. When he reached the second deck, I told him to move to his right, which would lead him to the portside bulkhead. Then he was directed to keep one hand on the bulkhead and move to his right approximately twenty feet until he felt the fire hydrant about waist high. The door to the disbursing office was next to the hydrant. The passageway was jammed with debris, but Bill reported few signs of damage in the area.

He found the safe almost immediately. It was secured to the deck with bolts that were inaccessible. Bill took an underwater lamp with him, and we turned it on. He waited a few minutes for the sediment to settle, then he placed the light about three inches from the dial on the safe and reported that he could dimly make out the numerals on the safe's dial.

The supply officer read Bill the combination, but Bill failed to open the safe. After trying for two hours, we had to admit defeat. I suggested that we cut a square hole through the deck around the safe and retrieve it as we had done on the *Utah*.

Tony was up for the next dive. He took two wire straps, a chainfall, and the cutting torch with him. He attached the straps to the safe and suspended the chainfall to an overhead deck beam. He took a strain on the straps with the chainfall, so that when the deckplate was cut the safe would not fall through the hole. Tony attempted to cut a hole in the deck, but there was so much interference on the underside that he never made much headway. Both Andy and Martin tried their hands at cutting, but without much success.

We eventually decided to burn a hole in the face of the safe around the dial. Somebody claimed that this would release the four arms that held the door closed. This did not work either.

We considered burning a hole through the top of the safe but we decided against this because the molten slag would probably destroy the paper money and records.

Pappy Haynes was in a hurry to start work on the *California*, so he told us to forget the safe for the time being. We could try again later if we had the time.

The *Arizona*'s Back Is Broken

The following Monday as we were pulling away from the dock, headed for the *California*, the yeoman from Haynes's office yelled to me that

Lieutenant Commander Haynes wanted to see me. The new commander waved me into his office with a big smile. I saluted and congratulated him on his promotion. Later, all of the men agreed he certainly deserved it.

Haynes told me the Salvage Unit had received orders from the Navy Department to confirm or deny the eyewitness accounts observing the bow of the *Arizona* jump out of the water after the magazine explosion on 7 December.

If we found a crack in the hull that extended to the keel, it would prove the ship's back was broken and she would not be worth the time or expense to raise her. Conversely, if none were found she would be raised.

I told him we had tried to check out the midship section, forward of the firerooms, but because of the extensive interior damage we couldn't make any headway.

Haynes said we should survey the *Arizona*'s outside hull in order to determine the overall damage from the mud line to the turn of the bilge, a vertical distance of forty feet. This meant tunneling through mud and crushed coral every four frames, or at sixteen-foot intervals, for the length of the ship.

"If we do find a crack and have to follow it to the keel, it means we'll be tunneling down forty vertical feet and then almost fifty horizontal feet to the keel. I don't know how we can prevent the tunnel walls from caving in on us," I said.

Haynes was silent a moment, then asked, "Can you do it?"

I was not about to say no, although I had my doubts about this job. "We'll give it a try, sir."

We moved the barges to the starboard bow of the *Arizona* and made ready to start the survey. The first tunnel began about sixty feet in from the bow. This starting point was selected because it was determined that if there was damage to the outer hull from the 7 December explosions, it would have occurred somewhere in the area forward of number two turret. Eyewitness accounts of the attack claimed to see the entire bow of the *Arizona* blown out of the water, while other witnesses disputed this. Much depended on what we would discover.

We began to discuss the best way to accomplish the vertical tunneling operation.

The divers discarded the idea of using the navy's Falcon washout nozzle, because we didn't think it was suitable for tunneling through coral and mud.

The *Arizona* rested in forty-five feet of mud and coral. The dangers in this operation were very real. Cave-ins at the sides of the shaft were likely. When this occurred the diver would be buried under hundreds of pounds of mud and coral.

Tony scratched his head thoughtfully. "I just remembered something. I was watching some civilian divers in Pedro one time diggin' around some pilings on a pier. All they used for a nozzle were some pipe fittings." He continued, trying to recall the details. "On one end was a short length of pipe, and on the opposite end was another pipe the same size. They were shooting about 350 psi of water to the nozzle, but since one end offset the other in pressure, the diver could handle the nozzle by himself."

When Bill asked what kind of a hose they used, Tony remembered it was a regular fire hose.

"I like it," I said. "If we can rig it so the diver can swivel the nozzle, he could ride the hose down the side of the hull. He'd be able to use his feet to guide the nozzle, and have his hands free to feel the hull."

We built a washout nozzle using those features. Vertical tunneling began on the starboard side of the *Arizona*.

Since I had been the most enthusiastic about using the tunneling system, I decided to try it first. As I descended through the mud, I manipulated the nozzle with my feet in semicircular motions, while keeping one hand on the hull to guide my path. Suspended two feet over my helmet was an eight-inch-diameter suction hose connected to a dewatering pump. Debris from the digging was sucked up to the surface and discharged clear of the tunneling operation. The surging, upward thrust from the water jet pushed me up toward the surface until I made myself less buoyant by reducing my air supply.

There was zero visibility because of the tons of mud and coral being pushed upward past my helmet. The first fifteen feet of tunneling went smoothly and fast. By holding the fire hose with one hand I could extend my other hand and feel the side of the ship for three feet in each direction. The hull was smooth and undamaged.

I finally reached the turn of the bilge, where the hull curves under in a horizontal plane toward the keel. This was at a vertical distance of about forty feet. Suddenly, one of the sides of the tunnel gave way and buried me under what felt like tons of mud and coral. I managed to keep one end of the nozzle pointed upward and soon the suction hose was pulling the debris out of the tunnel. After I tunneled below the turn of the bilge, I started to work my way under the ship in a horizontal direction. I tried to clear a path without using the eight-inch suction hose to remove the mud, but it turned into a disaster. As fast as I cut through the mud and coral the tunnel filled in behind me. Unable to secure the suction hose in a horizontal position, it was impossible to tunnel under the bottom of the ship for a distance greater than fifteen feet.

Every diver experienced the same problem. By the time the turn of the bilge was reached, wholesale cave-ins were common. The first cave-in was always a shock, but we learned to live with them during the two weeks it took to complete the survey.

Ben made the second dive. Straddling the fire hose at the mud line, he positioned the eight-inch suction hose two feet above his helmet.

"Okay, topside, turn on the water," he shouted.

Three hundred and fifty psi of water pressure surged through the hose from the fire pump.

"She's working like a charm. Keep lowering the washout hose as I take it and lay out the suction hose the same length."

"Wait a minute, Ben, the suction pump must be clogged. There's no water coming out of it," said Bill.

"Yeeow, no water is comin' out of it because the friggin' suction hose is stuck to the top of my helmet. Turn the damn pump off, the suction's got me hanging suspended like a goddamn puppet."

We did as he asked, and he tunneled down until he reached the turn of the bilge. We again heard one of his great bellows.

"Holy s— , topside, the whole damn bottom has fallen in on me. Take a strain on my lifeline and see if you can get me clear."

"We're pulling on your line now. Just keep the nozzle pointed upward. That will break up the mud so the suction pump can carry it away," directed Bill, trying to calm Ben.

Ben emerged, his diving dress and helmet caked with sticky, slimy mud from the bottom. After he recovered his composure, we asked if he was able to feel any damage to the hull.

"No," Ben said, cleaning his hands of the

gluelike mess. "It's as smooth as a baby's bottom all the way down. But it's a bugger of a job gettin' down there."

Four more treacherous tunnels were dug alongside the ship before Moon discovered the crack that sealed the fate of the *Arizona.*

He had descended ten feet in the mud approximately 120 feet from the bow. He reported that the hull in that area was wrinkled and warped but had no cracks.

"Make a big sweep with both arms across the hull. You're in the area where the biggest explosion took place," I called to him.

"Uh-oh. Here it is right before my nose. There's a crack all right, and it's a big one. Must be at least a foot across, jagged as hell, and it extends down below in what feels like a slanted angle."

"We've got it plotted on the plans. Keep following it down to the bilge keel," I said.

Moon traced the crack farther and farther downward, feeling the opening in the side of the ship. But suddenly his anxious voice came through the phone. "Topside, topside, the tunnel has caved in on me, and it's got me pinned right up against the crack. I think my hand is cut pretty badly. Can you feel me pull on the line?"

I told him we could feel his signal. I sensed the panic in his voice as the mud and coral crushed him in its stifling grip. I had been through a similar experience a few days earlier, and even though my air hose was furnishing me with oxygen, I felt as if I was suffocating.

I reminded him to keep washing with the nozzle, and to keep it in a vertical position so he could clear the mud above his helmet. With his good hand he worked his way out of the mud, and we brought him to the surface. He had lost a lot of blood from a nasty three-inch gash in the palm of his left hand. He was hurriedly undressed and taken to the dispensary at Ford Island. He returned later that day displaying his bandaged hand.

No more cracks were discovered in the *Arizona*. But the big opening in the hull was evidence that her back was broken. There was no way to raise her intact. We continued tunneling to frame 78, but when no further hull damage was found the survey was discontinued.

There were now three options open to the navy. The first was to sever the forward section of the ship using dynamite. This would take months to accomplish, but would allow the after section of the ship to be floated and probably salvaged. The second was to flatten the ship with dynamite and drive her deeper into the mud. This would clear the quay, allowing other ships to use it. This second option was never seriously considered because the graves of the crew would be desecrated.

The third option was chosen. The plan was to cut off the superstructure above water and construct a memorial in tribute to those who lost their lives on 7 December.

When the decision was finalized, diving work was suspended on the *Arizona*. The two barges were moved, and we soon began work on the USS *California*.

V

USS California

Blanking Portholes

The *California* had been hit by two torpedoes and one bomb. A near miss tore a fifteen-foot hole in the bow and caused leaks in the gasoline lines, which would cause major problems later.

As with the *Nevada*, Japanese bombs and torpedoes alone did not sink the *California*. Rather a lack of watertight integrity and uncontrolled progressive flooding were the culprits.

Ultimately, the *California* settled on the harbor bottom with a five-and-a-half-degree list to port with the port side of the bow five feet under water, and the stern seventeen and a half feet under. Initially, experts from the Bureau of Ships in Washington, D.C., recommended that steel pilings be driven around the ship and the water pumped out, leaving the ship high and dry. Later this plan was modified to include concrete patches over the torpedo holes.

Our crew moored the diving barges to the port side of the *California*. Pacific Bridge contract divers had already started work constructing a wood cofferdam (or fence) around the quarter-deck and bow area that was underwater. The wooden sides of the structure extended approximately five and a half feet above the deck. The sides were held in place by angle-iron braces. We made the cofferdam watertight by using four-inch-diameter fire hoses stuffed with caulking material. These hoses were placed between the bottom and sides of the cofferdam and the hull to seal the joints.

The naval shipyard removed heavy items that were accessible above water: conning tower, mainmast, catapults, anchors and chain, cranes, and boats. While this was being done, our diving crew was given the job of isolating the damaged areas by closing off all interior drain lines, piping, ventilation lines, manhole covers, and portholes. To do this, we closed operable valves, drove wooden plugs into holes, and bolted down loose manhole covers. This phase of the work progressed rapidly and removed the need for concrete patches over the torpedo holes because the surrounding bulkheads were made watertight.

Closing and making dozens of portholes watertight was a different matter. Initially, Andy tried to close the glass ports from inside the ship, but many of the covers were warped and damaged from the explosions or the intense fires that consumed the ship. Additionally, most of the threaded portions of the porthole hold-down bolts were damaged and inoperable. Andy was brought up, and the diving crew held a planning session on the barge. We had to find a solution to the problem.

I suggested that we blank off the portholes from the outside.

"How about using wooden patches on the outside of the hull and angle-iron strongbacks inside to span the opening?" Bill asked.

"That's good," Andy said, "but it has a big drawback. There are too many interior obstructions around the ports, and we'll have a devil of a time trying to fit a strongback inside."

"The shipyard could cut some round metal blanks, and we could fasten them from the outside with a stud driver," I said.

"That might work," said Andy. "But how will the diver hold the plate and also fire the stud driver?"

"We'll have them weld a short piece of round stock or pipe in the center of the blank so the diver can hold it in place and fire the driver with the other hand," Moon said. The crew agreed that this approach would work best.

"I'll ask Pappy Haynes to have the shipyard make the blanks," I told them. "But we'd better bone up on handling a stud driver tonight at the shack. None of us has used one since we were in diving school. Remember that guy who tried to fire a stud into a piece of cast iron? Shrapnel almost put his eyes out."

The operation of the underwater stud driver was reviewed later that evening at the diving locker. The driver unit weighed ten pounds and had a firing barrel twelve inches long. The projectile was a half inch in diameter; the pointed end was hardened, while the other end was threaded. The shell casing contained the powder charge of a .45-caliber shell. The projectile was fired by placing its point against the surface to be joined and pressing the driver sharply forward. It could penetrate half-inch-thick steel plate.

The next day the metal blanks were positioned over the portholes, and we fired the projectiles directly through the metal blanks into the hull of the ship. This method of attachment created a satisfactory seal.

One week later we had blanked off all the portholes. The dewatering of the ship continued rapidly.

Solving the porthole problem was but one of many that was handled through informal conferences among the divers. Our joint efforts and input were invaluable to the salvaging of the ships. Most of the innovations that we devised and perfected were adopted by others who came after us.

Our diving crew was so pleased with the progress we were making on the *California* that we decided to skip chow at the mess hall and treat ourselves to cheeseburgers, french fries, and malted milk shakes at the yard cafeteria. After stuffing ourselves we ambled over to the diving shack trading friendly insults as we went.

"Hey, guys, what did you think of that cute little Filipino behind the cash register?" asked

Jimmy. "I finally got her to speak to me tonight."

"Why the hell would she notice an ugly kid like you?" Ben roared. "When a handsome devil like me is available."

"Listen, you fat tub, if she wanted a hippopotamus, she would visit a zoo. . . ." The voices trailed off as we neared the shack.

I had promised myself to write a letter to my mother, so I begged off from the BS session and headed for the barracks. I loved my mother dearly, but after working from sunup to sundown, I had to force myself to write letters. Every week or so I would suffer pangs of guilt, and I would take time out and write to my mother. No one else ever received a letter from me.

I Get the Runaround

It was 1 March 1942, and I still had not heard any word about my request for aviation cadet training. During the lunch break I visited Lieutenant Crowe's office on Ford Island. I knocked on his door.

"Come in, Raymer, I expected to see you before this. Have a seat." He pointed to the empty chair.

"I knew you would contact me as soon as you heard something about my request, so I didn't want to bother you if there was no news, sir."

"It's no bother, Raymer. But the holdup might be one of jurisdiction. Best you check with your command."

I was puzzled by this possibility and left the office, eager to contact Haynes and get my request back on track. Two days later the opportunity arrived. I related my conversation with Lieutenant Crowe to Haynes.

"I think Lieutenant Crowe may be mistaken," Haynes declared. "There may have been a jurisdictional dispute over your status at first, but that was resolved a long time ago. You should be hearing from the Navy Air Corps any day now."

I thanked him and left after being assured that he would keep me informed of any new developments.

The Second Attack on Pearl Harbor

The work on the *California* proceeded on schedule. Our crew closed off all watertight doors in the compartments adjacent to the torpedo damage in order to isolate any leakage from the patches on the hull.

We used oblong wooden patches and strongbacks to blank off manholes whose covers were left ajar or had been blown off.

The new dewatering pumps from the mainland were pumping out the water faster than it was entering the ship. As the main deck rose above the outside water level, additional topside weights were removed. The *California* finally stirred and struggled out of her muddy bed. Work crews came aboard and began clearing debris and draining residual water from the interior of the ship.

Everything pointed to an early and successful salvage operation. Then two incidents occurred that nearly turned the operation into a major disaster.

In the early morning hours of 4 March 1942, the *California* was rising slowly, inch by inch, thanks to the pumps in operation twenty-four hours a day. Suddenly, air-raid sirens were activated and all electrical power in Pearl Harbor was shut down in order to extinguish the illumination generated by electric lights, electrical welding, or anything that might be seen from the air by enemy planes.

A light rain blanketed the entire island of Oahu, and a dense mass of clouds shrouded Pearl Harbor — dismal weather for the Japanese pilots of the attacking planes. The engine sounds from the two enemy aircraft could be heard somewhere up in the pea soup mixture of weather. Shortly thereafter, the faint sounds of exploding bombs were heard off the entrance to the harbor.

The officer who planned the 7 December attack, Admiral Yamamoto, was not satisfied with the intelligence reports he had received afterward. Before he could execute a planned attack against the Midway Islands he knew he had to find the U.S. Pacific Fleet aircraft carriers he had missed at Pearl Harbor. They were at sea on 7 December. He also wanted to assess the damage done during the December attack and test the United States' defenses.

Consequently, early in the new year, the admiral ordered two Kawanishi aircraft, nicknamed "Emilies" by U.S. intelligence, to get good visual sightings of the devastation at Pearl Harbor and to drop bombs as a harassing action. These were long-range, four-engine flying boats with a bomb load of up to two tons, a cruising speed of 160 knots, and a flying range of five thousand miles.

On 15 February 1942, the two Emilies left their Marshall Islands sanctuary and flew to French Frigate Shoals, just six hundred miles northwest of Hawaii. They landed there in rough seas inside the reef. All through the late evening they took on fuel from two submarines.

The pilots waited a few days for calm weather and then took off for Pearl Harbor under a full moon. The pilots were confident they would find good, clear weather over Oahu and would be able to answer Yamamoto's urgent question regarding the whereabouts of the U.S. aircraft carriers.

They cruised at fifteen thousand feet and soon picked up the coastline of Oahu, sighting a lighthouse at the western tip of the island. But a light drizzle began and, suddenly, dense clouds covered the island. Nothing was visible from the air.

Shortly after 2 A.M. on the morning of 4 March a frustrated pilot in the first "Emily" dropped his bombs in the water a mile off the entrance to Pearl Harbor. Twenty minutes later the second pilot released his bombs, and they fell harmlessly in an uninhabited forest area in the mountains. These bombs dug craters forty-five feet across and fifteen feet deep, and uprooted a number of monkeypod and eucalyptus trees.

Both pilots believed they were over the harbor.

Ineffectual as the second raid on Pearl Harbor turned out to be, the shutdown of critical electrical power to the pumps on the *California* almost caused the ship to roll over and sink bottom side up. Fortunately, power was restored in time, the pumps were restarted, and the battleship regained an even keel.

The story of the air raid was printed in island newspapers, but it was buried in the back sections and given only a few paragraphs. Censors prevented the news from leaving Hawaii.

Finders Keepers

After the *Nevada* was dry-docked and the *California* dewatered and cleaned, crews of sailors and civilian shipyard workers swarmed over the interior of these two battleships. The crew's personal lockers were picked clean either by their rightful owners, if they were still in the vicinity, or by salvage crews as they systematically cleared the compartments of debris.

Many in the salvage teams also looted jewelry and large amounts of "black dollars" (the term used for U.S. paper money, when the green ink turns black after being submerged over a period of time in salt water). Since none of the unclaimed money or jewelry could be identified as belonging to anyone, salvage crews reasoned it was "finders keepers."

The ship's armories, where small arms were stored, were opened and the looting of their contents was of the highest priority. The .45-caliber service sidearm became the most coveted item of all the "souvenirs" pilfered from the ships. Salt water had rendered all of the pistol's parts rusty and useless, but the frame, with its identifying serial number stamped thereon, could be reconditioned by reblueing. Also, the serial number could be used by gunner's mates to requisition new parts for the remainder of the gun.

Our diving team retrieved .45s from the armory on the Arizona. In a trade-off with an accommodating gunner's mate at the submarine base, we all had newly reconditioned guns for the price of one pint of our stashed alcohol.

Our crew made a solemn pact never to give away or sell our pistols to anyone. None of us considered the .45-caliber pistols we found on the *Arizona* to be stolen items. If we had not brought them up and reconditioned them, the guns would have been lost forever, we reasoned.

The U.S. government did not share this view with us and the salvage teams. The first inkling that there was a basic disagreement in philosophy came early at the end of the fourth week of work on the *California*.

We were summoned to the diving locker by Lieutenant. Commander Haynes. He was waiting for us in the company of two civilians dressed neatly in suits and ties.

"Men," Haynes began, "this is Mr. Smith and Mr. Matheson, special agents of the FBI. They are here to investigate the theft of .45-caliber pistols, which they have reason to believe might be in your possession."

I was stunned by this statement, and from the look on the faces of my shipmates, they were too. We had covered ourselves with the promise never to sell the guns, and I had no idea how the FBI could have singled us out for investigation. Several of the guys shook their heads in the negative.

After a gut-wrenching pause, Mr. Matheson stepped forward.

"Which one of you is James Willson?" he asked in his clear, cultivated voice.

"I am, sir," Jimmy answered, fear gathering in his eyes.

"I have a warrant for your arrest," Matheson announced simply. "You are charged with theft and selling government property, to wit, a .45-caliber automatic pistol. These are felonies under federal laws. You are advised that anything you say can and will be used against you in a court of law."

Jimmy blanched at the accusation. His young, innocent face turned pale. He stood very still, his back rigid, but his hands were trembling visibly.

The rest of us averted our eyes and studied our shoes or our oil-stained hands. It was a bad moment for everyone.

Alarming thoughts were racing through my mind. What had possessed Jimmy to sell his gun when we had all given our word we would not? When he was questioned further, he could very well implicate all of us. We were certainly guilty of retrieving them. But they would have rusted away on a sunken ship if we had not recovered them and replaced the parts.

Special Agent Matheson shifted his intense gaze from one man to the next. He cautioned us that if any of us had been foolish enough to steal government-owned pistols, now was the time to come forward and confess.

Toe studying became more concentrated, but no one spoke up or came forward. The silence was deafening.

Lieutenant Commander Haynes ended the meeting. "I have recommended that the Repair Unit's commanding officer conduct a barracks inspection the first thing in the morning," he said tersely.

Special Agent Smith stepped up to Jimmy, took him in custody, handcuffed him, and led him away. Jimmy dropped his head as tears welled up in his eyes. He looked back once at those of us he had worked with so long, knowing the days that had been filled with camaraderie were over. He appeared to be overwhelmed with fear and despair, as he walked, shackled, between the two agents like a common criminal.

After the door had closed, Haynes pulled out his handkerchief and wiped his forehead wearily.

He settled himself on the edge of the weathered table as our agonized crew shifted positions and waited for him to speak.

"Some of you probably think Willson's arrest was chickens— ," barked the old diving officer, "but serious implications go far beyond this one incident. A rash of lost ID cards has been reported among naval units, and this is a constant threat here in the islands. ID cards are missing, loose pistols are floating around . . . so we've got a dangerous situation that cannot be tolerated. Now, if any of the rest of you have mistakenly acquired a .45, get rid of it! I don't want to see anybody else arrested."

They could have arrested half the guys out here on worse charges, I thought. Why did they have to pick on one of our guys? We all felt a brotherly feeling for Jimmy. He had always seemed a little younger than the rest of us. Seeing his pathetic figure being led off in handcuffs like a common murderer produced a feeling of rage in all of us.

"The information the FBI gave me is rather sketchy," Haynes explained, "but it isn't confidential, so I guess I can tell you most of what I know about the case. Willson evidently sold or gave a .45 pistol to a Mr. Santos, a Filipino navy yard worker. Santos got drunk on his day off. He got into a fight with his wife and threatened her with the gun. It wasn't loaded, but she didn't know that, and she called the Honolulu police.

"When the police arrived, they disarmed

The author in late 1944 at the experimental diving unit, Washington, D.C.

Map of Pearl Harbor, Hawaii, as it looked on 7 December 1941.

My diving mate and friend Moon Mullen. I am on the right. Photo was taken in a night club in San Francisco in February 1943 while we were on thirty day survivor's leave as a result of the sinking of the *Seminole*.

Unidentified diver — probably taken aboard the *Oklahoma* after the ship was righted. This is a representative photo of what we oil-covered divers looked like while we worked to close off the fireroom uptakes.

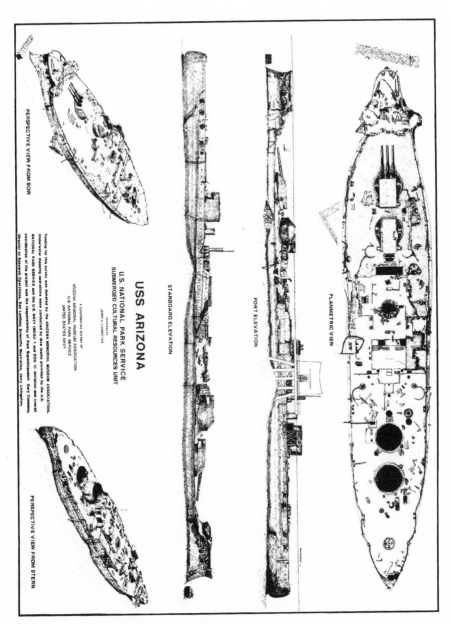

PERSPECTIVE VIEW FROM BOW

PERSPECTIVE VIEW FROM STERN

STARBOARD ELEVATION

PORT ELEVATION

PLANMETRIC VIEW

USS ARIZONA

U.S. NATIONAL PARK SERVICE
SUBMERGED CULTURAL RESOURCES UNIT

PREPARED BY
JERRY L. LIVINGSTON

A COOPERATIVE EFFORT OF
ARIZONA MEMORIAL MUSEUM ASSOCIATION
U.S. NATIONAL PARK SERVICE
UNITED STATES NAVY

Funding for this survey was donated by the ARIZONA MEMORIAL MUSEUM ASSOCIATION. Underwater mapping operations were conducted by dive teams provided by the U.S. NATIONAL PARK SERVICE and the U.S. NAVY (MDSU 1 and EOD 1). Initiation and overall coordination of the project was the responsibility of Park Superintendent Gary Cummins, Director of Research Operations, Dan Lenihan. Scientific illustration, Jerry Livingston.

Planmetric view of the USS *Arizona*.

USS *Arizona*, 12 December 1941.

USS *Oklahoma* righted to thirty degree position. Note hole (bottom, left) where smoke stack is broken off. Fireroom uptakes directly below stack. Ford Island Naval Air Station in background.

USS *Oklahoma* capsized. USS *Maryland* to the right.
(Courtesy USS *Arizona* Memorial, National Park Service)

Commencement of righting operations of USS *Oklahoma* at Pearl Harbor, 8 March 1943. (Courtesy U.S. Naval Historical Center)

USS *Nevada* showing bomb rupture on bow, forward of Number One turret. (Courtesy U.S. Naval Historical Center)

USS *Nevada* hull patch being delivered in February 1942 for use in repairing torpedo damage. Patch was later abandoned when it didn't fit. (Courtesy U.S. Naval Historical Center)

USS *Nevada* view taken 17 February 1942, salvage operations underway. (Courtesy U.S. Naval Historical Center)

Portside *West Virginia* in dry dock, cofferdam patches removed. Note damaged armor belt on side.

USS *West Virginia* sunk, pinning the *Tennessee* to the docking quays.

View showing the debris the divers contended with in USS *West Virginia*. Note dud fifteen-inch shell/bomb in foreground. (Courtesy U.S. Naval Historical Center)

25 May 1942, removal of the fourteen-inch guns of the USS *California* in order to lighten her draft prior to dry docking. (Courtesy U.S. Naval Historical Center)

View taken showing bottom of *Utah*'s hull after she capsized during the Pearl Harbor attack, 7 December 1941. (Courtesy U.S. Naval Historical Center)

USS *Utah* at the completion of first pulling period. Note entrance hole we cut to remove the ship's store safe. Ship is in about the 68-degree position. (Courtesy U.S. Naval Historical Center)

USS *Seminole.*

Eleanor Roosevelt greeted by admirals Ghormley and
Furlong. I was later introduced to her and took her on a
brief tour of the *Oklahoma* in September 1943. (Courtesy
Franklin D. Roosevelt Library)

Salvage operations on the USS *California* showing the cofferdam arrangement on the bow. (Courtesy U.S. Naval
Historical Center)

Santos and recognized the pistol as a military .45, so they turned it over to the FBI. They, in turn, sent the serial number in to the bureau in Washington, D.C., and discovered that the gun had been issued to the USS *Arizona*. And . . . since she was sunk, the only logical explanation was that a diver must be the culprit. When they confronted Santos with this information, he turned State's evidence and named Willson as the person who sold it to him. That's the story, and it is unfortunate. So I hope none of you are foolish enough to keep illegal money or guns in your possession." He looked around grimly, and we knew he felt as badly about Jim as we did. He turned abruptly and left the room.

A dejected diving crew returned to the barracks. The information about Jimmy's arrest and the subsequent barracks inspection spread like wildfire throughout the compound.

By dawn the next morning, the grounds outside the three barracks housing the Salvage and Repair Unit were littered with abandoned .45s, rings, watches, black money, and other looted items. The master-at-arms force was kept busy for hours stuffing seabags full of the contraband for disposal.

"Did you guys see all that crap come outta the barracks windows?" Ben asked. "A guy could get bonked by flying objects if he'd been wandering around out there last night. That Haynes is one pretty slick S.O.B. He got everybody to unload their loot without an inspection or another arrest, with no questions asked."

Another Luau

The next day was Sunday and our second party with the island girls had been planned for this date. The crew asked me to break the news of Jimmy's arrest to the girls, and as Moon and I rode together into town, we traded ideas how I could accomplish it.

The lead cab, carrying Ben, Bill, and Cameron, arrived at the Army-Navy Y first, and they were waiting impatiently across the street at the Black Cat Café, the designated meeting place. When Mullen and I arrived in the second cab, the girls still had not appeared.

"Have you decided what you're going to tell the girls?" Cameron asked.

I shook my head and said I didn't want to tell them the truth but that I hadn't come up with a good story.

"Lyin' is definitely the way to go. We sure don't want the girls to think we're a bunch of thieves!" Ben said emphatically.

"Yeah, I don't give a damn what Uncle Sam says, we didn't steal from nobody when we rescued them .45s. And we sure gave them back in better condition than we found 'em," Bronco exclaimed, each word punctuated with self-righteousness.

Cameron nodded in agreement. "You got a good point there, Bill, but it wouldn't convince the ladies. How about we say Jim is in the hospital with the clap?" He looked around for approval.

"Naw, they might think some of the rest of us got it, too," Bill said thoughtfully. "Maybe he ought to have one of those fatal noncatching diseases, like heart failure."

"Hey, I've got it," Moon said. "Let's have him transferred to a ship going to the war zone, then he'll be a big hero."

We all agreed this was the best story we could come up with, and we were embellishing on the details when the girls arrived.

Margaret was wearing a bright yellow muumuu with huge red flowers printed in the fabric. She was as exuberant as ever, taking charge of the group and herding us toward the bus.

We introduced Cameron to the girls and said he was taking Jimmy's place.

"So where's Jimmy?" Hattie asked.

"Old Jimbo got shipped out on a tin can last Wednesday, headed for the southwest Pacific," Cameron lied, not waiting for me to break the news. "Yeah, Jim's goin' to see the fightin' first-hand on that destroyer," he continued gravely.

"Oh yeah? Which one?" Margaret asked.

Cameron was at a loss. "Er, uh, uh . . ."

Moon took over smoothly. "Now, Margaret, you know that's a military secret. But listen, baby," he deftly changed the subject, "you better love me quick, 'cause I just might be the next to go." He laughed as he dodged the playful

179

punch Margaret aimed at him.

We piled into the bus, anxious to get the party going and forget Jimmy's arrest.

The bus traced its route around the island and dropped us off at the familiar beach. We trooped down the winding pathway as we congratulated the girls again and again on their choice of this secluded paradise.

A batch of the potent punch was put together with several of the girls taste-testing, offering advice for its improvement, and complaining a bit about the hoarseness they had experienced after the last luau.

"Don't complain, ladies, you may lose your voices, but it will clear your sinuses and keep you regular," chortled Ben, taking a great gulp from a paper cup.

The sun beat down on our little band of boozers as we refilled our cups time after time. The heat and alcohol soon produced a variety of emotions: mellowness in some, raucousness in others, and in Margaret and Moon a feeling of amour. The two of them wandered off together, leaning against each other for support. Moon spied a likely rock and backed Margaret up against it, probably hoping it would prop her up long enough to allow him to make love to her.

Margaret lifted her bright printed muumuu, cooperating, as Moon took aim with one eye closed to judge the target more accurately, he said later. Margaret was reverting to her native pidgin English. "Hey, you gonna diddle Mar-

180

garet so far away? You get closer mo' bettah see?" she jabbered. "Why fo' you got eye closed, you silly haole?"

"Cause, dammit, there's two of you when I look out of both of 'em. You gotta hep me, Margo."

"What you call me Margo fo'? Tha's not my name. You make fun of Margaret?"

She dropped her skirt and pushed Moon over backward in the sand. She flounced past me and headed down the beach taking two steps forward and one backward trying to find her way back to the party.

I followed her down the shore explaining that Moon was using a pet name and wasn't insulting her. But I could see she wasn't buying any such explanation, so I returned to the amorous arms of Hattie, who had suggested we cool off in the surf.

Hand in hand we staggered into the water and waded in up to our chests. I lifted her up as she clasped her legs around my waist. Our water games were going as I had hoped, and she was squealing happily when a huge wave crashed over the protective reef and knocked me off my feet.

I cursed my miserable luck and released Hattie, who disappeared into the froth of the wave. She surfaced, sputtering and swearing after swallowing a mouthful of salt water.

I splashed my way over to her, anxious to continue our liaison. But as I tried to embrace her she grabbed my arm and howled.

"What's the matter, baby?" I asked numbly.

"I stepped on some coral. My foot's cut, and it hurts like hell!" she wailed.

I helped her through the surf onto the sandy shore and examined the wound. There was a small gash on the sole of her left foot, and it was bleeding profusely.

I managed to find a clean handkerchief in my jumper and wrapped her foot in it as she watched me contentedly.

"When you get back to town," I said, "you'd better see a doctor. Coral can cause an infection pretty easily."

She gazed at me quizzically. "You really care what happens to me, don't you, honey? I'm not just another broad to you, am I?"

"Of course I care. You think I want you to bleed to death?" I laughed.

"Maybe . . ." she said slowly. "Maybe, if you could get overnight liberty you could stay at my house, and we would have a little more privacy." Her brown eyes searched my face beseechingly.

My mind was working quickly. An overnight liberty wasn't easy to come by, but I had a yeoman friend in the front office who might help me.

"I know you'll work something out, honey." She reached for my hand, and at that moment I thought she was the most desirable girl on the island.

The sun was low in the sky when the party

broke up. Moon had convinced Margaret of his innocence by telling her she reminded him of a beautiful screen star named Margo, and after grudgingly deciding this was truly a compliment, she accepted his explanation and apology. They kissed and made up and had a fine afternoon after all. After they boarded the bus with arms entwined, Margaret planted herself solidly on his lap and sat there during the ride back.

I lay on my bunk that night after lights out, the effects of the alcohol slowly wearing off. I pondered the vicissitudes of life and women in general. It had taken a piece of coral, a cut foot, and my concern over an injury to transform a casual beach party intimacy into something more promising.

I studied the possibilities of this happening on an island where the ratio was ten thousand males to each available female. The odds were so awesome, I fell asleep.

Early the next morning I contacted the yeoman and asked about the possibility of obtaining an overnight pass.

"Legally?" my friend asked. "Not a chance, but I'll tell you what I can do. I'll type out the form for you and leave the ink pad and signature stamp in the right-hand drawer of my desk. When you get in tonight after work, if you should find the overnight pass and stamp, I won't know a thing about it. If you get caught, I'm goin' to deny any knowledge of how you got the pass. Understand?"

Helping Jimmy

Three days later the crew was in the diving shack doing maintenance work on the diving gear: patching dresses, renewing frayed hoses, and checking the general condition of the equipment.

There had been a dark cloud hanging over the group since the arrest of Jim Willson, but no one had addressed the problem.

"I don't know how the rest of you feel, but I think we should get off our duffs and help Jimmy," I said.

"I agree," Ben said, "but I don't know what we can do."

We formed a plan. We decided to approach Pappy and confess, as a group, to taking .45s off the *Arizona*. We figured there was no way he would take punitive action against us, because we were vital to raising the ships. We thought he would find it unfair to punish Jimmy when none of us would be charged with an offense.

Ben said it sounded like good old-fashioned blackmail to him, and he was sure as hell for it.

I was sure that was true, but we felt we had to fight fire with fire. None of us felt it was a criminal act to recover the guns when we knew they would be lost to the elements if left on the sunken ship. We also knew that Pappy Haynes was our biggest supporter. He would help Jimmy if he had the opportunity to do so. We had to hope the federal court was over-crowded with cases and would send Jimmy's case back to our command for trial and punishment. Otherwise,

184

no matter what blackmail we used, Haynes wouldn't be able to influence the outcome of the case.

We trooped over to Haynes's office and offered our confessions. He heard us out and then said, with a twinkle in his eye, "I never heard a word you said."

Somehow, I knew he would do whatever he could to help Jimmy and that was all we could hope for.

Later, Ben and I walked over to the brig to visit Jimmy.

"How are they treating you?" I asked.

"Okay, I guess," Jim said. "But I'm not going to get fat on the food." He tried a small smile, then sobered and looked earnestly at us.

"I'm sorry as hell about this mess. I know what you guys must think of me, and that's worse than the punishment," he said.

"Forget it, Jim," Ben said. "We were just as guilty as you, but you got caught. The crew is grateful you didn't rat on us."

"Hey, I wouldn't do that. At least give me credit for doin' something right," he said.

We asked him why he sold his pistol. We pointed out that the crew would have loaned him money if he had needed it. He said he had not sold his gun, but had given it to the father of the Filipino girl he had been trying to romance. According to Jimmy the girl's father didn't want his daughter dating a sailor, but one of his hobbies was guns, so Jimmy decided to butter him

185

up by giving him his .45. Afterward, Jimmy said, he was taken into the family like a long-lost son.

Jim said the irony of the entire affair was the fact that the day he was arrested he had arranged to spend the night with the daughter.

"How's that for lousy timing?" he said.

On the way back to our barracks Ben said, "That's gotta be the most expensive piece of tail the poor devil never got."

Eventually the charges of stealing government property and selling it were reduced to a single charge of unauthorized possession of government property. After that, the U.S. Attorney in Honolulu declined to press charges. Jimmy was released from custody and was promptly transferred to new construction on the East Coast of the United States.

An Evening with the Divers

One evening after chow, Moon and I decided to walk over to the yard cafeteria and get a milk shake and a pack of cigarettes.

We walked lazily down the darkened navy yard road. The only illumination during the blackout conditions came from the blue-shaded lights marking the roadway. We reached the cafeteria entrance and walked through a zigzag maze that prevented the light from within reaching the street.

As we sipped our drinks, our conversation turned to the upcoming overnight dates with Hattie and Margaret. The two girls shared the same house. When Hattie told her roommate of our plans, Margaret had invited Moon to join us. Moon was apprehensive about the visit. He became such a worrywart about going that I finally told him if he didn't want to go I'd take care of both girls. He had a week to think it over. Our date was set for the following Saturday, and he finally decided the prospects were too good to back out after all.

It was early, so we wandered over to the diving locker to listen to stateside music on our old radio.

Ben and Bill were already there when we arrived. The radio was blaring out the music of Tommy Dorsey, and Sinatra was crooning "There Are Such Things." The cries and moans from the bobbysoxers were audible in the background. Ben shook his head disgustedly.

"Will you listen to those stupid little twerps swooning over that skinny clown?" Ben grumbled. "Why haven't they got his butt in the army?"

"I heard he's got a punctured eardrum," Moon said.

"Hell, half the divers I know have busted eardrums," Bill added.

The men continued to grumble over the talented vocalist, so Moon finally leaned over and twisted the dial until he picked up the sweet sounds of Glenn Miller's "Moonlight Serenade." The four of us relaxed as we listened to the nostalgic music broadcast from home. Each of us recalled where we were when we first heard the haunting serenade.

Later, as thoughts of home crowded my mind, we strolled the short distance back to the barracks. The moon was up now, silvery through the thin layer of cloud, and it lighted our way as the fragrance of plumeria blossoms filled the cool night air.

I tossed and turned in my bunk trying to overcome the feeling of homesickness. But the darkness and inactivity of the night only accentuated the longing for the pleasant days of the past. All my good experiences became great ones. Any bad experiences became comical. Girls who were only friends became lovers. Finally the ache of loneliness lessened, and I fell asleep.

A Replacement Diver

Jimmy's transfer created a need for another diver, so I received permission from Haynes to recruit and train a diver to replace him.

We selected Tom Cary, a shipfitter second class. Cary was a strapping twenty year old with a ready smile and a willingness to work that impressed us. For two months he had been hanging around the diving barge after he finished his regular work. He asked questions, observed the repair of equipment, and even helped us clean and store the diving gear for the night.

After attending a three-week diving course at the Pearl Harbor Submarine Base, Tom Cary was designated a second-class diver.

As usual, Ben had something to say about it. "Hope those pantywaist first-class divers over at the escape tank didn't ruin you, Cary. We'll teach you more about diving in one week than you'd learn over there in a year."

Martin Is Trapped

The work on the *California* proceeded on schedule. Our team closed off watertight doors in the compartments adjacent to the torpedo damage in order to isolate any leakage from the patches on the hull. We used oblong wooden patches and strongbacks to blank off manholes whose covers were left ajar or had been blown off.

Cameron's previous dive was devoted to closing watertight doors and hatches contiguous to the torpedo holes. He had been unable to dog two of the doors closed because the decks and bulkheads in the area were warped from the explosions and fires.

It was the last dive of the day, and it was Martin's turn. We sent him down with wedges and a sledgehammer to force the two balky doors closed. Ben manned the phones and was directing Martin to the site of the doors. Martin reported that he was encountering distorted bulkheads, and in one area the overhead was caved in to such a degree that he had to bend over to get past the damage.

He finally reached the forward-most door he was seeking and managed to force it closed by

189

driving steel wedges under the dogs of the door. As he moved aft to the next door, we heard a thump.

"What was that noise, Martin?" Ben asked.

"It feels like one of those big ventilation motors. Its fan housing has fallen off the over-head," Martin answered. "It didn't land on me, but it has me trapped in a corner."

"Are you hurt? Can you move it?" asked Ben.

"No, I'm not hurt, but this weighs a ton. The motor is pressing against my lower body, but I still have some feeling in my legs. Part of the housing is jammed on top of my helmet."

Ben had boasted previously that he could move anything with a wrecking bar, so we sent him down with the bar to move the motor.

Amid much swearing, huffing, and puffing, Ben was able to move the motor enough to relieve the pressure against Martin's legs. The housing and its attached ventilation line pre-vented moving the motor sufficiently to com-pletely free him.

It was now 10 P.M., and it did not appear that we could extricate Martin before morning. I sent Andy in to notify Pappy of the situation and also to request that he send out an additional air compressor as a backup air supply.

Both Haynes and the compressor arrived on the *Maryann* as we were lowering Bill to try his hand at freeing Martin. Ben seemed to think that if a chainfall was attached to the motor and pulled from the side, both the motor and housing would swing away and free the diver.

Bill tried this tactic, but instead of the motor moving out of the way, it rotated and pinned Martin tighter into the corner.

Finally, we realized that we had to cut the large ventilation line. Tension was maintained on the motor with the chainfall as Moon severed the line with the arc-oxygen cutting torch. The motor and housing tumbled on its side, and we were able to bring Martin to the surface at 4 A.M.

Again, it was apparent we had to use trial and error to solve many of the problems we encountered.

Explosion on the *California*

The closure of fittings and the isolation of damaged areas on board the *California* continued. Most of the residual water had been pumped out. She was readied to move across the harbor and into dry dock. Then a second disaster struck.

A violent explosion rocked the bow section of the ship below the third deck level. The blast blew open a hatch on the third deck, allowing water to flood the lower levels. In addition, a large patch covering a fifteen-foot by fifteen-foot hole in the bow was blown off by the force of the blast.

At first sabotage was suspected, because in those post–Pearl Harbor days most military men never quite accepted the fact that resident aliens of Japanese extraction were loyal to their adopted country. Bitter memories of the duplicity and the sneak attack by Japan were too vivid and recent for rational judgments. Resident Japanese in those days were not to be trusted.

It was finally concluded that gasoline vapors had accumulated in the space below the third deck from leaking gasoline lines. The spark that set off the explosion came from a short circuit in the temporary lighting system.

The explosion opened up the bow section of the *California* to the sea, and the bow of the ship rapidly sank almost to the bottom of the harbor.

Pacific Bridge divers had installed the outside bow patch, so they were called in to locate and retrieve the patch from the bottom. With the help of a floating crane, the patch was brought to the surface. It was badly damaged and bent out of shape from the force of the explosion, and obviously of no further use. The manufacture of another patch would take a week to complete and would disrupt the planned docking schedule for the *California*.

Since docking space for major ships was at a premium, it was essential that the schedules be maintained. Once in dry dock, a salvaged battleship's repairs were planned in such a way that it could be removed from the dock within seventy-two hours. This policy was necessary to keep the dry docks available for damaged ships of the active fleet, fighting the war. Salvage engineers made the decision to isolate the bow damage on the *California* at the third deck level.

This required closing and securing the distorted third deck hatch. The explosion had blown the hatch open and ripped the securing bolts that held the hatch closed from their mountings. The most logical course of action would have been to cut the hinges off the hatch, remove it, and have it straightened by the shipyard shipfitter shop. But this option was not available to us because one of the fleet battleships was damaged and due to arrive for extensive hull repairs, which would tie up the shipfitter shop.

Another method of making the hatch watertight was needed. It was decided to arc weld angle-iron strongbacks underwater across and above the warped hatch. Then we could drive wedges between the hatch and strongbacks to force the hatch down and make a watertight seal.

Our diving team performed this work within a twelve-hour period, and the bow of the *California* was pumped dry below the third deck level. But while Moon and I helped salvage the *California*, we sacrificed our Saturday date with Hattie and Margaret.

Martin was given liberty the next day to attend church, so I asked him to stop by Ernie's and apologize to Hattie for me and tell her I would get in touch later. Meanwhile the *California* met her scheduled dry-docking date in April 1942.

We moved our barges to the USS *West Virginia* and prepared to start salvage operations.

VI

USS West Virginia

Fire Phenomenon

On the day of the attack, the *West Virginia* was struck by seven torpedoes that opened a three-hundred-foot-long hole in her port side. A wall of burning fuel oil from the stricken *Arizona* surrounded her. The order was given to abandon ship.

Tugboats came alongside in a vain attempt to extinguish the flames. They were met with a fire phenomenon not seen before. As the flames were controlled in one area, fire broke out in adjacent spaces. The blaze was not contained for thirty hours, and it caused considerable damage to the interior of the ship.

It was later determined that this peculiar aspect of the fires was caused by burning oil-based paint on one side of a bulkhead igniting paint on its opposite side. The navy learned a valuable lesson in the future maintenance of naval ships from this disaster.

Warships were stripped of all oil-based paint and repainted with fire-retardant paint. This requirement saved many ships and lives that might otherwise have been lost to the ravages of fire.

We Get a Lesson in Diving

Our team began to survey the long gash in the *West Virginia*'s side to determine the best salvage method to raise her.

This preliminary survey would give Pacific Bridge engineers the information needed to plan the type of external patches needed and alert the shipyard to the magnitude of work that lay ahead.

We were getting ready to put the first diver over the side when I spotted Bosun McClung in a boat signaling us that he was coming alongside. Accompanying him was a huge chief petty officer. The two men stepped aboard the barge, and McClung introduced the chief.

"Men, this is Chief Duggs, master deep-sea diver. He was my diving instructor at the Deep Sea Diving School." The bosun continued, "He was one of the heroes from the submarine *Squalus* salvage job. I requested Washington to transfer him here to give us a hand, since he is an acknowledged salvage expert."

The chief was an enormous man, dwarfing most of us. He was six feet five inches in height and weighed 275 pounds. There were traces of gray in his brown curly hair, and his face was craggy, deeply tanned and weather-lined, clearly identifying him as a man who had spent much of his life out-of-doors.

"The chief will give us the benefit of his expertise, and he will be attached to the Salvage Unit at the shipyard. He will be directing the efforts to survey the damaged areas on the *West Virginia*. He'll be responsible for making a sketch of the underwater damage and will then submit it to me. You men have much to learn from the chief about salvage." So saying, the bosun boarded his boat and headed back to Ten-Ten Dock.

The successful salvage effort in raising the sunken submarine *Squalus* in 1939 was a heralded event throughout the U.S. Navy, and the circumstances of its salvage were known to every diver. Our diving crew felt privileged to have one of its bemedaled heroes onboard to give us the benefit of his experience.

Chief Petty Officer Willard Duggs spoke in his rich, low voice. "I'll make the first orientation dive," he said.

I sized him up and asked if a number three diving dress would be large enough for him.

He answered in the affirmative and directed us to dress him.

Bill and Ben got the suit down from the rack and Duggs struggled his bulk into it. He filled every inch. It took both assisting divers to pull the slack up on the suit bib.

"Doggone it, Chief, this dress fits you like a glove," remarked Bill cheerily.

The chief was in no mood for small talk. "Hurry it up now, and get me over to the diving ladder," he demanded.

He was led to the ladder while I manned the telephone.

"Topside, lower me down easy, there's zero

visibility down here, and I don't want to get impaled on some wreckage," ordered the chief.

"Did he expect searchlights and Benny Goodman down there? And what the hell does 'impaled' mean?" Bronco asked.

"It means getting a stanchion jammed up your butt," Ben answered. "Ed, tell the chief to use a little more air. He's heavy as two tons of s— . Bill, give me a hand tending his lines."

"I'm not going to give the chief any instructions on diving," I said. "He's a master diver. He knows what he's doing."

"Topside, take me up about four feet. I'm in the wreckage now," ordered the chief. "There, that's good. Now lower me a couple of feet."

The directions kept coming for ninety minutes, though the diver did not progress more than ten feet in any direction. Ben and Bill were sweating profusely from the exertion of tending the mammoth weight of the chief, and they were muttering obscenities to themselves and each other.

"Topside, take me up another two feet, I think I can see something."

This was too much for Ben's temper. With a bellow of rage he exploded. "Damn it, Ed, you either tell him to lighten himself up, or I'm gonna yell down and tell him to start acting like a diver or get his butt up outta there."

Reluctantly, I gingerly suggested that the chief might want to lighten his weight by inflating his suit.

"Topside," came the answer, loud and clear, "when I want your advice, I'll ask for it. Now take me up about four feet so I can clear this wreckage."

We all wondered how long this could continue. The chief had been down two hours and Ben commented that he had never given any estimate of damage. He figured this was the longest orientation dive in history.

"Be patient," Moon said. "He'll have to pee pretty soon, then he'll surface."

"Knock it off, you guys," I said. "He may not be able to teach us anything about handling ourselves underwater, but he did play a key role in salvaging the *Squalus* in his younger days."

"Yeah, and remember, he taught Bosun McClung everything he knows about diving," Mullen added sarcastically, recalling the bosun's one and only dive on the *Utah*.

"He was probably a pretty good diver in his day," I said, trying to make a case for the chief. "He's not a kid anymore. Probably thirty-five years old."

Bill said there was an old Kanaka shipyard diver who was old enough to be his father, and he was still diving. He maintained the chief had been sitting around the diving school drinking coffee for so long he had forgotten how to dive.

To Ben's relief, the chief finally gave a signal on his lines to bring him to the surface.

Duggs laboriously climbed the diving ladder, stumbled over to the dressing stool, and sat down wearily. Ben and Bill removed his helmet and breastplate as he sat hunched, breathing heavily.

"I think I may have had an accident," he said finally, eyes directed off into space. "I haven't done that since the *Squalus* job."

"That can happen to anyone after a three- or four-hour dive," I broke in quickly, hoping to head off any snide remarks from Ben.

"There's a bucket of soapy water and a brush you can use to scrub out your suit, and a barrel of fresh water to rinse out your diving underwear."

"What did you find down there, Chief?" Moon asked, trying to sound serious and keep a straight face.

Duggs just shook his head and mumbled that there was a hell of a lot of wreckage.

During a two and one-half hour dive, Chief Duggs discovered the great difference between diving on an undamaged submarine and working on a torpedoed, sunken battleship.

The Plan to Raise the *West Virginia*

During the following four days, our diving team surveyed the entire port side of the *West Virginia* and plotted the damaged areas on the ship's plan. Chief Duggs was not seen again aboard the diving barge. We surmised that, like Bosun McClung, he had found the administrative duties at the yard salvage office more to his liking. This was disappointing to Ben. He had few other people he could make light of in the intervening months of arduous work.

In addition to the huge gouge in her side, the survey showed that a torpedo had exploded in the steering engine room and had torn the rudder off. The rudder was located lying in the mud and a line was attached to it with a buoy to mark its location for future recovery. Raising the *West Virginia* would be far more difficult than either the *Nevada* or *California* had been. It would test the ingenuity and salvage expertise of every faction involved in the operation.

Based on the results of the survey, a salvage plan was developed to raise the ship. We planned to construct and install a huge cofferdam over three hundred feet long, which would cover the torpedo holes. We would pour six hundred and fifty tons of underwater cement to seal its sides and bottom.

We would then open all doors and hatches to allow the trapped water to flow down to its lowest level, where it could be pumped out. Next we would reestablish watertight integrity throughout the ship by closing all openings we had previously opened, thereby isolating the damaged areas.

As the ship was refloated, all weights would be removed as they became accessible.

Civilian Pacific Bridge contract divers were assigned the outside job of attaching the enormous cofferdam patches to the hull over the torpedo holes. Our diving crew was given the task of opening and closing watertight fittings and repairing closures within the ship.

We had slowly worked our way up to the third deck level, closing all watertight openings as we went.

Although it was thought there were approximately sixty-six bodies within the West Virginia, we had not found any as yet. That was soon to change.

Tony was the scheduled diver. He lowered himself down to the third deck. Martin was on the telephone, and he had directed the diver to the watertight door at frame 55.

"Topside, I'm here at the door ready to undog it, but there is a — a body wedged in the top part of it, and I can't budge him."

This was Tony's first encounter with a corpse underwater. He was trying not to show his uneasiness, but most of our crew had experienced anxiety in dealing with the dead men in the darkness, and we understood his nervousness.

"Feel around his body — his belt must be caught on one of the door bolts," Martin suggested.

Tony struggled with the mass and said the body seemed to be clear of any obstruction but he couldn't pull him away from the door.

"Well, grab him by one of his arms or legs and pull him away."

It was obvious that Tony was having a bad time coping with this situation. Martin asked me to take the phones; he said he thought I might handle the communication better.

Tony was mumbling under his breath, beseeching the cadaver to come free. All at once his voice became a sharp cry. "Oh God, I just pulled his arm off. What should I do with it?"

In a measured tone I said, "Just drop the arm where you're standing. When the water is pumped out they can put it and his other parts in a bag and bury him just like the others. Is the body free now?"

He said it was. He was calmer at that point but said he felt sick with revulsion.

"I know how you feel, but you'll run into more of those poor guys before you're through. You'll never get used to it, but it won't be quite as bad next time," I said, remembering my own first experience on the *Arizona*.

Things proceeded smoothly until a three-day delay halted diving inside the ship until cofferdam patches were manufactured.

When the cofferdam patches were ready to be secured to the hull, it was my turn to dive. I started my dive on the first platform deck level to establish an area of watertight integrity. This proved impossible because there was so much damage that all the road marks were wiped out. I could not identify or determine what remained in that part of the ship.

We solved this problem by establishing a boundary nearer the center line of the ship, where the damage was minimal and water-tightness could be achieved. We soon learned that when we thought everything was under control, something was sure to change it.

Bill began a new survey near amidships, and his route was being duly recorded by topside. He had just finished saying that he was stepping through the door at frame 97 when he screamed into his phone that he was falling. His phone faded in and out intermittently, but his last transmission was loud and clear.

"Something is wrong with my air supply."

We were not able to get an answering pull on his lines, so we knew they were hung up somewhere. Moon was hurriedly dressed and sent down to follow his lines. We tried to contact Bill, but we could not get through.

In a matter of minutes Moon reached the watertight door Bill had fallen through. He reported that Bill stepped into a compartment where the deck had been blown away by a torpedo. He found Bill, a little dazed from his twenty-foot fall, lying in the midst of shards of decking, but none the worse for wear. Later, Moon said he could not understand how Bill was not impaled on some of the wreckage.

"God must love all dumbheads," Moon teased.

Bill's airhose was slashed, and the air was leaking from it. The telephone wires in his lifeline were also nicked, which had caused the lapses in communication.

Divers Are Persona Non Grata

"Hey, Eddie, my boy, let's take advantage of the

next couple of days off and go over to Hattie's house." Moon was putting his freshly laundered whites in the footlocker at the foot of his bunk. "Margaret told Martin to tell me she 'borrowed' two quarts of bourbon from the restaurant store-room, so we can have a few shooters on Ernie. Apparently Ernie stashed it away before prohibition."

It sounded like a fine idea to me, so we decided to ride into town the next day and arrange a date with the girls.

Ernie's was filled to capacity with a sea of white navy uniforms and a sprinkling of army khaki. As usual, the enormous figure of the owner could be seen sitting at the front door on his bar stool regulating the number of patrons permitted to enter.

We saw Hattie and Margaret serving customers behind the bar. Our turn finally came, and we were motioned to a table. We ordered steaks, and when Hattie took her break she joined us.

"Do you want something to eat?" I asked her.

"No, thanks," she said. "I've got a tooth that's killing me. It's an abscessed wisdom tooth. I can't get an appointment with a dentist till Monday, and I'm having a hell of a time with it."

She said her dentist told her that she, like many Hawaiians, would probably lose her teeth before age fifty because she did not drink enough milk, and the water supply lacked the necessary minerals to build strong teeth.

Moon thought that was a rather grim prediction and joked about it being another reason to end prohibition, which was still in effect on the island.

I told her we had the weekend off, but we would certainly understand if she didn't want to party.

"I'm not going to let a toothache keep me from partying," she declared. "The only time I feel good is after I have a few drinks. Plan on Saturday. Margaret's off work at five, and she's got some good whiskey for us."

Moon and I took our time and arrived at Margaret and Hattie's small frame house at 6 P.M. The house was raised on concrete pilings to protect it from Oahu's heavy rainfall and numerous insects. Both girls were in a jovial mood.

Hattie broiled the island's famous Ono, or wahoo fish, using a highly seasoned Portuguese recipe. The fish and fresh salad and bread were delicious. As we were finishing the home-cooked food, a sudden shower dropped rain on the corrugated tin roof, making conversation difficult. Moon helped Margaret with the dishes, as Hattie and I settled on the rattan couch in the small living room.

"How is the tooth?" I asked sympathetically.

"Not so bad now that I've had a few drinks. I may not even go to the dentist," she declared defiantly, helping herself to another generous glassful of Jack Daniel's.

Moon and Margaret joined us, and we sat around chatting comfortably as the second bottle was opened.

"So we're drinkin' courtesy of old Ernie, eh?" Moon was savoring the smooth liquid, so different from the harsh alcohol we had provided.

"Hell, no," Margaret replied. "This is just a small payment for all the crap he passes out after I tell him to keep his paws off me."

"Why don't you quit if he gives you such a bad time?"

"Tips are too good to give up, and besides, all my friends work there. We're the only place in town with such high-class employees — all Portagooses." She giggled.

"Let's drink to fat old Ernie." Hattie slopped more of the whiskey in everyone's glass and held hers high. "Here's to his generosity and his ugly face." Her words were slurred, and she laughed shrilly as she leaned her head on my shoulder.

"I think you girls are ahead of us in the drinking department." I laughed.

"I only drink for medicinal purposes," hiccuped Hattie, "and I just hope we don't run out of medicine before I'm cured."

"Speaking of medicine, that island beer has got to be the worst tastin' stuff I ever drank," I said.

"S'bad all right. I suspect they brew it with dog s— and sewer water. Don't know how you poor guys were able to sit at the bar and sop it up all day long." Margaret shook her head sadly.

"I sure as hell hope that brewery goes out of business before prohibition is over," Moon said. We finished off the bottle, and Hattie yawned. "Honey, I gotta get up early tomorrow. S'time you helped me into my little ol' bed."

Moon was happily covering Margaret with noisy wet kisses, and she finally shoved him away. "Sorry, Moon, baby, but you ain't goin' to get nothin' tonight. Ol' Margaret's got her 'monthly'."

Not to be discouraged, he announced, "Well, darlin', there's other ways to satisfy this Irishman."

She struggled to her feet and looked down into his hopeful face. "Save that crap for those whores on Hotel Street," she shouted at him, eyes flashing.

"Okay, okay, don't get so huffy. We'll go to bed and just snuggle. All right, baby?"

She flounced out of the room, and he followed her into the small bedroom.

After they left, Hattie and I staggered unsteadily down the hallway into her room.

Hattie lay close in my arms, her full, round curves pressed against me. She was breathing heavily in her passion, and the halitosis from her abscessed tooth drifted into my face. While the large amount of Jack Daniel's I had consumed made me immune to the lumpy mattress and the hot, muggy night, I could not concentrate on making love to this girl with her bad breath.

I considered my options. I didn't want to hurt

her feelings or disappoint her, but the situation rendered me incapable of making love. If I pretended to pass out from too much booze she might leave me alone and turn over. But I wasn't sure I could fake unconsciousness. I finally decided if I held my breath while I kissed her, and pressed my nose against her cheek during the sex act, maybe I could perform the job expected of me.

While contemplating this plan, my partner's body grew more and more relaxed, and I realized that she had drifted off to sleep and was snoring sonorously.

I was hungry for a cigarette and moved into the living room looking for my lighter. I saw the shadowy figure of Moon sitting dejectedly in one of the armchairs.

"Is Hattie out of commission too?"

"No, she's asleep, thank goodness. I couldn't stand her breath another second."

Moon asked what I was planning to do. I told him I was getting out of the house, pronto, before Hattie woke up. I planned to hide in the thick shrubbery near the back of the house until daylight and then hightail it back to the base. It would not be the best way to spend my liberty night, but I didn't want to be caught violating the curfew between 9 P.M. and sunrise.

In a drunken, befuddled voice Moon asked me if I'd mind if he sneaked into Hattie's bed while she was asleep. "She'd never know I wasn't you in the dark," he said.

I told him he was crazy as hell. She would know who he was in a second. I warned him not to try it. I got dressed and left the house. I huddled outside in the bushes to avoid the cruising shore patrol and the Honolulu police patrols. I had just settled into a fairly comfortable spot in the shrubbery when I heard Hattie's bloodcurdling scream and a stream of profanities. Margaret was awakened, and I cringed as I heard both the girls yelling at the top of their voices, accusing Moon of every crime ever committed against women, except perhaps that of robbing Hattie of her virginity.

Moon was trying his best to make a joke of his evil deed but neither girl was buying his story.

Hattie's last words emphasized that she never wanted to see him or me ever again, and she was very explicit about what each of us could do with our body parts.

Moon staggered out the front door in his skivvies, carrying his folded uniform in his hands. He found his way to the back of the house, peering in the bushes and whispering my name.

When I first heard the commotion inside the house, I was afraid the neighbors would call the police thinking a murder was being committed. But when I pictured what was taking place inside, I started laughing and couldn't stop.

"Izzat you, Ed?" Moon asked, parting the shrubbery.

"Yes, you dumb clown. Get dressed and climb in here before the cops grab you."

"Guess I messed up royally with the girls." He sighed remorsefully. "No more beach parties or anything."

He looked so pathetic I told him to forget it. "I should have dragged you out when I left the house," I said. "Besides, if my flight training doesn't come through, I'm getting off this rock some other way."

"If you go, I'm goin' too, buddy," Moon declared, and he gave me a comradely punch on the shoulder just before he fell backward into the shrubbery.

So ended the relationship between our diving crew and the lively Portuguese women. Our disappointment was twofold, since we could not enjoy another steak at Ernie's, fearful of having to face the embarrassing recriminations we were sure would be forthcoming from Hattie and Margaret.

Tragic Deaths

As soon as the two main patches on the port side of the *West Virginia* were made reasonably watertight, the water level within the ship and the cofferdam patches was reduced five feet, but at that point the inflow of water equaled the pumping capacity and no further headway was made in dewatering. Most of the leakage was found to occur in the areas contiguous to the patches from leaking seams, shrapnel holes, and loose rivets.

The leaking seams were repaired, using underwater arc welding, while the larger shrapnel holes were plugged using wooden patches drawn up tight against the hull with J bolts. Smaller holes and loose rivets were made watertight by driving wooden plugs into them.

After five days of continuous work patching leaks, the pumps were able to overcome the ingress of water and the *West Virginia* was refloated. However, problems related to lightening her load were far from over.

Originally Dry Dock Number Two was designated for docking the *West Virginia*, because her docking sill was forty feet deep. However, the number two dry dock was reserved for the repair of major fighting ships, especially aircraft carriers, that might sustain combat damage. This precluded its use for the battleship, leaving only the much smaller number one dry dock with its thirty-six-foot-deep sill.

As dewatering continued, the ship rose higher and higher. Work crews from the ship's force and the Salvage and Repair Unit began unloading oil, ammunition, and stores from the accessible areas. In addition, sixty-six bodies in an advanced state of decomposition were recovered and placed in canvas bags for burial.

Three bodies were found in a completely dry storeroom. They were dressed in blue uniforms. The three had emergency rations stored at their battle station, and they had ample water, since they had removed the cover to an adjacent freshwater tank. They also had battle lanterns available for their use. Two of the men wore wristwatches, and one of them carried a wallet-size calendar, which had the days checked off from 7 December to 23 December. It was believed their deaths were due to lack of oxygen.

The discovery of these three men in an unflooded compartment caused a profound sense of anguish among our divers. Especially shaken were Moon and Tony, who had sounded the *West Virginia*'s hull on 12 December and reported no response from within the ship.

Both divers were positive there were no answering sounds from their hammering on the hull. The *Tennessee* was jammed up against the *West Virginia*'s starboard side so tightly that nothing could slip between them. It had been impossible to sound that area. They had sounded the damaged port side, but there was so much wreckage jutting out that the sounds of their hammering probably were not transmitted through the hull.

I sensed that Moon and Tony were suffering from guilt feelings that were unjustified. I assured them that they had done everything humanly possible to find the trapped men. The fact that they had been imprisoned in that particular location was a cruel twist of fate.

"In any event, it's extremely improbable that we could have rescued them even if we had known they were there," I said. "I'm no engineer, but given the depth of water over the battle station's access hatch there must've been tons of water pressure on top of it. Neither the men inside pushing up on it nor the divers pulling could have opened it. So let's forget the guilt trip. We did our best to find all the men."

"We might have saved them if we had had our underwater arc cutting torch in those early days. We could have punched a hole in the top of the compartment and allowed water to flood the space," Moon said thoughtfully. "When the water level got high enough, and the water pressure inside and outside were equalized, the men could have undogged the hatch and opened it."

"For crying out loud, that rescue scenario has got so many holes in it and so many *ifs* and *maybes* it's ridiculous. The fact is we didn't have the cutting torch and even if we had, we probably would have killed them with the fumes from the burning red lead paint. The men are gone. There wasn't anything we could have done about it," I stated firmly.

"I know you're right, Ed, but I feel lousy," Tony said. "I was the one that sounded the hull." He walked slowly away to the end of the barracks where his bunk was located.

I watched him as he lay prone on his bed, eyes staring at the ceiling, and I realized he was far more affected by this situation than I would have believed. He had always been such a loner, someone that none of us could reach, and one who rarely showed emotion. This incident brought out a quality I had not seen before. He seemed devastated by his feelings of guilt and grief, and it was many days before he seemed free of those feelings.

Diving Seabees

During the first few months after Pearl Harbor was attacked, navy divers received the sum of ten dollars a month in additional diving pay. Congress finally recognized the hazards involved in wartime diving, and we began to earn five dollars per hour, or any portion thereof, for dives certified to be extremely hazardous.

Dives in and around sunken ships were deemed to meet this criterion. While the pay was still less than that of the civil service and Pacific Bridge divers' pay scales, it was nevertheless a vast improvement, and morale soared. On average our divers earned 10 to 20 dollars a day in extra pay. I was making as much money as a full commander in the navy.

Shortly before the *West Virginia* was ready for dry-docking, two Seabee sailors, Matt Wiley and Roscoe Cole, were sent by their unit to be trained as salvage divers. Both men were in their mid-thirties and had been journeymen steel workers in civilian life. They attended second-class diving school, and in a very short time handled themselves well underwater. They proved within the first month to be valuable additions to our diving crew on the *West Virginia*.

The day following their first payday as salvage divers they showed up on the barge with long faces.

"What's the matter, Roscoe? You look like you lost your best friend," I said.

"No, but we're out of a good-paying job. The old man is recalling us from temporary duty," Roscoe lamented.

"Is your outfit pulling out?"

"Hell, no. According to our disbursing officer, the skipper asked to see our pay records after a month's diving pay had been entered. When he saw how much we earned he blew his stack. He said we were making more dough than he was as a lieutenant commander."

"Doesn't he know that you're risking your neck for that extra dough?" Moon asked.

"Damn it, we need you guys. We'll be short-handed without you and that means we'll just have to train somebody else. I'm going to talk to Haynes. Maybe he can scotch your recall," I said.

After I explained the situation, Haynes called the office of the Seabee's commanding officer.

"Commander Larder, this is Commander Haynes, diving officer of the Salvage Unit. I'm calling regarding your command's recall of two of your divers, Wiley and Cole."

I listened attentively as Haynes used his "buttering up" technique on the other officer. I wondered if it would be effective in charming the Seabee officer out of his men.

"Well, Commander, I can appreciate that you need their services, but we need them desperately here. We are on the front lines, so to speak.

It's vital that we get these ships raised and back with the fighting fleet," Haynes said.

There was a short pause as Haynes's brow creased into a frown, and he listened impatiently to the man on the other end of the line.

"No, I'm not saying your unit isn't important, too, but it's more a question of work priorities. Don't you agree? If you could just spare them until we get the *West Virginia* in dry dock, I'd truly appreciate it." His voice became more strident as the frown increased.

"Not even for that short period? Is that your final decision, Mr. Larder?" He drew out the "mister," and he scowled as he drummed his fingers impatiently on the desktop.

"Dammit, Larder, that is the flimsiest excuse for recalling those men I ever heard. You and I both know that's a bunch of crap." He was yelling now, and he smacked his fist on the desk.

He looked over at me, suddenly aware that his conversation was being monitored, so he quickly motioned me out the door.

As I exited I overheard the angry voice of Haynes: "And one more thing , Larder, you can damn well take your excuses and jam . . ."

I returned to the diving barge and related the heated telephone exchange to the team.

"Well, I'll be damned," said Ben in amazement. "You mean to tell me Pappy got all over another officer to help out an enlisted man?"

"I wonder if he'll get himself in trouble insulting that Seabee C.O.?" Martin asked.

"Are you kiddin', Martin?" I said. "Pappy was an officer before Columbus discovered America. He's plenty senior to that miserable Seabee officer. He may not be able to keep Wiley and Cole on the diving crew, but I sure gotta give the old buzzard credit for trying."

After this experience with the petty jealousies of an outside command, only volunteer divers from the Salvage and Repair Unit were selected and trained. A tremendous amount of salvage work still remained to be accomplished on *Oklahoma*. Therefore, an additional ten navy divers were accepted and joined the diving crews.

Prohibition Rescinded

A few weeks later, on a Saturday, Pappy Haynes sent for me as the team arrived for work. He informed me that since our work on the *West Virginia* was completed, he wanted me to move the diving barge to the *Oklahoma* on Monday. He wanted the crew to start cutting into the magazines and removing the 5-inch shells. He also told me the salvage engineers planned to leave the 14-inch shells onboard as ballast during the righting phase.

He finished his instructions with an unexpected surprise. "Tell the men to take the weekend off."

I hurried off to tell the guys about weekend liberty. But the prospects of liberty without the company of feminine companions produced scowls and gripes, all targeted toward Moon and his misbehavior. They couldn't look forward to a steak at Ernie's, our alcohol supply was depleted, and the island brew was so lousy they wouldn't consider going into town for a drink of it.

We spent Saturday morning lounging around the barracks, reading books or writing letters. Moon said he was tired of his grumbling companions, so he walked over to the administration building to visit a friend.

Noon chow went down, and we ambled listlessly over to the mess hall, went through the chow line, then sat dejectedly eating the tasteless food.

As we were finishing, Moon burst through the door and bounded over to our table. We didn't even bother to look up.

"I got great news, you guys," he said eagerly.

"Yeah? You shipping out to Tokyo?" Ben asked.

He finally got our attention when he announced he had it on good authority that the U.S. Army had just rescinded their prohibition order for Hawaii.

This meant we could finally get a decent mixed drink in a Honolulu bar. It didn't take us long to return to the barracks, don our uniforms, and head for Honolulu and Waikiki.

Ben, Lover Extraordinaire

Sunday night found a barracks full of men nursing

hangovers and lamenting the fact that while booze was plentiful, women were not. In fact, the end of prohibition had caused the few available women to become even more cautious about appearing on the streets of Honolulu, and no one could really blame them.

We were casting off the lines to the sampan on Monday morning when Haynes arrived on the pier, face flushed and out of breath. He said plans had changed for the *Oklahoma*'s salvage. Recent soundings of the harbor bottom around the exterior of the battleship revealed that the amidships section was resting on solid coral, but the bow was partially afloat in soft mud. It was believed the mud would allow the bow to slide rather than rotate during the righting operation. They needed to deposit thousands of cubic yards of coral under the bow area. A pile of crushed coral one-third of a mile long, one-third of a mile wide, and one-third of a mile high was moved under the bow for support. Since our diving barges would be in the way of this work, Pappy told me to leave the barges tied up to the *West Virginia*. He ordered us to perform progressive maintenance on our equipment for the next two weeks.

After a few days of the very dull but necessary chores of repairing torn diving dresses, assembling new lifelines and air hoses, and replacing parts of damaged equipment, the crew became restive.

Moon, who somehow managed to get information from sources all over the base, told us that the Royal Hawaiian Hotel was not completely occupied at the present time. The guys asked me to approach Pappy Haynes and request his help in getting us some R&R at the hotel.

Haynes told me he would check out the possibility with one of his contacts, but he said not to count on it. Heretofore, the only men allowed to use the hotel were aviators and submariners who had been in combat or who had finished a war patrol. So we felt privileged when a day later Pappy informed us that we had reserved rooms at the famous pink hotel in Waikiki.

Andy, Ben, Cary, and I were the first to go, and we were assigned single rooms. Each room was furnished with a double bed, a large dresser, and two easy chairs.

Andy was content to bask on the beach and compose letters to Enid, his girl in the Midwest. Cary, on the other hand, explored the wonders of tidal pools and hiked up the crater of Diamond Head until the army caught him one day and drove him off.

Ben spent most of his waking hours prowling the bars of Waikiki looking for his favorite type of women, those with "big hooters and broad rears," but without much luck.

I spent much of my time in the lovely hotel, hoping to find a higher class of female companionship, also without much luck.

It had been a dull and relaxing six days, but

our stay was nearly over, since this was our last evening. Ben wanted a good Chinese dinner and asked me to join him. I wanted to refuse his invitation, but he looked so forlorn I decided to go along. The two of us headed for the famous Chinese restaurant Lau Yee Choi, more commonly nicknamed "Lousy Chows" by the military.

Ben and I sat in the bar waiting to be seated when a tall sailor, too thin for his height, came up behind Ben and slapped him on the shoulder.

"Hey, you tub of lard, how the hell you been?" the sailor asked.

Ben introduced me to his old friend Joe. I sat there and laughed at their sea stories and humorous reminiscences. They had been stationed together on the USS *Medusa*. Joe was in mid-sentence when he glanced up and stopped abruptly, his eyes wide.

"Ben," Joe whispered, "don't fall off your stool, but a couple of beauties just came in the front door. They don't have nobody with them, and if we hurry over there maybe we can buy 'em a drink."

We watched closely as the two women walked to the bar and sat down. One was a tall blonde wearing a green jersey dress that emphasized her bony frame. A severe overbite made it difficult for her to close her lips tightly. Her large teeth dominated her thin face.

Her friend was much shorter and heavier. As she swiveled around on the bar stool, I noticed that her generous derriere covered and overlapped the leather seat. She wore a very large picture hat of black straw, decorated with multi-colored artificial flowers clustered on the under-side of the brim. This giant masterpiece of millinery diminished the small, white face, which had a red Cupid's bow painted on it.

"Which one looks good to you, Ed?" Joe asked. "It's your pick. Ben and me don't care which one we get, we can always share her."

"I appreciate your generosity, guys, but count me out. I'm going to hit the sack early."

"Well, I'm partial to blondes," Joe said. "I'll take the tall one with the yellow hair."

"Good Gawd," Ben whispered to me, "times is tough! I never thought anything like them two would ever look good to me. I'm glad Joe wants the blonde. With that set of choppers, she could chew corncobs through a picket fence." Ben got to his feet as Joe declared he would engage the two cuties in sparklin' conversation.

"You're a smooth talker all right," said Ben, eyes rolling skyward. "But if I let you do the talking, we'll both miss out for sure."

As the two sailors approached the women, I moved to an empty table within earshot, anxious to observe this encounter. It went something like this:

"Hi, girls," Ben started, smiling his brightest smile. "My buddy, Joe, and me been admiring you ladies, and we wondered if we could buy you a drink?"

"That's nice of you boys. I'll have a gin and

tonic," answered the blonde in a low, husky voice.

"And I'll have bourbon on the rocks," piped the lady in the hat, her tiny lips parting into a smile as she squinted myopically at the two sailors.

Things seemed to be going very well.

"I'm Ben, and this here's Joe. And what might your names be?" said jolly Ben.

"I'm Thelma," the blonde answered, baring her large teeth further with a smile.

"And I'm Mimi," said the hat.

"Pleasure to meet you." Joe entered the conversation as he slid up on the bar stool next to Thelma.

"Where you girls from?" asked Ben, taking the empty seat beside Mimi. "We don't see lovely ladies like you by themselves very often."

The two girls basked happily in the warmth of Ben's compliment.

"We live inland up near Schofield. Both our husbands were ordered out to Midway Island last month," answered Mimi, her eyebrows dipping in a forlorn little frown, an obvious attempt at expressing her sadness.

"Geez, that's too bad. Guess it gets pretty lonely out there without a husband." Ben sighed sympathetically.

"Yeah, and if we tried to take a little break like this around there, some nosy witch would be sure to start nasty rumors about us," Mimi said. "And we're not the kinda wives who would . . ."

"You got that right, Mimi," sniffed Thelma. "Every time we meet up with some dog faces, the first thing they want to do after they buy us a drink is to get us into bed. . . . and we just ain't those kinds of girls."

"Hell, no, you ain't! It's easy to see that. If you were, Joe and me wouldn't want nothin' to do with you. We're lookin' for a couple of nice girls to spend a pleasant evenin' with. Right, Joe?"

Joe nodded enthusiastically.

The girls consumed four more drinks in short order, and I noticed Mimi was slurring her words and giggling uncontrollably at everything Ben said.

"What say we all go over to the Royal Hawaiian and dance?" Joe suggested.

"Tha'sa great idea, honey," Thelma replied.

"I'd go for that, Benny," Mimi said. "But I heard that's just for R & R, and they probably won't let us in."

"I got a surprise for you, little lady. I'm staying there," Ben declared triumphantly. "And I can take anybody in there I want."

The girls smiled happily. "Are the rooms as pretty as we've heard?" Mimi asked.

"Can we take a peek at your room?" Thelma smiled coyly.

"Hell yes." Ben beamed. "As a matter of fact, we can even have a drink up there. I've got a full bottle of Jack Daniel's just waitin' to be opened."

"Oh goody, I'd druther drink then dance any

ol' day." Mimi giggled.

As Ben walked past my table he leaned over and asked me if I wanted to have a nightcap with them. I declined, knowing that a fifth wheel might hamper this romance. I told him I would follow them to the hotel, but I'd keep a discreet distance away. I said I would meet him for breakfast in the morning and would expect a full report of his conquest.

The two couples wended their way through the garden to the front entrance of the hotel. Ben raised his hand and stopped them. I hid behind a tree waiting for them to enter the hotel. The last thing I heard from the group made me smile.

"Joe and me will go in the front way and open my room. You two girls wait outside the emergency exit door until I come and let you in. That way nobody'll see you and get the wrong idea."

I was finishing my second cup of coffee the next morning when a bleary-eyed Ben arrived and sank into his chair with a deep sigh.

"Don't tell me the 'Hat' was too much for you, Bennie boy? You look like she put you through a wringer."

"You wouldn't believe what happened last night." Ben launched into the story of his romance with the Hat.

Ben said he and Joe got the two girls safely into Room 107. They broke open a bottle of whiskey and each had a few snorts.

The girls asked if the workbench was comfortable, and then proceeded to try it out by bouncing up and down on the double bed.

He said Joe and the girls used the bathroom and then it was his turn. When he finished, he flicked off the light and opened the bathroom door. The room was dark except for a glimmer of light showing through the transom over the door, providing just enough illumination to make out the figures in the bed.

Joe had mounted Thelma and was banging away solidly. The bedsprings were squeaking, and the two participants were breathing heavily. Thelma's raucous voice cried out noisily from time to time. Ben tiptoed over to the far side of the double bed and slipped out of his skivvies. He pulled back the sheet and fell into the arms of an eager, amorous Mimi.

Mimi grabbed him, and he entered her ample body. His mouth met hers in a long, passionate kiss. Then, as the lovemaking progressed, he pressed his left cheek affectionately against hers and felt his nose grating against a coarse-textured fabric.

He thought a classy hotel like the Royal Hawaiian would have a better grade of linen. Shifting his head to the other side of her face, he continued humping, happily.

Ben was near climax when he realized his nose was breathing noisily into a wad of rough material. What the hell is this? he wondered vaguely, as he worked steadily on Mimi, completing the act.

Ben and Joe finished their lovemaking at about

the same time, and finding no room in the bed, rolled off their respective partners onto the floor.

"Oh, that felt so goooood, honey!" Ben mimicked the Hat's voice. He said he had agreed with her as he lay panting and prostrate on the floor, where he had time to wonder again why the hotel would use straw in their pillows. He extended his arm to check the pillowcase. His hand encountered what he was sure was the brim of a hat. Yes, and there were those damn fake flowers he remembered. He could hardly believe it. This crazy broad had worn her hat to bed. She'd actually been f— with her hat on.

Ben said he was so amazed, he asked her if she knew she was still wearing her bonnet.

"Well, what was her answer?" I asked, trying to stop laughing.

"She said, 'of course, silly, you wouldn't want me to get my hair mussed, would you?' "

Sayonara to Flight Training

I was concerned that I had not been contacted about my application for cadet training, so once again I visited Lieutenant Crowe on Ford Island.

I approached the yeoman and asked to see the lieutenant. The yeoman went through the office door and closed it behind him. He emerged and told me Crowe was preparing for a conference and would prefer that I come back another time.

I sensed a runaround, and I was angry. I stood my ground. I was determined to find out what had happened to my application.

Previously, Lieutenant Crowe had been anxious to see me and had assured me the navy cadet program was desperate for men of my caliber. The fact that another sailor in the Repair Unit received orders to flight school heightened my feelings of uneasiness.

I told the yeoman I could not return to Ford Island for at least another week, so would he please ask the lieutenant to see me now. I was finally allowed into his office. He pulled my application out of his pending basket and studied it for a minute and then handed it to me. The request showed that Pappy Haynes had approved it, but showed a notation by Lieutenant Commander Arnold, which read: "No further action is to be taken on this request until notified by this command."

Crowe shrugged his shoulders and said there was nothing further he could do about my status. My first thought was to confront Arnold, but I changed my mind and decided to let Haynes carry the ball for me.

I met with the diving officer that afternoon.

"Raymer, I just hung up the phone after talking to Lieutenant Crowe, so I know why you're here. I was not aware of the notation Mr. Arnold added to your request, but I intend to find out if this was Mr. Arnold's idea."

"I don't know why Mr. Arnold would give me the shaft unless he blames me for losing one of his boots," I blurted out in anger and despair.

Sensing my frustration he advised me to calm

down and think rationally about my situation. He explained that Arnold was probably ordered to add the notation to my request by the commanding officer, because the command needed all the experienced divers it could muster for the remaining salvage work on the *Oklahoma*, *Utah*, and *Arizona*. He told me to consider the decision as a compliment and to be proud of the fact that the command recognized my worth as a diver and leader.

I knew he was conning me, but even so, it was balm for my ego.

Pappy ended the conversation by dismissing me. "That's all, Raymer. What were you saying about Mr. Arnold's boots?" he asked vaguely.

"Nothing, sir." I decided nothing would be gained by embarrassing Arnold about his missing boot.

That evening when I talked with Moon, my anger and frustration had dissipated and were replaced by common sense. If all the doors to flight school were closed to me, then I'd better forget about it and get on with my life.

Diving was interesting and challenging, the pay was great, and the men in the diving crew were good joes. Things could be worse, I told myself, and I finally pushed the dreams of flying from my mind.

But after expressing this rationale, I knew that I wouldn't be satisfied until I had experienced the adventure and excitement that duty in the war zone would bring.

"I don't know about you, Moon, but I'm volunteering for the first duty in the South Pacific that comes along," I said.

"Me too, buddy."

VII
USS Oklahoma

Ben Proves His Mettle

The *Oklahoma* was struck amidships on her port side by seven torpedoes. A gash two hundred feet long was opened in her hull, and she rolled over upside down. Four hundred men were trapped inside. Two hundred feet of her starboard bottom was above water. At its highest point her hull was twenty-six feet above mean low tide.

A salvage plan to right the ship was developed by teams of engineers. The first phase of this plan required the creation of an air bubble in the tanks and compartments along the starboard side. This bubble would give the ship an additional 20,000 tons of lifting buoyancy. One million gallons of fuel oil were scheduled to be pumped out, and hundreds of tons of shells needed to be removed from the magazine storage spaces.

After our sojourn at the Royal Hawaiian Hotel, we began work on the *Oklahoma*. Things had gone so well for us on the *West Virginia*; we were confident that raising the *Oklahoma* would be a breeze. Little did we realize she was destined to become a millstone around our necks.

Raising her became an undertaking filled with agony and death! Our first assignment was to cut into the five-inch projectile magazine. This was a job we had performed many times before on the *Arizona*, but one the crew nevertheless dreaded because of the subsequent explosions associated with the work. The penetration of the magazine on the *Oklahoma* differed somewhat from the *Arizona*, because she was upside down. It was necessary to enter those areas through the bulkhead rather than the overhead. Access holes had been burned in the bottom of the ship, and a twenty-eight-foot-long wooden ladder led down to the water level inside the ship.

This arrangement forced us to descend the length of the ladder with 196 pounds of diving gear on our backs before reaching the water.

First Andy and then Bill tried the return trip up the ladder. They managed to reach the halfway mark before succumbing to physical exhaustion, and we lifted them up the remaining twelve feet.

Ben, the bull of the team, was dressed. He had been strutting and bragging about his strength for some time and was sure he could descend and climb the ladder without help.

He finished his work on the bottom and started up the ladder. One third of the way up he yelled into the phones, "This is a snap. You bunch of sissies better go back to Mama. Andy, if you'd quit droolin' over Enid all the time and concentrate on the business at hand, you'd make it up this ladder too."

"You better save your breath, fat stuff. You're not as far as we were when we gave out, so don't give us any advice yet," Bronco replied resentfully.

Ben reached the halfway mark, his labored breathing heavy and raspy over the phones. "Dammit, keep a heavier strain on my lifeline," he roared as he struggled to lift one eighteen-pound shoe to the next rung of the ladder.

At the three-quarter mark, he was obviously in trouble. He was muttering obscenities to himself. He cursed the rivulets of sweat that were running down his forehead and burning his eyes.

"You guys are doggin' it up there," he gasped. "Keep a heavy strain on my lines. Who the hell's tending me, anyway?"

"Now who's the sissy, Benny baby?" Bill needled gleefully. "Do you want us to send Andy down to help you up the big ladder?"

With a bellow of rage, Ben summoned his last ounce of strength and clumped up the remaining few rungs of the ladder. He sank wearily onto the dressing stool, his head and body bathed in sweat. He was quickly undressed, but he sat there for a few minutes while he cooled off.

"My damn legs are still quiverin' so's I can't stand up. But I showed you guys it could be done, didn't I?" Ben said, seeking a modicum of admiration from the divers.

We all agreed that since Ben was the only one

strong enough to climb the ladder, he was elected to make all the dives. That suggestion cooled Ben's bravado.

Different members of the crew made suggestions about how we could do the work and also be able to climb the ladder without killing ourselves. Andy suggested we use a shallow-water mask and a tank suit. But we rejected that idea because electricity from the cutting torch would be coursing through the diver's unprotected body.

"The first time you struck an arc underwater," Ben commented, "you'd light up like a Christmas tree. Also, those electric bolts would make you sterile as a steer, and Enid sure wouldn't want that."

After several other suggestions, Cary proposed a solution to the problem. A solution that, ironically, would later cause his death on the USS *Utah*.

Cary proposed removing half the lead weights in the diving belt, and leaving off the lead-weighted shoes. This reduced the weight of the diving gear by seventy-eight pounds. To help compensate for the top-heavy condition of the diver, the belt would be worn below the diver's hips and cinched tightly with a leather strap.

This worked well, and we were able to make our way up and down the ladder with a minimum of exertion. The only remaining problems were the explosions that occurred as we cut through the magazine bulkheads.

We removed approximately fifty tons of anti-aircraft shells without further incident. But our next job, blanking off the fire room uptake openings, presented a more difficult and dangerous challenge.

Blanking Off the Fireroom Uptakes

The opening and closing schedules for watertight doors, hatches, and manholes were drawn up by the engineers as a means of controlling the effects of the air bubble when the ship was rotated to an upright position.

Almost overlooked were the large fireroom uptake openings leading to the smokestack. These openings measured approximately thirty feet by thirty feet, and had to be made airtight before starting the righting operation. Otherwise, the air bubble would escape when the ship was rolled over to the ninety-degree position.

Another hole was burned in the bottom of the ship, and a wooden ladder was installed that led down to four feet of water covering the uptake openings. Once the diver entered the water, he proceeded through a door into the firerooms, a distance of fifty feet.

Since it was not practical to use the standard deep-sea diving rig on this particular job, we wore tank suits, or coveralls, and used light-weight shallow-water belts and diving masks. There was no oral communication with topside, since telephones had not been developed for use in a shallow-water diving mask. A standard gas mask was modified and adapted for use as a diving mask. Air was supplied through a standard oxygen hose and in turn the hose was secured to a lifeline of two-inch manila rope.

The diver and topside communicated with a series of sharp and distinct tugs on the lifeline. One tug on the line from topside meant "Are you all right?" An answering tug meant "Affirmative." Two sharp tugs from the diver signaled "Give me some slack in my line." As sufficient slack was received, a single tug was given to stop feeding the line. Three tugs by the diver ordered topside to take up his slack, and four tugs indicated he was coming up and to take up his slack slowly as he advanced.

Since underwater cement had been used effectively on the *West Virginia*'s cofferdam patches, we decided that this method of closing off the uptake openings would be the best one to use. Great physical strength was necessary to handle the building materials needed to construct the cement forms over the uptakes. Two divers worked together as a team to complete the job.

The teamwork required to achieve such an undertaking while working in total darkness was difficult to master at its inception. Finally, a method evolved wherein a working model of the cement form was built topside, and the divers were given exact instructions to follow during their upcoming dive.

Communication between the two men

working together underwater was established by one simply grabbing the other by the arm, which meant, "Come to the surface, I want to talk to you." Both divers would then stand up with their heads above water and shout back and forth through their face masks.

The free air space within the fireroom contained a high concentration of odorless hydrogen sulfide gas. This fact was unknown to us until the day Bill and Cameron were working on the cement forms.

According to Bill's account of the incident, Cameron had shaken his arm to signal a surface conversation. Both men popped their heads above water.

"What'sa matter? Is somethin' wrong?" Bill shouted through his mask.

"My mask is leaking under my chin, and I'm gettin' a mouthful of crappy water. I gotta readjust it," said Cameron.

"Want me to tighten it for you?" Bill asked.

"Naw, I'm going to take it off and check the head straps," Cameron replied.

"What's the air like in here?" Bill asked, and receiving no answer, he yelled louder, "Cameron?"

He lurched over to where Cameron was crumpling and grabbed him just as his head went underwater. Bill remembered the accidental deaths aboard the *Nevada* caused from breathing a high concentration of hydrogen sulfide gas, so he quickly felt around for Cameron's mask and put it over his face. Cameron's body jerked convulsively, and he started to breathe normally once again. He involuntarily vomited into his mask, but he later said he was so frightened of the consequences of washing out his mask, that the mess remained sticking to his cheeks and mouth until he reached the diving station.

In the meantime, Bronco signaled that both divers were returning to the surface. This incident marked the first time we had encountered lethal doses of gas on the *Oklahoma*, but it would not be the last.

We constructed cement forms over the uptake holes using wooden timbers. These were floated into the fireroom, then weighted with sandbags and sunk into position around the perimeter of the uptake openings. The timbers were held in place by wiring them to the uptake grillwork. Heavy expanded metal was stretched over the grillwork and attached to the timbers to support the weight of the cement. Fine wire-mesh screening was laid over the expanded metal to retain the cement.

Because the uptake openings were on a steep angle, the cement forms were terraced with divider planking at two-foot intervals to prevent the wet cement from running to the lowest end of the patch. Finally, the cement forms were completed and the pouring of cement began.

Given the viscosity of the wet cement, and the long path the mixture had to travel to reach its destination, modifications were required to deliver the mixture.

A large pressurized cylinder was used and the hopper filled with wet cement. The top cover was fastened and compressed air applied through the top of the hopper. Air pressure forced the mixture down through the stiff rubber hose to the divers stationed by the uptake forms. Tons and tons of cement were delivered to the uptake patches. This method effectively sealed off the uptake openings, so little air escaped as the ship was later rotated.

VIII

South Pacific Theater of War

Tonga Islands

After we closed off the fireroom uptakes, diving operations were halted for a few days. Salvage engineers pumped compressed air into the *Oklahoma* to test the hull for leaks and to determine the size of the air bubble needed for buoyancy during her righting operation.

It was during this lull that a secret dispatch arrived in the Salvage Unit. It was from Commander Service Force, Pacific, and it requested the services of two divers and a five-man salvage team to volunteer for duty aboard the USS *Seminole* (ATF65). The *Seminole* was scheduled to depart for the war zone within the week. I told Moon this was my chance to get out of Pearl Harbor, and I was taking it. I remember saying, "If I don't go now the war will be over before I ever hear a shot fired in anger." Mullen would later remind me of those last words. He was also anxious to leave the oil and filth of Pearl Harbor for the clean waters of the Pacific. He suggested that we hurry down to Haynes's office and fill out our requests before any of the other divers heard about the dispatch. But our fears proved to be groundless. We were the only two divers who volunteered, which left Pappy no alternative but to approve our requests.

On 15 August 1942, Moon and I and the other five salvors reported aboard fleet tug *Seminole*. She was 205 feet long, 38 feet wide, and carried a crew of 110 men. Her top speed was sixteen knots, and her design and powerful engines proved ideal for towing and ocean salvage work.

She got under way and arrived in Tongatabu, Tonga Islands, on 29 August 1942. Her stated mission was to provide emergency salvage and repair services to damaged vessels in the war zone.

Tongatabu

Our first diving job was to retrieve two barge loads of army-owned cranes and bulldozers resting in one hundred twenty-five feet of water. The barges had been anchored in the harbor earlier, but a violent storm had hit the area, swamped the barges, and spilled their cargo on the bottom.

My first dive in the harbor of Tongatabu was an amazing experience, since almost all of my diving was done in zero visibility within the interiors of sunken battleships.

Once on the bottom of the harbor, I did not need to hunt for cranes and bulldozers, I could see and identify them from a distance of one hundred feet. Contributing to this excellent visibility was a pale coral bottom and an absence of mud. Thousands of colorful fish darted in and

241

out of coral formations in their search for food. Hungry sharks, moray eels, and bigger game fish prowled the edges of the coral. None of the denizens was large enough to give me pause for my safety.

Moon and I rigged wire straps to the cranes and bulldozers, and the *Seminole* hoisted them aboard waiting barges. Work on this project was halted for two weeks when the aircraft carrier *Saratoga* and battleship *South Dakota* arrived requiring emergency diving services.

The *Saratoga* had been torpedoed and large sections of her hull plating hung down twenty feet below her keel. It was feared the damaged plating would tear off, swing back, and damage the ship's propeller while under way. Moon and I cut the damaged plating away while our salvage team and a repair team from the USS *Vestal* reinforced the damaged hull plating above water. These repairs permitted the carrier to sail twenty knots without danger of crippling herself from the damaged plating.

The *South Dakota* developed a similar problem when she hit a submerged coral head. This accident ripped off two hundred feet of her side and bottom hull plating. She was repaired in the same manner as the *Saratoga*. Without these repairs, both the *South Dakota* and the *Saratoga* would have been easy targets for enemy submarines or airplanes lurking in the area.

The crystal-clear waters of Tongatabu Harbor made our repair efforts easier to accomplish on the aircraft carrier *Saratoga* and the battleship *South Dakota*. For example, we could clearly see the arc-oxygen torch and the cutting electrode. We did not have to fumble with the electrode to try to insert it in the torch, as we did diving in total darkness in Pearl Harbor. Ironically, the only time I injured myself was while I was working on the *South Dakota* under perfect diving conditions.

Mullen and I were cutting away huge sections of the battleship's torpedo blister, which had been damaged. I crawled out on part of the blister and was leaning forward to cut a portion of steel plate that was hard to reach. Just as I finished the work I lost my balance. The cutting torch was in my right hand, and somehow in my scramble to hang on to my perch I stabbed myself in the hand. The red-hot end of the electrode punched through my left glove and penetrated the fleshy palm of my hand. Fortunately, the hot electrode cauterized the wound and did not become infected.

After finishing diving on the *Saratoga* and the *South Dakota*, the remainder of September was spent retrieving the sunken bulldozers.

Survivors

On 15 October, the *Seminole* received a high-priority dispatch from the commander of the South Pacific ordering her to get under way and proceed with all possible speed to a point seventy-five miles northwest of Guadalcanal, in the

Solomon Islands. We were ordered to rescue survivors from two sunken ships, the destroyer *Meredith* and tug *Vireo*, and to retrieve a one-thousand-ton barge and tow it into Tulagi Harbor, across the channel from Guadalcanal. The dispatch also ordered the destroyers *Gwin* and *Grayson* to help rescue survivors and then escort the *Seminole* and barge to Tulagi.

Our three-day voyage to the rendezvous with the barge and survivors began with calm weather. At approximately 0100 on 18 October, we encountered rough seas and intermittent heavy rain squalls. This weather condition persisted throughout the next twenty-four hours. While heavy seas hampered our efforts to retrieve the barge, the inclement weather also protected us from detection by patrolling enemy planes.

When the *Seminole* arrived on 18 October, we were met with a nightmarish scene. Only 97 men out of 236 from the destroyer and tug had survived the three-day ordeal. Terribly burned men, their flesh hanging in tatters, many of whom had swallowed fuel oil, lay retching inside the rafts. Other more able-bodied shipmates clung to the outside of the rafts with ropes.

The sea around the life rafts was alive with marauding sharks. The water boiled in their frenzy to attack the men in the water. The attrition rates inside and outside the rafts were enormous. Ten of us on the *Seminole* lined the rail with .30–'06 rifles and killed a number of huge tiger sharks. But we soon discovered that the dead fish only attracted more sharks, so we stopped shooting them.

The two accompanying destroyers rescued most of the survivors while we pulled the remaining eleven out of the water. Shortly after getting them aboard, the lookout shouted down that he had spotted the drifting barge about a mile away. We headed for it at full speed.

The recovery of the adrift, fully loaded barge in the open sea was a masterpiece of ship handling and seamanship by the captain, Lt. Comdr. William G. Fewel. Mountainous waves tossed the *Seminole* and barge together with shattering blows. Even with large ship fenders between them, the *Seminole* suffered a dished-in hull and many cracked ribs. As the barge and ship smashed together, the force of the blows knocked us off our feet.

Our first job was to cut away the tons of chain bridle and hundreds of feet of three-inch towing wire dangling from the barge. Once the old towing assembly was removed, we could connect the *Seminole*'s towing rig.

The clearance work was given to Moon and me because we were experienced in cutting with the oxygen-acetylene torch. Two crew members accompanied us on the barge to help attach the *Seminole*'s tow wire, and also to tend our lifelines while we cut away the old towing rig.

The four of us tied ropes around our waists and crawled out on the bucking barge on our hands and knees, dragging the cutting torch and hoses. Crewmen from the *Seminole* tended our lines from the safety of the ship, ready to rescue any of us unlucky enough to be knocked over the side. Circling the barge were great numbers of tiger sharks, snapping, biting, and waiting for someone to fall overboard. After a few hours of trying, failing, and trying again to sever the old tow wire and chain bridle, we finally completed the job shortly before sunset. We attached the Seminole's tow wire and took the barge in tow. Then the ship headed for Tulagi Island, approximately seventy-five miles away.

The badly injured survivors were cleaned of fuel oil and their wounds treated by the ship's only hospital corpsman. All eleven of them had suffered serious burns and other injuries and were in great pain. Some were unconscious or delirious. We heard them screaming in agony as they relived the horrible three days after their ship was sunk. One man kept having nightmares about the monster shark that jumped into his life raft and tore off a wounded man's leg. Apparently he watched the shark swim away with the leg in its teeth, only to see another shark tear the leg from its mouth. Other survivors told of witnessing delirious comrades who imagined seeing missing shipmates swimming back to the raft. In their delirium they slipped out of their life jackets and swam out toward the nonexistent shipmates, never to be seen again.

Sometime during the early evening hours of

18 October, one of the survivors died. None of the crew had handled a dead body before. The executive officer assigned two of the permanent crew members to prepare the body for burial at sea. The corpse was carried from the berthing area to the crew's washroom and placed on the tile deck. As the muscles in his body relaxed, large quantities of fuel oil were excreted. The oil had been ingested by the deceased as he floated in a sea of fuel during his tragic three days in the water.

The two young crewmen told the executive officer they did not have the stomach for handling a dead body and begged him to relieve them of the onerous task. The executive officer asked Mullen and me if we would complete the job. He knew we had handled many bodies while diving in Pearl Harbor.

We agreed to do it even though neither of us had any experience preparing a body for burial. We had seen a burial at sea depicted in a movie, so we tried to duplicate what we remembered.

We wrapped the body in canvas and added about twenty pounds of scrap iron below his feet. Then we sewed the canvas shroud closed. The body was placed on a wooden plank and draped with an American flag. The captain said a prayer, the plank was raised, and the body slid from under the flag into the ocean. There were few dry eyes during the ceremony, even though none of us even knew the name of the sailor we buried. But his hellish last hours of life deeply affected all of us.

Later when the *Seminole* was blown out from under me and I was in the water with only a life jacket keeping me afloat, the images of the shark attacks came back to haunt me.

Tulagi

The *Seminole* arrived in Tulagi Harbor during the early morning hours of Monday, 19 October. We transferred the ten survivors to the *Gwin*. Then the two destroyers departed the area. The Solomon Islands are an archipelago in the southwest Pacific Ocean located five degrees below the equator. There are eight large islands and forty-odd islets and atolls which lie in two parallel chains separated by a wide channel, nicknamed the "Slot."

Florida was one of the large, mountainous islands with dense jungles. Off its southwest coast was the small island of Tulagi, which had been the capital of the British Solomon Islands before the Japanese captured it five months after the Pearl Harbor attack. Tulagi Harbor was well protected, and ships and boats could moor directly to the banks of both islands and remain hidden from enemy aircraft. Two smaller islands dotted the harbor, Gavutu and Tanambogo. The Japanese had used these two islands as repair bases to service their ships and facilities. Fortunately for us, they left behind a supply of telephone poles and metal shapes, which we would later use to build a new rudder for the *McFarland* and steel I beams to reinforce the damaged stern of the *Portland.*

Geologically the islands could be described as coral deposits on an underwater mountain range that had been pushed above the surface of the water by past volcanic action. This created rugged, mountainous country marked by sheer cliffs and deep valleys above and below the surface of the water. Centuries of hot, humid climates had blanketed the islands with lush jungles — jungles so thick with foliage that sunlight never penetrated. The topographical features helped save many of our ships from detection and destruction.

The captain moored the *Seminole* and the barge directly to the banks of Tulagi Island. We tied our mooring lines to the trunks of trees. Dense foliage extended over the ship and barge. Netting was draped over the exposed areas of the ship, and then camouflaged with branches from trees and bushes.

The other occupants of Tulagi included two PT boats and an old WWI destroyer, USS *McFarland.* The foliage kept us hidden from enemy planes during daylight hours.

Most days we experienced ten to fifteen flyovers by enemy planes trying to spot our positions. I'm sure they knew we were there, but they were never able to find us.

We arrived in Guadalcanal when morale was at its lowest ebb. From Admiral Nimitz down the chain of command, there was grave doubt U.S. Forces could prevail. According to Admiral Nimitz's report to Washington: "It now appears that we are unable to control the sea in the Guadalcanal area. Thus our supply of the positions will only be done at great expense to us. The situation is not hopeless, but it is certainly critical." Mid-October 1942 marked the nadir of misery for American forces in Guadalcanal.

The navy and marines were hanging on by their fingernails. The U.S. Navy ruled the sea from sunup to sundown, thanks largely to our Cactus Air Force, who protected the ships when they had gasoline enough to fly. Surf boats met the supply ships offshore, unloaded them, and landed the cargo on the beach.

But when night fell, our big ships ran like scared rabbits, and small craft holed up in Tulagi Harbor or were beached on Guadalcanal. From dusk to dawn the Japanese navy owned the area. They landed troops, equipment, and supplies, and shelled Henderson Airfield and our positions without fear of opposition. This situation finally changed for the better after Adm. William Halsey assumed command of the South Pacific.

USS *McFarland*

In the predawn hours of 19 October, the *Seminole* sneaked out of Tulagi Harbor with the barge in tow, headed for Guadalcanal approximately twenty-four miles away. We reached the middle of Sealark Channel, but then we were ordered to return to Tulagi with all possible speed.

An enemy submarine had been sighted near Savo Island and enemy aircraft were headed for Guadalcanal to bomb Henderson Field. It was no time to be out in the channel with a barge loaded with gasoline, bombs, and ammunition.

We returned to Tulagi without incident, and we moored the ship and barge to the island.

We had just secured the last line when the commanding officer of the *McFarland*, J. C. Alderman, and the engineering officer, Lieutenant Chambers, came aboard and asked our captain for the assistance of our salvage unit to help repair the *McFarland*.

Mullen and I and members of the five-man salvage team went aboard the *McFarland*. The first order of business was to plug holes and split seams in the underwater hull section of the ship in order to keep her afloat. Next, it was decided to lighten the ship aft by removing one three-inch gun and the deckhouse.

The *McFarland* had received a bomb hit in her stern two weeks earlier. The blast had blown off twenty-five feet of her stern, including the rudder, but miraculously had left undamaged her two propellers, and their shafts and strut bearings.

The engineering officer had assembled three abandoned Japanese telephone poles approximately thirty feet long and two steel beams. He had a vague idea how he was going to build the rudder, but he didn't know how he was going to hinge the rudder to the stern of the ship.

The *McFarland* was moored to the bank of Florida Island. The sheer banks of both Florida and Tulagi Islands dropped straight down one hundred feet or deeper. Battleships or carriers could moor to the islands without danger of going aground.

Enemy air raids on Guadalcanal were predicted and the enemy submarine had not cleared the area, so on 20 October at 0830 we went alongside the *McFarland* and removed the deckhouse and gun using the *Seminole*'s crane. Moon and I were also diving, plugging the shrapnel holes in the ship's bottom hull.

Mullen and I decided not to wear a hard hat diving outfit while we repaired the *McFarland*, because it was too cumbersome. Instead we used a shallow-water mask and swim trunks. Visibility under the ship and in Tulagi Harbor was only fair. After I had been underwater for an hour, Moon signaled that he was bringing me to the surface. I came up and asked why. He pointed up the inlet between Tulagi and Florida Islands, a look of fear on his face. About one hundred yards upstream were two of the biggest crocodiles I had ever seen, lying on the bank sunning themselves. We suspended diving for the day.

Meanwhile, the *Seminole* crew worked the remainder of the day and into the night transferring hundreds of barrels of gasoline and tons of bombs from the barge to the open decks of the

Seminole. We spent the night aboard the *Seminole* and the next morning before daylight we headed for Guadalcanal and our baptism of fire.

We arrived a few hundred yards off the beach and were met by approximately thirty Higgins boats that circled our ships waiting to be loaded.

The boat crews were unrecognizable as U.S. Navy sailors. They were a ragged bunch, sporting unkempt beards and wearing combinations of filthy marine, navy, and Japanese attire.

We loaded all thirty of the boats, and they made a beeline for the beach. Suddenly a hidden Japanese howitzer in the hills started firing at us. We went to battle stations, and shortly thereafter our hull was damaged by a near miss explosion. Shrapnel from the shell punched a few small holes in our side. All the rest of the shells zoomed harmlessly over our heads.

We moved out of range of the enemy howitzer, which had been nicknamed "Pistol Pete" by the marines. The marines had often tried to destroy Pete by bombing and shelling his location, but without much luck. The big gun was mounted on railroad tracks and was well hidden in a cave. The Japanese never rolled the gun out of the cave or fired at our forces when any of our planes were in the air for fear our pilots would discover their hiding place.

The remainder of the morning was spent unloading our cargo. We returned to Tulagi in the afternoon, and the salvage crew continued working on the *McFarland*.

Because the enemy submarine was still on the prowl in the channel, 22 and 23 October were spent in Tulagi. In addition, we were exposed to daily flyovers by enemy planes looking for juicy targets.

The crocodiles were gone by 22 October, so I decided to finish the patching job. I was unaware that the underwater banks of the island were home to large areas of stinging sea nettles. The nettles gave a painful sting when they came in contact with a bare body. I felt a sharp pain on my foot and bare leg, which I was sure came from the teeth of a crocodile. I came up as if shot from a cannon, almost afraid to look and see if I had a whole leg. Moon and I were stung many times after that, but we never gave much thought to crocodiles again.

By the time we finished the underwater repairs, the *McFarland* crew and our salvage team had bolted the telephone poles together and were attaching the steel beams to both ends of the rudder. Lieutenant Chambers's rudder creation had grown from its original twenty-foot length to more than thirty feet. From then on we always called him "Rubber Ruler Chambers" — behind his back, of course. The nickname wasn't meant to be cruel, because we all agreed that he had worked many long hours on the project, but the name did afford us a little levity in an otherwise grim situation.

Up to this point, no one had devised a plan to hinge the rudder and attach it to the ship. All of us in the salvage crew got together with the engineering department of the *McFarland* and came up with a solution. We rounded up some two-inch-diameter steel round stock that the Japanese had left behind. We cut the stock into eighteen-inch-long sections. These pieces were heated to a red heat and bent in U shapes.

When we were ready to attach the rudder to the ship, we flooded the bow of the *McFarland* with water and assembled as many of the crew on the bow as we could crowd in the space. This had the desired effect of raising the stern about three feet out of the water. Two U shapes, one top and one bottom, were welded to a vertical steel beam attached to the vessel's stern.

The rudder was floated into place, the U shapes passed through the welded ones on the vertical beam, and then the shapes were welded to one end of the rudder. We attached two wires to the other end of the rudder and ran one to the port side and the other to starboard of the stern. The wires were connected to a winch, and the rudder was controlled by taking a strain on one wire while slacking off on the other. The ship was capable of making thirty-degree turns with her new rudder.

Both the captain and the engineer praised our salvage team for the outstanding job we had done for them. The captain asked our skipper for our names, ranks, and serial numbers because he said he wanted to recommend us for commendation medals, but we never heard from him again.

Seminole **Is Sunk**

Finally, on Saturday, 24 October, the coast was clear for transiting Sealark Channel. The *Seminole* was loaded with gasoline and munitions, and we delivered our cargo to Guadalcanal without incident. This second load almost emptied the barge of its deadly cargo.

Sometime late on 24 October, the *Seminole* received word that two old World War I four-stack destroyers, USS *Zane* and USS *Trever*, would be arriving in Tulagi from Espíritu Santo early on 25 October. Their mission included: towing four PT boats to Tulagi, delivering 300 fifty-five-gallon drums of aviation gasoline, conducting a shore bombardment of Jap positions on Guadalcanal, and escorting the *Seminole* to a new assignment.

During the early morning hours of 25 October, all the gasoline drums from the barge and destroyers were loaded aboard the *Seminole* and *YP-284*, a wooden-hull ex–tuna boat.

In addition to the gasoline, the *Seminole* also carried a few hundred rounds of 75mm ammunition, four howitzers, and one hundred marines returning to the front lines on Guadalcanal. In the last-minute confusion caused from having marine passengers aboard, I forgot to bring our diving mask and cutting torch aboard. This turned out to be a stroke of luck.

The *Seminole* arrived off Guadalcanal and off-loaded the marines, howitzers, and about three hundred drums of gasoline. Suddenly, general quarters was sounded and the ship went to battle stations. Enemy planes were over Henderson Field, but they attacked neither the airfield or our ships, for some unknown reason. We received orders from Guadalcanal at 1000 to return to Tulagi with all possible speed because three enemy destroyers were sighted rounding Savo Island heading for Guadalcanal. As we neared mid-channel, the enemy destroyers changed course and it was obvious they would cut the YP and our ship off before we could reach the safety of Tulagi Harbor. The captain changed course and headed for Lengo Channel.

In the meantime, the *Trever* and the *Zane* came charging out of Tulagi Harbor steaming south at about twenty-nine knots. The three enemy destroyers gave chase and opened fire at a range of five miles. Soon the *Zane* was hit with a 5-inch shell, which knocked out one of their guns and left three men dead and four more wounded.

The *Zane* and *Trever* ducked in a shallow channel, which the destroyers were not willing to enter. The enemy ships then turned and headed for the *YP* and the *Seminole*. The three destroyers mounted twelve 5-inch guns with a range of at least fifteen thousand yards. The *Seminole* had one 3-inch gun which had a range of about ten thousand yards. We also had a couple of .30-caliber machine guns. Without a level playing field on which to compete, we knew it was useless to fire at the Japanese ships.

The *YP-284* became the first casualty, because she was the closest to the destroyers in mid-channel. She was hit with a salvo of 5-inch shells and sank almost immediately.

The *Seminole* changed course and ran parallel to the beach, hoping that we were not seen. This maneuver put us outside the protective umbrella of our marine howitzers ashore.

The enemy ships headed directly for us, firing as they came. At first the distance was so great, I watched the shells lose their spiraling motion and tumble end-over-end over my head, then fall harmlessly into the sea.

Hiding behind drums of aviation gasoline and watching shells flying overhead made Moon and me wish we were back in Pearl Harbor. We grabbed life jackets and used them as shields, as we peered through the armholes at the fireworks. Strangely enough, even this completely useless protection gave me a feeling of safety. Moon said he felt the same way.

Moon leaned over with a smile on his face and shouted, "What was that you said about never hearing a shot fired in anger?"

He got an expletive for an answer.

Three salvos pounded the *Seminole* in her forward area. At least fifteen armor-piercing shells tore through her thin hull plating without exploding. Shrapnel flew. I heard a cry and saw a seaman drop dead from a shrapnel wound. Three others in the crew suffered wounds.

Moon, the ship's chief carpenter's mate,

Henry Buhl, and I were huddled on the open fantail, expecting the ship to reach shore. We looked over the side, and to our surprise, saw members of the crew floating by in life rafts and life jackets.

"What the hell's going on?" yelled the chief to a life raft crowded with men.

"Abandon ship. Get the hell off there," came the answer.

Whatever the reason, the order to abandon ship never reached the three of us on the fantail. Probably the public address system was destroyed from the numerous shell hits in the forward part of the ship. The three of us did not need a second invitation. We were surrounded by fires. The boat deck was burning fiercely, and gasoline drums were exploding. The forward part of the fantail was ablaze, and the flames were licking at our heels as we hurriedly donned life jackets and jumped over the stern.

The wounded ship continued down the channel, discharging fuel oil and burning gasoline. The *Seminole* was approximately two hundred yards downwind from us when she exploded with a thunderous roar, spewing burning gasoline over a wide area.

Sealark Channel between Tulagi and Guadalcanal was a favorite feeding ground for large numbers of sharks, because of the thousands of enemy and allied sailors who died there when their ships were sunk. The channel was nicknamed "Iron Bottom Sound," because more than fifty ships from both sides met their end in its waters.

Etched in my mind were the grisly pictures of the shark-bitten survivors from the *Meredith* and the *Vireo*. As I looked warily about, I saw Moon's dark head bobbing in the water near the chief's, so I called to them to stay close together as I swam toward them.

No sharks were seen during the four hours we were in the water. I think they were driven off by the many explosions and fires from the *Seminole*'s demise.

After sinking our two ships, the enemy destroyers began firing machine guns at the life rafts, while their crews fired rifles at our heads bobbing in the water. The three of us slipped out of our life jackets and ducked underwater.

Two bullets whizzed over my head, and one hit my jacket.

We later found out that during this period of the Guadalcanal campaign, neither side was taking prisoners, which I'm sure accounted for the enemy strafing us in the water.

Finally, the Japanese destroyers came within range of the marine howitzers and our gunners hit one destroyer and scored near misses on the other two. Also, two of our F4F aircraft from VMF-212 squadron arrived and strafed the destroyers, driving them away. The Higgins surfboats came churning out and picked up the survivors from the *Seminole* and *YP*. Moon, the chief, and I did not realize we were swimming directly toward the beaches that were occupied by Japanese troops. Fortunately, we were rescued before we reached shore.

Later that day we cheered when we heard our forces had paid the Jap destroyer back in spades. The attack on the *Zane, Trever, Seminole,* and *YP* by the three enemy destroyers had far-reaching implications.

The Japanese task force that entered Sealark Channel on 25 October consisted of eight destroyers and one heavy cruiser. Their mission was to bombard Henderson Field and put it out of commission. The cruiser, *Yuri,* and five destroyers waited for the three destroyers to finish chasing the old World War I destroyers and sinking us before they assembled to bombard Henderson Field. This was a grievous error on their part.

This delay gave our pilots time to gas up their dive-bombers and take off. The planes damaged most of the destroyers and forced the cruiser to run aground. At the end of the day's engagement, we clearly had won more than we lost.

Guadalcanal

Moon and I reported in to the commanding officer of the Naval Station, Guadalcanal, for orders. Our navy work clothes were torn and oil soaked, so we were issued one marine khaki pair of pants, shirt, and field shoes, but no socks.

The *Seminole* survivors were assigned makeshift tents in the naval station compound.

Behind our tents we were required to dig shallow foxholes, approximately two feet deep, for ourselves in case of air raids.

During this period of the campaign in Guadalcanal, enemy snipers infiltrated our navy and marine camps at will. The snipers hid in the dense jungles by day and positioned themselves in palm trees at night.

A few of our people were killed by snipers when they lit their cigarettes at night. We quickly learned never to smoke or light cigarettes out in the open.

I'm sure the Japanese military didn't plan on winning in Guadalcanal by the use of snipers. Our intelligence forces thought it was part of their overall psychological warfare plan of harassment. There is no question that their use of snipers made our lives more miserable.

Our roving sentries around the camps managed to kill most of the snipers, but new Jap recruits soon took their places.

When the pitch-blackness of the night blanketed the island, none of us ventured outside our tents. The only exception to this rule was when the call of nature was very strong. When it was necessary to sit down and answer the call, we had to walk approximately five hundred feet in the darkness to the latrines. During this journey, we would be challenged by roving sentries demanding the password to identify ourselves. Stand-up calls of nature were answered against the tree nearest to our tent.

Our passwords changed daily and always had the letter *L* in them because the Japanese couldn't pronounce the "ell" sound. It always came out sounding like an *R*.

Later in November when the 8th Marine Division landed, snipers abounded in the trees near their encampment. Guadalcanal was the baptism of fire for these marines and they reacted accordingly. The first few nights after they landed sounded like the Fourth of July and Chinese New Year all rolled into one. Steady bursts of BAR machine guns, rifles, and even hand grenades thundered through the night air. None of us dared to go outside our tents at night until the marines moved inland to the front lines. Although the marines killed many of the hated snipers, they also killed a few hapless cattle that wandered into their line of fire. The natives were later reimbursed for the loss of their livestock by the U.S. government.

Moon and I were each assigned a small landing craft and issued boxes of dynamite, with orders to blow up any obstructions on the beaches that could be used by the enemy to hide behind. The beaches were littered with approximately one hundred wrecked and abandoned boats, tanks, and large pieces of debris that washed ashore after the fierce naval battles offshore. We were successful in blasting apart most of the obstructions after we discovered where to place the dynamite charges to get the maximum results. Once we reduced the wrecks to manageable proportions, we pulled the larger pieces into deep water and sank them. This assignment took us three weeks to complete. Later the *McFarland*'s skipper sent the naval station a message that requested the services of *Seminole*'s divers for two days to help finish repairs to the ship. Moon and I completed the job and returned to Guadalcanal.

At night we operated with a convoy of boats, resupplying the marines fighting the Japanese 230th Regiment, located between Koli and Taivu Points. This assignment was fraught with unseen terror and danger for marines and sailors alike.

U.S. troops had surrounded the Japanese on three sides and were pushing them into the sea. The assigned mission for our convoy of boats was to ferry replacement troops and supplies to our forces on the northern and southern flanks of the enemy. The GI's favorite acronym, SNAFU (situation normal all fouled up), must have been conceived to describe our resupply campaign.

Our nightly trips were made on moonless nights and under tight security measures. But somehow the Japanese knew all about our movements.

Our convoy of boats came under attack from friendly and enemy fire for most of our three-hour trip. We arrived near the area where the designated marine signalman was supposed to give us the secret signal to land, by blinking his flashlight. Not one but dozens of flashlights up and down the beach beckoned us with the correct secret signal. At least six different boats were conned into landing on Japanese-held beaches and were forced to fight their way clear.

Despite assurances that security and communications between headquarters and units in the field would improve, nothing ever changed during this ten-day period.

During the first week in November, Moon and I discovered firsthand why the marines referred to the jungles of Guadalcanal as a "living hell." Eight of us surfboat coxswains were ordered to transport a contingent of marines up the Tenaru River in search of enemy soldiers. Natives, who hated the Japanese, reported seeing many enemy troops near their village.

We arrived at the designated area and the marines headed into the jungle looking for the enemy. Our orders were to secure our boats to the riverbanks and wait for our troops to return. This assignment stretched into a two-day, two-night affair, but thank God I wasn't exposed any longer than that to the miseries of the Guadalcanal jungle.

Foul-smelling swamps and bogs surrounded us. Lagoons hid hungry crocodiles in fetid waters. We saw huge snakes, enormous spiders, scorpions, and lizards three feet in length. We encased ourselves in netting after some of us were stung by three-inch-long wasps and bitten by ants whose poison caused large red welts and felt like we were being burned with lit cigarettes.

I ventured into the jungle only once, on my first day there. As I walked beneath the foliage, I felt what I assumed to be branches and leaves brushing against my head and shoulders. When I emerged from the jungle darkness and returned to my boat, Moon rushed up to me and started to slap and brush me on the back. He was dislodging a strange type of voracious leech that lived in trees and dropped down on their victims as they walked beneath.

Of all the crawling, squirming, flying creatures I encountered in the Solomon Islands, none made my flesh crawl as much as the blood-sucking leeches did.

Guadalcanal was not a place for fun and games. There were no books to read, no movies to watch, no sports to play, and no females to romance. Our only recreation was of our own making.

One of our favorite games was the crab horse race. We would draw a circle twelve feet in diameter. Everyone who wanted to join in the game caught a coconut crab and marked its shell with a symbol for identification purposes. Bets were collected from each contestant, and the crabs were released in the middle of the circle. The first crab that crossed the circle won all the bets. The bets were usually made in cigarettes, because no one had any money.

The largest wager that was ever won centered around the least likely outcome. Two cartons of sea store cigarettes were the prize. Twenty crabs were released in the middle of the circle. With deliberate exertion they began to grasp each other with powerful claws. Crabs were torn apart in slow motion. Some contestants lay inert while others continued their deadly combat. On the sidelines, the bettors were alternately exhorting and cursing their entries in the race. Severed legs and claws were building in mounds, reminiscent of a beachside barbecue. From beneath one such mound a very small crab emerged in apparent confusion. He clawed his way out on the far side of the continuing battles. He had lost a claw and two legs during the skirmishes. He hesitated for a minute, then turned to look back at the battle-field. Contestants continued to separate each other into cocktail-size pieces. After due deliber-ation, the weary veteran corrected his direction and slowly limped across the finish line. He was the only contestant able to do so.

The other source of diversion for us was our weekly betting pool. Once again the prize was in the form of cigarettes, but the game was much more bizarre. Only seven bettors could enter the pool. We divided toilet paper into seven squares and marked them for each day of the week. Then each contestant drew a square out of a hat. The game was won and bets were collected by the person who drew the day of the week that had the greatest number of dead or alive Japanese soldiers delivered by the Guadalcanal natives.

The natives of Guadalcanal had suffered

greatly under the Japanese occupation of their island. They hated the Japanese with a passion. Woe unto the Japanese soldier who was captured by a Guadalcanal tribesman. He would be sure to end up with a spear through his body, strapped to a pole, and deposited in front of the naval station. Natives were paid by our military for any enemy soldiers they brought in. Our intelligence people wanted them for interrogation, but the natives seldom delivered any Japanese alive.

The second week of November began uneventfully, but then all hell broke loose. A small convoy of merchant marine ships, escorted by destroyers, arrived off Guadalcanal and began unloading their cargo of food and materials. At a time when tobacco was used almost universally, we had no way to obtain cigarettes on the island. There were no navy exchanges, and we had no money to buy cigarettes if they had been for sale. So the days of unloading cargo from ships became special events for surfboat coxswains. Unloading meant that at the end of the day we could be rich in cigarettes and maybe a few candy bars.

We did not beg or even ask for such wealth from our benefactors on the navy and merchant ships, but Moon and I devised a subtle approach that got our message across.

Mullen and I tied our boats close together alongside a ship discharging cargo.

I would shout to Moon, loud enough to be heard on the deck of the merchant ship, "Hey, Mullen, you got a smoke?"

"Naw, I ran out of cigarettes last week."

This short exchange would usually elicit sympathy from the crewmen aboard ships. Hard as life might be at sea, sailors knew it did not compare to the dangers and hardships encountered on Guadalcanal. We could frequently count on a carton of sea store cigarettes being tossed into each of our boats. Once in a while a generous soul would lower a whole case of cigarettes to us and ask us to distribute them, which we did.

The marines seemed to have an unlimited supply of tobacco. I think cigarettes were shipped to them disguised as kitchen utensils, or some other innocuous label, to prevent theft of the contents. One of the small eighteen hundred–ton cargo ships, the SS *Majaba*, was torpedoed by an enemy submarine as she rode at anchor about five hundred yards offshore. The *Majaba* started sinking slowly, and her civilian crew quickly abandoned ship.

Moon and I were circling the *Majaba* in our boats. She didn't appear to be sinking quickly, so we decided to board her and cut the anchor chain, which would allow the tide and surf to push her up on the beach. As soon as she was safely beached, we climbed aboard and carried off dozens of cans of fruits and vegetables. Our diet up until this time consisted of cans of corned beef from Australia, three times daily.

We gorged ourselves on canned peaches and pears. We also gave away cans to crewmen from the *Seminole* and swapped some of our treasures for baked goods dreamed up by cooks from the 1st Marine Division.

The next day we returned in our boats to finish unloading cargo from the merchant marine ships. One of the crew members told me his ship was leaving for Seattle as soon as they finished unloading. I asked him if he would mail a letter to my mother when he arrived in the States, and he assured me he would.

When I returned to the base, I tried to find a piece of paper I could use to write my letter on, but without success. Finally one of my marine friends said he would give me what he thought was a Japanese telegram that he found when he first hit the beach on the day of the U.S. invasion.

I told him I didn't want him to give me his souvenir, but he insisted it was for a good cause. I wrote my mother in Riverside and told her if she heard any disquieting news about the *Seminole* that she was not to worry because I was all right. I took the letter out to the ship and prevailed upon the crewman to use his envelope and his stamp to mail it.

When I visited my mother in early 1943, during my thirty days survivor's leave, she told me she had received my letter almost a week before getting a telegram from the navy informing her I was missing. No one could read the message written in Japanese on the back of the telegram. Until her death, my dear mother treasured that letter I sent her forty years before.

The Joy of Socks

The sun rose early, and I awakened from the brightness of the island sky. I sat up in my makeshift bed aboard my landing boat and reached for my marine shirt already caked with salt. It was stiff and felt scratchy on my chest and shoulders. I think I'll sleep in it tonight, I thought, because perspiration will make it softer. I felt around in the bottom of the boat for my marine field shoes. I pulled one of the high-top shoes on and grimaced with pain as the rough leather interior and exposed stitching rubbed against my raw ankle-bone. I groaned and pulled on the other shoe as well.

Fresh water and soap for bathing and laundering were luxuries unavailable to us on Guadalcanal. Also, socks were in extremely short supply. Socks were only issued to marines on the front lines, and rightly so. Marines slogging through swamps and bogs hunting for Japanese suffered bouts of "jungle rot." Jungle rot was the name given to a disease that infected feet, which were immersed in contaminated water over long periods of time. It is a debilitating condition, which if untreated sometimes requires amputation of the feet. The only prevention was to keep the feet warm and dry. Extra pairs of socks were vital as prevention tools.

I got to my feet and looked over at my buddy Moon, still snoozing in his boat. I felt a terrible urge to scratch the dozens of red welts above my shoe tops left by swarms of hungry mosquitoes. Damn, I thought, if only I had a pair of heavy woolen socks, I'd be able to stuff my pant legs inside. Then I'd be protected from those murderous varmints.

I decided to wake Moon. "Hey, Moon. How many cans of peaches do we have left in your boat?"

Moon sat bold upright and rubbed the sleep from his eyes. "How do I know this early in the morning? I'll count them when I'm awake."

"As long as we have at least two cans, I'm going to try and barter one for a pair of socks," I said. "Get dressed and let's go see your cook friends at the 1st Marine Division. Maybe there is someone who might swap peaches for socks."

"Yeah, okay. But give me a chance to get my eyes open."

We walked through the palm trees to the marine mess tent near Henderson Field. I had a gallon can of peaches under my arm. We told the cooks about the business transaction I planned to make. Moon and I were just finishing our coffee when one of the cooks walked up and pointed to a corporal buddy of his who owned three pairs of socks. He seemed a likely candidate for my proposition.

I approached the corporal and asked him if he was interested in a swap. He jumped at the deal and said he would pick up the socks from his tent and be right back. He returned shortly with a rolled pair of socks, and our swap was consummated.

Moon and I returned to our boats, and I hid the socks under the floorboards of my boat.

During the next three days, a convoy of supply ships arrived offshore and began to discharge their cargo. All available surfboats worked from before daylight until sunset unloading the ships. I didn't have time to think about my socks, let alone try them on.

Finally, when the three hectic days were over, I retrieved my socks from their hiding place and unrolled them.

"You lucky son-of-a-gun," Moon said as I pulled the first sock on my right foot. The sock stretched to my knee and my foot still hadn't reached the toe of the sock.

Moon let out a whoop of laughter, hooting and hollering.

"What's so funny?" I asked.

"That marine took you to the cleaners, my friend. Those socks don't have any feet in them. They probably rotted out from being in the water too long."

I trudged back to the marine cook tent only to learn that the corporal and his outfit had gone back to duty on the front lines the night before.

Despite this setback, I managed to tie a piece of twine to the bottom edges of the socks, which formed stirrups and prevented them from slipping out of my shoes. While the twine was a little uncomfortable to walk on, the socks protected my ankles from chafing and kept the mosquitoes from draining my blood.

The Naval Battle for Guadalcanal

November also ushered in increased aerial activity by two Japanese irritants. The first was nicknamed "Washing Machine Charlie." Charlie was a twin-engine seaplane dispatched at night from an enemy cruiser. His mission consisted of flying over our positions and dropping flares and propaganda leaflets. He acquired his nickname because the plane's engine sounded like an old Maytag washing machine chugging and laboring overhead. A greater irritant was "Louie the Louse." Louie was a single-engine seaplane that also was based aboard an enemy cruiser. But when we heard Louie coming we knew we were in for a night of terror. He always accompanied the "Tokyo Express," a group of cruisers and destroyers who steamed offshore, throwing tons of screaming shells aimed at Henderson Field. Louie started the festivities by dropping flares over our positions around midnight, then he dropped fragmentation bombs indiscriminately. After that, the intensive shelling from the ships began. While the attacks were not always successful from a military standpoint, they did cause us many sleepless nights. So Louie was aptly named "the Louse."

On their nightly runs, the Tokyo Express

started to bombard the beaches in addition to the airfield. Moon and I received word from headquarters to return inland where we could seek the safety of foxholes when the bombs began to fall.

We reluctantly left the comfort of our boats for a tent. The bombing and shelling continued unabated and forced us to spend long hours in our foxholes. But the explosions themselves didn't evoke the dread many of us felt as we crouched in a dank, black foxhole. It was the many unwelcome visitors that climbed into our holes with us that I minded. Thousands of big rats and coconut crabs, driven out of their nests by the earth-shattering explosions, scurried about in a frenzy as they tried to escape the noise and eruptions. This experience ranks as my second least favorite one while in Guadalcanal. The leeches remain in first place.

Moon and I endured this situation for a few nights, and finally decided we would rather face enemy shells than do battle with rats and crabs and God knows what else in the dark. So we sneaked back to our boats and rigged up hammocks and slept in them for the remainder of the time we were on the island.

Almost every day, Moon and I swam in the ocean in order to cool off and also to wash our sweat-soaked clothing. Most days I would rinse my one pair of marine khaki pants and shirt and hang them out to dry while I swam around in the nude. Swimming in the tepid tropical waters was relaxing and cooling, but without fresh water to rinse my body, the harsh dried salt from the sea-water caused an itchy rash to form between my legs and under my arms.

These itchy areas, combined with the ones from the four-inch band of mosquito bites around my ankles, kept me scratching in one place or another day and night. Sometimes at night I would wake up clawing at my crotch, only to awaken other areas of my body to their need for attention. Nothing could be more frustrating than to have five areas of your body clamoring for a good scratching, and only two hands to satisfy the demand.

Shortly after midnight on 13 November, we were awakened by the sounds of heavy and sustained gunfire coming from offshore. I was sure that the Tokyo Express was paying us another visit.

We waited expectantly for the incoming mail, or shells, but none arrived. The distant rumble of big guns became a continuous muted roar. The skies to the north of us were brilliant with orange, yellow, and red flashes. It looked like a huge Fourth of July fireworks display. At first we had no idea what was happening, but then we realized that our navy was finally challenging the dominance of the Japanese navy after sundown. Finally, about 0215, the gunfire and flashes stopped and were replaced by drifting masses of flames that marked the dying ships.

Moon and I did not sleep much that night,

wondering who had won the battle and what we would find at dawn. Just before first light we saw five burning ships visible on the horizon. We decided to take my boat out and see if we could be of help.

Hours later we approached the first ship. It was one of our destroyers, the USS *Cushing*. The ship was burning violently amidships on the main deck and on the fantail. We saw four bodies sprawled on deck, so we went alongside and Moon jumped aboard to see if anyone was alive. No one was, so we left hurriedly because we were afraid the unexploded ammunition, scattered about on deck, might go up at any moment.

We headed for the next destroyer, but then we spotted two men clinging to some floating debris. They were floating in a patch of thick bunker oil, and their heads and faces were covered with it. We pulled them from the water and wiped the oil from their faces and eyes only to discover they were the enemy! Moon grabbed his rifle and motioned them to lie facedown on the deck.

"If either of you two bastards move as much as an eyeball, I'll plug you. Understand?" he said in his best James Cagney/Edward G. Robinson voice.

I'm sure they didn't understand him, or me either, when I shouted to Moon that he'd better club them, since shooting them might put holes in the boat and sink us. But they lay facedown for a full four hours while we held them captive.

Shortly after picking up our prisoners, we saw a large ship in the distance that appeared to be traveling in circles. I thought it looked like one of our heavy cruisers, but in the morning haze I couldn't be sure. Suddenly it fired its big forward guns, and I could see a red and yellow cloud of smoke appear.

"Hell, they're shooting at us," Moon yelled.

I quickly changed course to dodge the shells, then as we looked beyond the firing ship, we saw huge explosions and fires erupt from direct shell hits.

The heavy cruiser USS *Portland* gave a good account of herself on the morning of 13 November 1942. She drew first blood by sinking a Hibiki-class destroyer with two 8-inch salvos. Shortly thereafter she received a large-caliber shell hit in the starboard hanger, which wounded the executive officer and twelve other men.

The *Portland* fired eighteen 8-inch shells at a cruiser and scored several hits, which started a number of fires.

At 0158 hours, the *Portland* was torpedoed in her starboard side by a Jap destroyer. The *Portland* began circling to the right in tight circles as she finished her first complete circles. Soon she spotted a Haruna-type battleship and blasted her with twenty-four 8-inch shells, which caused many fires that burned out of control. The *Portland* received two hits from 14-inch shells, but they didn't do much damage to the hull because they were bombardment shells and didn't penetrate her side. The other enemy battleship's salvos flew over the *Portland* without hitting her.

At 0630, the *Portland* commenced firing at a Shigure-class destroyer near Savo Island and sank her with a couple of salvos. This last shelling was the one that Moon and I thought was coming straight at us when we headed out Sealark Channel in our Higgins boat.

USS *Portland*

We finally recognized the firing ship as one of ours and we headed for her with full speed. She was the heavy cruiser USS *Portland*. She had been crippled by a torpedo hit in her starboard quarter. It had opened up a fifty-foot hole in her side. Her two forward propellers had been blown off, which left only the after port and starboard screws available for propulsion. The rudder was jammed to starboard, and this, combined with the fifty-foot-wide hole in her starboard quarter, forced her to travel in right circles only.

I brought our boat alongside the *Portland*'s bow and yelled up to a khaki-clad figure and asked if we could help. The figure turned out to be the commanding officer. He pointed to a damaged and sinking ship a few hundred yards away and directed me to proceed with all possible speed and see if we could be of help to them.

The ship was the light cruiser USS *Atlanta*. When we arrived, she was slowly sinking despite the valiant efforts by her crew to save her. We passed a towline to her bow and began to pull her inch by inch toward the northern end of Guadalcanal. The officer on the bow who was directing the towing effort said that they hoped to get the cruiser in shallow water before it sank, so it could be salvaged at a later time.

Shortly after we began towing the *Atlanta*, the harbor tug *Bobolink* arrived and relieved us of our towing assignment. We returned to help the *Portland* attempt to steer a course for Tulagi Harbor. The *Portland*'s commanding officer told me to place the bow of my boat against his starboard bow and push, as he tried to steer by using his engines. Unfortunately, our boat didn't generate enough pushing power to be of much help.

Hours later a YP craft joined us in pushing, but it wasn't effective either. That afternoon the tug *Bobolink* returned after she finished towing the heavily damaged *Atlanta* to Guadalcanal. The *Atlanta* was subsequently abandoned and scuttled in deep water to keep her out of enemy hands.

After the *Bobolink* relieved the YP and us, I informed the commanding officer of the *Portland*, Capt. Lawrence DuBois, that Moon and I were salvage divers and we could get the ship's rudder operational if he could get us some diving equipment. He told me to meet the ship as soon as they arrived in Tulagi with a list of diving equipment we needed. He said he would send a message and have the equipment flown in immediately. We turned our two prisoners over to the YP and headed for Tulagi.

We arrived in Tulagi about 9 P.M. We tied up our boat to one of the PT-boat piers. We were dead tired, so we hit the sack. We were awakened about 11:30 P.M. by an LTJG (lieutenant, junior grade) who asked us to volunteer to fill in as crew members on his PT boat. Moon and I rubbed the sleep from our eyes. We told him he could count on us, even though the nearest we had been to a PT boat was to watch one go by. The lieutenant said he was short one gunner and one engineman. Moon spoke up first and said he would man one of the twin .50-caliber machine guns. This left me belowdeck to help run the engines, which I had never seen before. The LTJG explained his predicament, saying that most of the newly arrived boat crews were in the sick bay with dengue fever or malaria and too sick to get out of bed. He told us that the attack they had planned to mount that night could have used all six boats, but they were lucky to get two under way because of sickness. The urgency came from a report that a strong Tokyo Express, consisting of heavy cruisers and destroyers, was on its way to attack the airfield and its planes on Guadalcanal. The LTJG emphasized that we couldn't allow this to happen even if it meant sacrificing the two PT boats. There was also concern the enemy might attack Tulagi and sink the wounded *Portland*. Moon and I hurried aboard the lieutenant's boat, eager to ride a PT boat on an attack mission. The boats were eighty feet long and constructed of plywood. They carried two twin-mounted, .50 caliber–machine guns and four torpedo tubes. The torpedoes were launched by the skipper from the cockpit. Three twelve-cylinder Packard engines drove the boat through the water at forty miles per hour or better.

The regular engineman was already aboard when I arrived and was standing by to start the engines. He pushed the *start* buttons and the engines coughed and sputtered, and as all cylinders fired together a rumbling roar reverberated throughout the jungles of Tulagi and Florida Islands, setting off a cacophony of noises from the inhabitants of the jungles. As the boats came alive, we cast off our lines and headed out to Sealark Channel to challenge the huge armada of enemy ships. Nights in the waters off Guadalcanal were darker than the inside of a cave. In the early evening hours after sunset the glimmer of light from the setting sun behind the island helped outline the tallest peaks and sloping sides. But once that light was extinguished, total darkness enveloped the area. Once we cleared the harbor the skipper pushed the throttle to flank speed. The bow sprang high in the water, the stern sat down low, and the surge of power knocked me off my feet. I soon learned to hang on to something solid when those powerful engines revved up. A few minutes after midnight we received a friendly recognition signal from the *Portland* and the *Bobolink* as they inched their way into Tulagi. Approximately halfway across the channel we slowed to one-third speed and applied the muffler system. The full-throated roar of the engines was reduced to a purr as we snaked our way closer to Guadalcanal. The enemy ships were laying down barrage after barrage of shells into the airstrip. The enemy was oblivious to our presence at first. We headed for two of the ships that appeared to be firing the biggest shells, judging from the size of the muzzle blasts. The LTJG had told us earlier that it was always safer to attack a cruiser than a destroyer because of their slower speed and less maneuverability. Our skipper fired all four fish, as did the other boat, when we were a few thousand yards away, but none of them hit their target; at least none exploded. At about the time of our torpedo attack, the Japanese stopped firing at Henderson Field. Apparently one or more of the enemy ships spotted the torpedo wakes and realized they were under attack. We had turned tail and headed for Tulagi at flank speed. Soon enemy searchlights were sweeping the skies in search of the torpedo planes who weren't there. By the time the lights were directed across the water, we were out of sight. About the only thing our foray accomplished that night was to confuse the enemy about our ability to attack him with torpedoes from a hidden platform.

The *Portland* arrived in Tulagi shortly after

midnight on 14 November. We arrived back in Tulagi about 3:30 A.M. The next morning we made out a list of diving equipment we needed and Captain DuBois broke radio silence and ordered our equipment flown in from Espírito Santos.

I made the inspection dive on the *Portland*'s damaged stern at 1445 on 14 November. I used the shallow-water mask I had left on the *McFarland*. Unlike the murky water conditions under the *McFarland*, the visibility under the *Portland* was perfect.

I began my dive at the stern of the ship, and the first item I noted was the rudder, which was jammed against its stop to starboard. This meant it was at least thirty degrees to starboard.

Next I inspected the four rudder arms. Each arm was approximately twelve inches in diameter, solid in construction, and made of cast steel. The arms were attached to the rudder head and swiveled as the rudder was moved from side to side. The other ends of the four arms were attached to electric hydraulic motors, located in the steering engine room, which provided the power to move the rudder arms. The four arms had been bent sharply inboard to port from the force of the explosion. Looking at their condition, I knew that our first diving job would be to cut the rudder arms at the rudder head in order to allow the rudder to swing freely from side to side.

I checked the aftermost port and starboard

propellers, shafts, and struts, and they all seemed to be in excellent condition. The forward two shafts were sheared at the flange just outboard of the hull, and the shafts and struts were blown away.

There was little damage forward of bulkhead 129, but aft of that was complete devastation for about sixty feet. Bulkheads, overheads, and decks were blown away. All voids and compartments aft of bulkhead 129 on the starboard side were either completely destroyed or flooded.

In the same area, the starboard shell plating was blown away for a distance of fifty feet. The main deck was also blown upward, which destroyed the number three turret and its three eight-inch guns.

My last area of concern was to check the shell plating below the fifty-foot-wide hole in the hull. I wanted to determine if any damaged plating was hanging down that could dislodge and damage the propellers while the ship was under way. None was detected.

The shipfitters from the *Portland* and our salvage group began repair measures immediately. The only disruptions to their round-the-clock work were the constant appearances of enemy planes trying to locate the crippled *Portland*.

At 1630 Sunday, 15 November, a PBY seaplane from Espírito Santo landed in Tulagi with our deep-sea diving outfit. Mullen and I went aboard the *McFarland* and retrieved our underwater arc-oxygen cutting torch and cutting electrodes.

While Moon and I cut the four rudder arms, the shipfitters welded sixteen-inch I-beams across the gaping hole in the ship's side. These beams were reinforced from below and above by welding heavy angle iron to them.

While repairs progressed on the *Portland*, work was stopped momentarily on 18 November when the crash boat was called away. The PBY airplane that had flown in our diving gear crashed on takeoff. The plane sank before it could be saved, but the crew was rescued by the *Portland*'s boat and delivered to Tulagi Island.

Moon and I severed the twelve-inch-diameter rudder arms with our underwater arc-oxygen cutting torch, which allowed the rudder to swing freely. Then, as we had done in a similar manner on the *McFarland*, we attached wire cables to the rudder and led the cables up to chainfalls on deck. This arrangement permitted the crew to move the rudder manually from left to right.

Moon and I finished our work on the rudder first, so we went up on deck and watched the crew complete their repairs. I suddenly slumped down on the deck, unconscious. I awakened the next morning to a sea of bright lights and sterile whiteness. I was lying in the *Portland*'s sick bay with a temperature of 106 degrees and a diagnosis of malaria.

On Guadalcanal, prior to working on the *Portland* job, we were required to take daily doses of

Atabrine to ward off possible malaria germs carried in the bite of the female mosquito. The torrential rains that flooded the islands daily created muddy bogs and stagnate pools, and in turn nurtured an already overcrowded mosquito population. The hungry predators carried malaria, dengue, and dozens of lesser-known diseases.

Because of the emergency situations we encountered on Tulagi, I forgot to take my medication. Of course, I was not the exception to this oversight, because many more marines and sailors were incapacitated from diseases in the Solomon Islands' campaigns than from action with the enemy.

On 21 November, the sister ship of the *Seminole*, USS *Navajo*, arrived in Tulagi to escort the *Portland* to Sidney, Australia, where she could get emergency repairs to her steering gear and hull plating.

The *Portland* got under way for Australia at mid-afternoon on 22 November. The *Navajo* used her towing engine to guide the *Portland* through the narrow waters surrounding the Solomon Islands during the first two days.

As we steamed out of Tulagi Harbor, I left my hospital bed and staggered up on deck. I waved good-bye to Moon in his boat as he escorted us on our way. I heaved a sigh of relief to be leaving Guadalcanal behind. But there was also sadness in the farewell to my buddy with whom I had shared so much and the others who were left to finish a hellish job on those islands.

I took one last look at Guadalcanal as we steamed by. I marveled at the view. Even though I knew the miseries of the island, it appeared to be a Hollywood-inspired tropical paradise: beautiful white sandy beaches, lush, green vegetation, and rows of coconut palms swaying in the wind. I could almost picture Dorothy Lamour dancing the hula in her sarong. But once ashore, the scene changed drastically. Inland from the beautiful beaches, the gates of hell opened for us Americans. No amount of training could have prepared us for the horrible conditions we would experience.

Perhaps my most vivid memory of Guadalcanal was its stench. The malodorous smell of decayed and rotting plants, animals, and human remains was real and unrelenting in its intensity and longevity. More pronounced was the smell of death. Death was ever present for us on the "canal," especially its nearness. It walked with us in the jungles and swamps, rode with us in the water and the air, and slept with us under the palm trees and on the beaches.

I was lucky to be one of the living, I thought, as I stood at the rail looking down at the darkness of the water and the dancing phosphorescence whipped up by the wake of the *Portland*. I thought proudly of the role the *Seminole* played in helping turn back the Japanese conquest of Guadalcanal.

The loss of the *Seminole* was not in vain, I

assured myself. She had delivered more than ninety thousand gallons of precious aviation gasoline and thousands of scarce rounds of 75mm ammunition and bombs to the desperate aviators and troops. These crucial supplies arrived in time to thwart a Japanese assault on Henderson Field. The gasoline also permitted Wildcat fighters of the Cactus Air Force to defeat a large flight of enemy bombers that attacked U.S. transports off-loading troops and supplies near Lunga Point in early November 1942. This fuel was also used by marine fliers to bomb and sink the crippled battleship *Hiei*, and then go on to sink eleven enemy transports and massacre the embarked twelve thousand elite enemy soldiers of the Hiroshima Division.

Celebrities of Sidney
Two days out of Guadalcanal, the *Portland* cast off the *Navajo*'s tow wire and proceeded to Sidney, Australia, under her own power. She was able to maintain her course by steering with her engines and the makeshift rudder arrangement.

The USS *Portland* arrived in Sidney, Australia, at 1130, 30 November 1942. We moored to the Cockatoo Island dock. Shipyard workers began repairing the ship immediately. I had heard someone say that Australian society and technology were at least twenty years behind ours. If that statement was accurate, then thank goodness for the difference, especially with respect to Aussie shipyards and their workers.

I marveled at the efficiency, effectiveness, and can-do attitude of the shipyard workforce as they ripped the *Portland*'s stern apart and repaired the damage. Unlike our shipyards, Aussie workers could perform three or four different jobs. Thus the repair work on *Portland* was finished in record time.

I was finally pronounced cured of malaria and discharged from sick bay upon our arrival in Sidney. Members of the crew were making plans to go ashore amid much anticipation and jubilation. I hadn't planned to go on liberty because I was still a little wobbly on my feet, and I didn't have a dress uniform or a farthing in my pocket. When the *Seminole* sank, all my pay and service records were lost.

My entire wardrobe consisted of the clothes on my back. The executive officer ordered small stores to issue me an undress blue uniform so I wouldn't look like a ragamuffin. I was considered a passenger, and as such I had no duties, so I had nothing but time on my hands. I spent the first few days sitting around the shipfitter shop. I volunteered to help with a couple of small jobs, because I was bored. The chief of the shop, Jake Hoar, and a few of the other shipfitters such as Al Lucas asked me if I wanted to go ashore with them. They offered to take up a collection, or even loan me the money out of their pockets, so I could buy a set of dress blues and have spending money on liberty. I really appreciated their offers, but I was too proud to take a handout.

But then pride took a backseat when stories began to filter back about fabulous, fun-filled liberties. Stories about love-starved Sidney girls who asked for American sailors' autographs and treated them like movie stars. While I suspected there might be some exaggeration in these accounts, I reasoned that if there was even a modicum of truth involved, I certainly couldn't take a chance and stay aboard. I told the shipfitter crew that I had changed my mind, and if their offer was still open, I would accept it. I suddenly became a rich celebrity with a new set of tailor-made blues and five hundred dollars burning a hole in my pocket. The shipfitter shop had ensconced themselves in one of Sidney's small mom-and-pop hotels. The older couple who owned it doted on their newfound Yankee sons. We joked with them and treated them with great affection. I corresponded with them after the war for many years. The stories about the lovely women of Sidney were mostly valid. Most of the eligible Aussie men were in the army, and off fighting Hitler's army in North Africa. They were the so-called Tobruk Rats, a formidable fighting force. Their departure left the home guard army to defend Australia.

The home guard was not highly prized by the lovely damsels, but they were all they had until our arrival. The guard consisted of old men and 4F types. American sailors were the virile, adventurous young men the girls were looking for. To make matters worse for the home guards, their pay was about one quarter that of ours. A big Saturday night date for them consisted of a ride around Sidney on the tram or streetcar. Into this milieu, so ripe for a takeover, rode the big-spending Sir Galahads in white hats from the *Portland*, anxious to rescue the fair ladies from boredom. The damsels of Sidney were ecstatic, while the home guard fulminated. In retrospect, I don't blame the guard for resenting us. I'm sure if the roles had been reversed I would have felt the same way. During the time we were there, we spent money lavishly on the ladies to show them a good time. We wined and dined them in the finest restaurants. We took them to movies, amusement parks, and to dances. We bought them mixed drinks, entertained them, romanced them, and loved them. But never once did we take them for a tram ride around town. We always traveled in taxicabs, although at times automobiles weren't the most dependable means of transportation. Gasoline for cars was unavailable in Australia during the early part of the war. Automobiles were fitted with large metal tanks measuring two feet in diameter and four feet long. These steel tanks were attached to the backs of the cars, and they burned propane for fuel. The cars managed to chug along fairly well on level roads, but when they came to a hill they usually couldn't climb to the top. More often than not, we had to get out and push the taxis while our girlfriends walked alongside to the crest of the hill.

After a very short five weeks, the *Portland* was repaired and sailed for the United States. The dock was crowded with comely, weeping females, waving soggy handkerchiefs and swearing undying fidelity and love for us forever. For our part, we could be proud of the fact that we had raised the consciousness of Sidney's women to new heights. So high in fact that they probably wouldn't be satisfied to spend another Saturday night date riding on a tram. We also were thankful we didn't have to face any disgruntled home guards again. The *Portland* stopped in Samoa and then sailed directly to Mare Island Naval Shipyard, where I started my thirty days survivor's leave. The disbursing office reconstructed my pay records and decided I had nearly five thousand dollars owed me. I returned to the *Portland* and repaid the shipfitter crew who had so unselfishly helped me. I caught a train for Riverside, California, and visited my mother and family for a few days, and then returned to the bright lights of San Francisco. Shortly after arriving, I suffered a recurrence of malaria. I was hospitalized for twenty days, and then I returned to Pearl Harbor and my old Salvage Unit.

IX

Return to the Oklahoma

Righting the *Oklahoma*
When I arrived in Hawaii on 1 April 1943, Moon was on hand to welcome me. I arrived in time to witness most of the righting phase of the *Oklahoma*.

Moon quickly filled me in on the changes that had been wrought in Honolulu while we were gone.

"Man, you won't believe what it's like here," he said. "They had Bob Hope and his troupe over here awhile back. We've got good movies every night at the naval station submarine base and the shipyard. The beaches are open for swimming. They even have Saturday afternoon dances at the Royal Hawaiian Hotel and complimentary dance hostesses, for God sakes."

"Wow, lead me to them," I said.

During my absence, Martin and Tony had received orders to attend Deep Sea Diving School, and they left before I arrived. But I was happy to find Ben, Bill, Andy, Cary, and Cameron still on the job. Also a number of new divers had been qualified and were working in other diving crews on the *Oklahoma*.

Divers had made the interior of the Oklahoma as airtight as was humanly possible, and the righting plan was on schedule.

Pulling power to right the ship was supplied by twenty-one winches implanted in concrete pads on Ford Island. Each winch exerted twenty tons of pulling power. A series of huge hauling blocks were connected to the winches. It took more than forty-two miles of one-inch-diameter steel wire cables to connect these blocks.

Leverage was increased at each of the twenty-one stations, during the pulling operation, by passing three-inch-diameter cables over pulleys atop forty-foot-high A-frames. The ends of the cables were attached to pads welded to the exposed bottom hull of the ship.

Moon then described the events of the first few days of the righting operation to me. He said everything was in place and ready to begin on 8 March 1943. The twenty-one electrically driven winches on Ford Island took heavy strains on their wires in unison. With a lurch and a groan the *Oklahoma* started her slow but steady rotation.

Everyone was jubilant. They cheered lustily as they observed the ship's movements, drowning out for the moment the sounds of metal being crushed and torn.

As the ship continued to roll over at the rate of three feet per hour, the distinct sounds of metal creaking, popping, grinding, and snapping became louder. Moon said observers offered opinions as to the origin of the noises. Most of the divers thought it came from masts and smokestacks tearing away as the ship turned over. The significance of these sounds was not realized until much later in the salvage operation.

When Bill heard the cacophony, he gleefully concluded that the ship was rolling over on schedule and would soon be raised. Then he would be on his way to Deep Sea Diving School. "Each one of them noises means I'm one step closer to gettin' me a babe in D.C.," he announced.

Later he would curse the day he made that remark.

I finally went back to work, and as the ship was rotated, we cut away the structural wreckage from the portside hull so measurements could be taken by Pacific Bridge divers, and the shipyard could begin fabricating the enormous cofferdam sections. Each panel section was built thirteen feet wide, fifty feet in height, and weighed twenty tons.

The righting movement continued until the *Oklahoma* came to rest in an upright position with a three-degree list to port on 16 June 1943.

Two Divers Die

Meanwhile, ten monstrous twenty-inch-diameter deep-well pumps arrived and were placed in position to dewater the ship down to the first platform deck level. These large pumps dewatered a flooded compartment in a matter of minutes. The suction forces generated by these newest pump additions were awesome, as debris of all types was routinely sucked up through their cylindrical-shaped maws and discharged overboard.

As the water level was reduced in each compartment to the two-foot level, the pumps were stopped and floating bodies were recovered and placed in canvas bags for burial. This method of recovery was used to prevent the pumps from sucking up the corpses along with the debris. Hundreds of decomposed bodies were saved for burial in this way.

Pacific Bridge divers attached the sections of cofferdam patches over the gaping two hundred-foot-long torpedo wounds in her port side. In order to ensure a watertight fit of the cofferdam patch, more than one thousand tons of under-water cement was poured on each end of the patch and along its bottom side.

The extra weight of the patches and cement created an unstable condition. Therefore, the salvage engineers decided to correct this by attaching four submarine salvage pontoons, each with eighty tons lifting capacity, along the port side. No one could have foreseen that this decision would result in the death of two divers, one navy and one civilian.

Before loaning the pontoons to the Salvage Unit, the Submarine Force divers were required to inspect them for their material condition.

Chief Smyth, master diver, and his two assistants were assigned this routine job.

Submarine salvage pontoons are steel cylinders approximately thirteen feet in diameter and thirty feet long. They are encased in wood sheathing and weigh fifteen tons. Bolted manhole plates in the top sections allow access to their interiors.

Safety precautions forbid personnel to enter the interior of these pontoons until the spaces are adequately ventilated by mechanical blowers. The person entering the interior is required to have a lifeline attached, and the line must be tended by someone outside. These stringent precautions were written to prevent the serious hazard of oxygen deficiency.

Rusting, or oxidation, within the cylinder consumes all oxygen in the compartment. This condition kills silently and quickly.

The chief and his two assistants arrived at the shipyard where the pontoons were stored, and prepared to conduct their inspection. The chief sent his two assistants to obtain portable ventilation blowers while he unbolted the manhole plates.

The chief apparently became impatient waiting for his helpers to return, so he elected to inspect the interior of the pontoons by himself. When the two helpers returned they found the chief dead.

What prompted him, a seasoned master diver, to ignore all safety precautions will never be known, but the navy lost a fine chief petty officer, needlessly.

Another diving fatality occurred with a veteran civilian diver from the Pacific Bridge company.

The four lifting pontoons were secured to the midship section of the *Oklahoma* just outboard of the main cofferdam patch. Each pontoon had large anchor chains secured to the bottom of the pontoon fore and aft. The chains were passed from the port side underneath the ship's hull and secured to bitts on the starboard side. This belly-band arrangement of the pontoon chains permitted each pontoon to lift a maximum of eighty tons.

Since the four pontoons were afloat and riding up against the main patch, extreme precautions were taken to insure that boats and ships passing the *Oklahoma* did not exceed five miles per hour. This reduced speed allowed the ships to maintain steerageway without throwing up a wake, which would cause the pontoons to bang against the patch and damage it.

One morning as we approached the port side of the *Oklahoma* on our way to the diving barge, Moon waved his hand at a figure sitting on the deck. He yelled a "hello" and told me the man's name was Joe Valdez. "He's been a diver with Pacific Bridge for a hundred years, I guess. He had a bad session with the bends a few years back and now he's all crippled up. He doesn't dive anymore, but they use him as a tender."

"Is there anybody you don't know, Moon?" I laughed.

"Well, I try to be sociable," he joked. "But old Joe and me go back a long way. I used to see him in Art's Bar in San Pedro. We've hoisted a few together. The guy must be more than seventy-five years old by now."

I slowed the sampan to three miles an hour, noticing the diver working in the water. As we sailed slowly by, I saw Joe get off his haunches, pick up his coffee cup, and limp off out of sight, leaving the diver's lifeline and air hose dangling over the side of the ship.

"Holy Moses, Moon, did you see what your friend did? He just walked away and left his diver unattended."

Moon shrugged. "Yeah, he sure did. But most of those civilian divers are so much at home in the water, they probably don't even need a tender. They don't wear weighted shoes and hardly any weights on their belts. I've seen 'em going up and down those cofferdam forms like a bunch of monkeys."

"Maybe so. But don't you ever leave me dangling without a tender. I kinda like the navy's safety rules on that subject," I said.

Later in the day bad news reached us. A civilian diver had been killed. The Pacific Bridge diver was down forty feet inside the main patch, his lifeline and air hose trailing over the side between the patch and a pontoon. The wake from a passing boat caused the pontoon to crash against the patch and the diver's lifeline and air hose were severed.

Old Joe had been getting a fresh cup of coffee when the accident occurred, and he did not even know about it until it was all over and the diver's lifeless body was brought aboard.

Presumably the diver did not realize what had happened until it was too late to save himself. Once his air hose had been severed at the depth of forty feet, the remaining air in his suit escaped in seconds, leaving him without buoyancy to reach the surface.

When we heard of the accident, Moon and I were sickened by the results of what we had witnessed earlier. We had seen Joe Valdez thoughtlessly wander off, forgetting his obligation to his diver.

When Moon sought out his friend later that week, he reported that the broken old man was crazy with grief and guilt. He had been fired and was drinking himself into his grave, unable to face the fact that he was responsible for another man's death.

Commander Haynes summoned me to his office the next morning to find out if safety instructions were followed when we worked around the pontoons. We were always scrupulous about our responsibilities to our fellow divers. I told him this tragic lesson in carelessness would make us even more aware of the dangers involved.

As I reached the door, Pappy called out to me.

301

"One more thing, Raymer. A newspaper correspondent will be here next month to tour the
Oklahoma, and I've selected you as his guide."

I'm sure he felt this was an honor, but I was
not as anxious to conduct tours on the *Oklahoma*
as he might have imagined.

Plugging the Leaks

Dewatering of the ship continued as holes were
cut in the platform decks and the pumps were
sunk into the bilges. We were kept busy opening
up previously secured watertight doors and
hatches in order to allow the trapped water to flow
out to central locations where the pumps could
pick it up and discharge it overboard.

The draft of *Oklahoma* was now at the
forty-five-foot mark and it was predicted that
within a week the required thirty-six-foot draft
would be reached and the ship could be
dry-docked. This good news excited the diving
team, all of whom were scheduled to return to
the States.

Bill was especially enthusiastic about the news
and remarked loudly, "I hear them babes in
D.C. are crazy about sailors. They say there are
ten babes to every guy. Hope that don't change
till I get there."

Unfortunately, he was not going to see any
babes for a long time to come.

The *Oklahoma*'s mean draft remained at the
forty-five-foot level despite all the extra
pumping capacity that had been employed. The

source of the voluminous leaks in the hull was finally discovered in the bottom area of the ship.

Moon was sent below to investigate the area in question and to make a report.

"It's a mess down here. All I feel is a rumpled, twisted surface. The bottom plates are folded over each other like an accordion. The rivets are popped out, and it's leaking like a sieve. I just put my hand over a rivet hole and the suction almost pulled my finger off."

When I asked if he could find a way to stop the leaks, he had no idea how we could get between the crumpled plates to fill the rivet holes. Wooden plugs could be inserted in the holes we could reach, but there were many thousands of hidden leaks that we needed to plug.

After two hours of surveying the bottom of the ship, Moon surfaced and finished his report.

"There's just no way we can repair those bottom plates. They're just going to have to use bigger pumps."

"The engineers told me the pumps in operation are the largest they could find. Get dressed and we'll report to them. Maybe they'll have some ideas," I said.

"Do you remember all the noise of metal grinding when they were righting the ship?" Andy asked Moon.

"Yeah, that's about the time it was rolling over on its bottom," he replied.

"Right. We all thought it was wreckage breaking away as the ship rolled over, but it must have been those bottom plates breaking and folding over and the rivets shearing off."

After hearing the damage report, the engineers had no answers for us. As we had done many times, we met at the diving shack that evening to put our heads together and try to come up with our own solution to the problem.

Cameron was blaming the engineers for miscalculating the amount of buoyancy needed to roll the ship over without damaging her. I let him talk for about a minute, then I interrupted.

I said we weren't qualified to make a judgment call on where the fault lay. Our job was to figure out how to repair the leaks.

Ben questioned how we would be able to float up under the *Oklahoma*'s bottom in a deep-sea diving outfit and work effectively while suspended there.

"Maybe you could get yourself some water wings or maybe a kapok life jacket to hold you up. But I doubt we'd find anything to float a ton of lard like you, Ben." Bill laughed.

Ben let out a whoop. "You punch-drunk swabby, you may have come up with the answer."

"What the hell you talkin' about?" Bill asked.

Ben explained that it might be possible for a diver to wear a shallow-water outfit and a kapok life jacket and float up against the ship's bottom. This would allow him to move around a lot easier and faster than if he was burdened by a deep-sea outfit.

Then Moon chimed in. If we released hand-fuls of kapok near the creases and folds in the bottom plates, the pumps would automatically suck the kapok into the hidden rivet holes and seal them.

We didn't know if this would be effective, but we could not come up with anything better. We all decided it was worth trying.

A Tour of the *Oklahoma*

The next morning I headed for Haynes's office anxious to explain our plan for plugging the bottom leaks. But before I could be announced by the yeoman, Pappy burst through his door, red-faced and out of breath.

"Where the hell have you been?" he yelled. "They're looking for you out on the *Oklahoma*. That news correspondent arrived, and you're supposed to greet him." He wiped beads of sweat from his upper lip.

"But you told me the reporter would be here tomorrow."

"Somebody must have screwed up on the dates, then. Get out there on the double and report to the salvage officer."

I caught a motor launch and was soon aboard the *Oklahoma*. One of the salvage officers had the correspondent in tow and was explaining the righting operation to him. I waited respectfully until the commander addressed me.

"It's Raymer, isn't it?"

"Yes sir, metalsmith first class."

He introduced me to the correspondent, Mr. Eugene Burns, from the Associated Press. He directed me to give Burns a guided tour through the interior of the ship and show him anything he desired to see.

Mr. Burns shook my hand. He was middle-aged and slight of build. His grip was firm though, and his pale blue eyes were piercing as he studied my face.

When I asked him where he wanted to start the tour he told me to lead the way. I decided to begin on the third deck level. The salvage crews had not cleaned these areas, and I wanted Burns to see and appreciate the magnitude of the job required to salvage a battleship.

I led him forward to the ladder. I warned him to hang on to the chain handrails because the steps were slippery from muck and fuel oil.

We reached the third deck, and Burns asked me about dead bodies: how many had been found, what was done with them, how they could be identified.

I explained that the medics sorted through all the sludge and debris for bones. Then they placed approximately two hundred bones in a bag, which represented the number in a human body. The bag was sent to the army hospital, where a chaplain performed services for the remains. According to the *Oklahoma*'s muster records, four hundred of the crew perished aboard her. I finished by saying I was glad it wasn't my job to explain to the sailors' families why their loved ones remained unidentified. The reasons could seem very offensive to them.

Slithering through the ankle-deep filth, Burns caught himself as his foot struck something on the deck. He cried out in revulsion when he found it was part of a human body. "My God, I've stumbled over a leg. It even has a shoe on what's left of the foot."

I picked up the filthy shoe and a few small bones fell out. Scratching the sole, I discovered it was white rubber.

"It must have belonged to an officer or a chief. They're the only men who wear white shoes," I said.

Burns was visibly shaken, and we paused a moment as he regained his composure.

I was curious about Burns's request to have a senior enlisted man show him around when he could have chosen an officer to guide him, so I asked him for the reason.

His answer surprised me. He said he had been told by some of his contacts that senior petty officers were the backbone of the navy, and they were usually very knowledgeable and willing to be up-front in describing a situation . . . good or bad. He wanted to write a column without frills or fables, and he thought an enlisted man would present it that way.

The lights flickered and dimmed suddenly.

"What's happening to the lights, Raymer, and the ventilation? It's stopped." His eyes widened anxiously as the darkness closed in and the stillness enveloped us.

"Probably the portable generator went dead," I answered calmly. "Here's an extra flashlight. The lights should be coming back on soon."

The stale air was becoming heavy and foul, and I could see that Mr. Burns was nervous.

"Let's get the hell out of here," he said. He threw the beam of his flashlight up a ladder, searching for an exit. The light shone on a breastbone and skull caught in the hatch.

"My God, we can't go up that ladder," he gasped, obviously shocked by the scene.

I tapped his arm and pointed to a ladder farther down the deck. "Come this way, and we'll get out of this mess."

A moment later the lights were restored and the cool, sweet air from outside began flowing through the canvas ventilation sleeve flapping in its tethered position.

"When we're working down here in the debris and slime, knowing there is death all around us, it's almost like being in a tomb. I've often wondered what would happen if the ship turned over again and sank during one of those moments," I said, slightly amused at the reporter's discomfort.

"I think the tour is over, Raymer. Let's go topside and get some fresh air."

I answered his questions as we went topside. When he finally felt he had enough information he again extended his hand to me.

"I want to thank you for a grim but informative tour. I've seen and learned a lot this morning, and I have a much greater respect and appreciation for what you fellows are doing out here. It's something we're all interested in on the mainland, and I'll write it the way you've explained it today," he assured me.

True to his word, Burns wrote a two-column account of his tour exactly as I have recorded it in these pages. The story was carried in every major newspaper in the nation, and my mother in California received telephone calls from friends as far away as Maine.

That afternoon, after the tour, I returned to the diving barge. The divers were curious about what had transpired, and I swaggered with mock self-importance as I related my encounter with the well-known correspondent.

Ben brought me back to reality. "If his highness ain't too tired to take his turn after his arduous morning tour, then get your butt in a suit and make the next dive. We've rigged two hogging lines [or belly-bands] under the ship. Now you can pull yourself across the ship's bottom hand over hand. Do you want to use a shallow-water or deep-sea outfit?"

I opted for the shallow-water rig and a kapok life jacket. The crew had found a few oil-soaked life jackets and had removed the loose kapok from them, then transferred the kapok to canvas bags.

I descended the hogging line underneath the bottom of the ship. I got in position, and signaled for them to send down the canvas bag of kapok. I received the bag and reached out to feel the damaged bottom. There was a tremendous suction coming from the rivet holes hidden within the mass of folded steel bottom plates. It felt exactly like a huge metal accordion bellows.

I pulled out handfuls of kapok and floated it near the crevices and folds. Immediately it was sucked into the damaged areas. I moved eagerly along the hogging line, dispensing the remaining kapok with the same results. The leaks were plugged! I could hardly wait to tell Pappy Haynes that our experiment was successful.

Death of Salvors

For the next two weeks we stuffed hundreds of pounds of kapok into the cracks and crevices of the ship's bottom, working carefully, aware of the danger from the pumps' suction. Some headway was gained against the ingress of water but progress was slow. Additional steps were required to improve the draft of the ship, now at the forty-two-foot level.

Water was drained from the storerooms that lined the outboard side of the third deck level. Teams from the Salvage and Repair Unit burned drain holes in the storeroom bulkheads with an oxygen-acetylene torch as close to the deck as possible. The released water poured out into the passageway, where it was funneled down through drain holes cut in the decks to the lowest point of the hull. From there the water was ejected by the big twenty-inch pumps.

The next requirement was to burn holes through the bilge into the double bottom. This was necessary to lower the suction pumps as deeply as possible. Since the bilge plates were covered with three feet of water, an underwater cutting torch was used to penetrate the deck.

Moon and I were working on the bilge. I was wearing a shallow-water diving suit, and Moon was my tender. Suddenly the electricity was cut off, and we were left in darkness. Immediately the ship lurched and shuddered, as if in its death throes, and I heard the all too familiar sound of a muffled explosion. Then a ghostly silence settled over the ship.

"Where's the battle lantern?" I asked worriedly.

"It's here," Moon called, breaking the overwhelming silence in the ship. "God, I wonder where the explosion came from?"

"I don't know, but I'm sure as hell not going to stick around here to find out."

Moon shone his light on the surface of the rapidly rising water as I gathered up my tools. Without electricity to work the pumps the water level had already risen six inches. We hurriedly climbed up to the dry third deck, and I discarded my diving suit. A shaft of daylight coming from an open access hatch penetrated the darkness, and we headed toward it.

"You go to the salvage station and find out what happened, Moon. I'll take the lantern and work my way forward."

"That was a mean blast. It could have caused a hell of a lot of damage. Be careful what you're doing," Moon warned.

"You better get a doctor. There's bound to be somebody hurt," I called back as I moved forward along the third deck.

A sudden stench of rotten eggs assailed my nostrils, and I knew it was hydrogen sulfide gas. I finally reached the midship section and entered the mess hall compartment. As I played the light along my path I noted that on my right was a line of commissary storerooms and on my left was the ammunition conveyor belt, which was used to transport shells from the magazines to the ship's guns. The conveyor belt was supported by heavy metal sides that stood three feet high above the deck.

Scanning the deck ahead I saw that I was entering a dead end. I peered through the pall of smoke and settling dust. It appeared that the storeroom bulkhead had been blown inboard and jammed against the conveyer belt housing. As I approached the place where they met, I heard moaning coming from somewhere within the labyrinth of twisted and torn wreckage.

The moaning stopped and an anguished voice cried out. "Help me. Oh God, help me."

I directed my light over the distorted wreckage, hoping to see the man, but I couldn't.

"Hello in there, can you hear me?" I called out in the gloom.

Silence. A maddening quiet descended upon the unearthly scene, broken only by the steady dripping of water coming from above.

Eerily, the soft moaning began again, raising hackles on the back of my neck. I worked my way around the end of the rubble until I discovered a narrow opening between the torn bulkhead and the deck. It was just high enough to wiggle under.

I discarded the lantern, and lying on my stomach, I found I could inch my way along fairly easily toward the sound of the injured man.

As I groped my way along the conveyor housing, my outstretched hand encountered the texture and shape of a pair of rubber boots. I shifted my body so my hand could follow the line of the boots upward. My heart quickened as I felt a leg extending upward from the boot. I stretched my reach further along the leg and past the hip, where it terminated abruptly — where the bulkhead and housing merged tightly together in one grisly union.

The sound of moaning was now directly over my head.

I recoiled in horror and withdrew my hand as I realized the man's body had been severed at the waist when the explosion had thrown the bulkhead against the conveyor housing. I felt my throat constrict, and I fought off a wave of nausea.

I struggled to regain some composure as the question filled my mind: How could this man be cut in half and still be alive?

Sick with the knowledge of my ghastly discovery, I called out to the unknown victim.

"I'm right below, can you hear me?"

The moaning ceased and was replaced by sobbing.

"Are you in pain?" I asked stupidly.

"No," came the weak reply. "I can't feel anything. But I know I'm hurt bad. I can't move my body and I can't feel my legs." He made strangled, choking sounds.

I swallowed hard, trying to keep my voice calm. "The doctor will be here soon."

"I'm scared. Please don't leave me," he sobbed.

I searched my mind desperately for words that would help both of us through the terrible moments I knew lay ahead.

"Do you have a flashlight?" the man asked.

"No, I'm sorry. I had to leave my lantern behind when I crawled through the wreckage. I needed both hands to pull myself along on my stomach."

"I wish there was some light. I hate the darkness."

"The doctor will bring a light when he comes," I said. "Can you tell me a little about what happened down here? Was anyone with you before the explosion?"

In slow, halting sentences, the voice related what he knew of the accident. Three men from the Repair Unit were with him. He was cutting drain holes in the bottom of the storeroom bulkheads with a torch. The other men were clearing wreckage away from the passageways. He had just begun a cut when there was a blinding flash, and he woke up pinned to the bulkhead.

"What happened to the other guys?" he asked.

"I don't know," I answered, but I was sure they had perished in the blast.

"I'm getting sleepy. I don't want to fall asleep. Keep talking to me, will you?"

"Sure, sure, I will," I assured him. His voice was becoming weaker, and I felt he had only a little time left. I was desperate to do something more than just jabber inanely.

"I'm going to see if I can reach you. There's a little space on this side of the bulkhead. I'm going to squeeze my arm up through it and try to find you," I said.

I found a jagged hole just large enough to jam my arm through. Scraping my skin on the rough surface, I pushed upward until I was able to grasp the cold hand of the dying man. The physical contact created a human bond between us that I hoped would comfort him.

He cried softly now, thanking me over and over for finding him and pleading with me to stay until the end.

I couldn't speak, I was so choked with grief and compassion.

The sailor's grip on my hand slowly relaxed, the pressure lessening little by little until it went slack.

I knew he was dead but I continued to hold his hand. . . .

Sometime later, voices and lights appeared and a navy doctor spoke to me.

I finally released the limp hand and pulled my arm away.

Almost an hour had elapsed since I had discovered the stricken sailor, but it seemed much longer. I was deeply moved by this man's death. Even after fifty years, as I relive this experience, I am deeply saddened.

Later, the doctor explained that the sailor's upper torso had been pinched so tightly that his blood continued to flow through the arteries and veins in his upper body sufficiently to sustain life for a short time.

Salvage teams were finally able to extricate his body and those of three other men who died in the explosion. A memorial service was held at the base chapel, and the men were buried in Red Hill Cemetery. I attended the service, and I knew I would never forget the young sailor whose hand I held in death, but whose face I never saw.

Andy's Accident

The weeks passed and the diving team made great strides plugging the leaks in the bottom of the *Oklahoma.* Nearly two-thirds of the hull had received the kapok treatment as we crawled under the ship's bottom, inching our way over the unseen surface like so many flies on a ceiling.

As we worked aft toward the midship section of the ship, we began to encounter areas more heavily damaged than we had heretofore felt. On one of Moon's dives he reported finding big cracks and holes in the bottom plates. He had put his hand over the edge of one of the holes and suction pulled his work glove off. He said some of the holes were large enough to swallow an arm or a leg.

He said he'd been thinking of some way to protect the divers from the dangerous suction, and thought if we carried long fabric streamers on the dive the suction force would pull them in and direct the divers to the holes.

It sounded like a workable solution to the men, so we rounded up some old bed sheets and cut them into two-inch wide, seventy-two-inch-long strips.

"Too bad we don't have old Arnold's ragbag of uniforms anymore," said Ben. "There's nothin' I'd like better than tearin' those friggin' pants of his into little strips. Wonder if the cheap S.O.B. will ever find that other boot of his when they turn the *Utah* right side up."

"Hell no, he won't," Bill retorted. "How could he when you buried it in the mud?"

"How do you know that?"

" 'Cause you can't keep your big mouth shut. Everybody heard you over the phone when you was cussin' and stompin' it."

The following day, Moon volunteered to make the first dive and try out the experiment he had suggested. After he had been submerged an hour he called and told us the streamers worked perfectly. As he moved along the hogging line, he allowed a streamer to float outward. When it got near a hole it was pulled into it with a strong suction. Then he followed the streamer to the hole and, depending upon its size, either plugged it or stuffed kapok into it.

Moon said the procedure reminded him of fishing for largemouth bass. If the fish didn't pull the rod out of his hand, he could then reel him in. We thought this was a good simile.

"Very poetic, Moon, but don't forget to let go of the pole if you have to. If you get caught in the suction you'll be dead as a mackerel," Cameron remarked.

The next day Cameron was the scheduled diver, and Ben was standby. Cameron announced that he was not going to dive. He said he had a crick in his neck, and he'd developed a terrible pain in his lower back. He headed for sick call on Ford Island.

The divers gave him a hard time, jeering and casting aspersions. We thought it was another ploy by Cameron to escape an arduous dive.

Andy was the only one who believed that Cameron was hurting, so he volunteered to take his dive. Andy was dressed in a deep-sea outfit, and he descended into the darkness of the underside of the *Oklahoma*. We sent down many bags of wooden plugs and wedges as he repaired dozens of holes.

Andy was ordering another bag of plugs over his diver telephone when he suddenly cried out in panic. "I'm caught in a hole. It's sucked my arm up to my shoulder. I'm hanging by my right arm. It's killing me."

We hurriedly finished dressing Ben and led him to the ladder. Ben took the rungs two at a time and dropped down to the hogging line. We knew Andy was in deep trouble. He wasn't the type to cry wolf. He had always done more than his share of work without complaint. His anguished voice was more than enough proof that he was in grave danger. I called to him that Ben was on his way.

"Hurry, hurry," he screamed. "I don't have any feeling in my arm. What's wrong with my air? I can't breathe."

I could hear Andy moaning as Ben arrived at his side.

"Andy is hanging here by his arm. I've turned his air on full blast, but the pumps are sucking it out faster than it's coming in. His suit has collapsed against his body."

"Can't you pull him free?" I asked.

"No. If I yank any harder I'll pull his arm off. Stop those damn pumps!"

I jumped up the Jacob's ladder leading to the main deck of the *Oklahoma* and raced to the pump control station.

"Stop the pumps," I yelled at the yard workman manning the station. "I've got a diver in trouble."

"Can't do that without permission from the salvage officer."

I knew an explanation wouldn't budge the Kanaka workman from his bureaucratic duty. I wasn't about to waste any more time with him.

"Get the hell out of my way. I'm turning those pumps off."

I punched the red Stop buttons on all the pumps, and they came to a whining stop.

Lieutenant Commander Arnold, the duty officer, rushed into the control room. "What happened to the pumps? The ship will sink. Get those pumps going immediately." He turned and saw me for the first time.

"I turned the pumps off, Commander. One of my divers is caught in a hole, and the suction from the pumps is holding him there."

He asked me why I didn't shut down one pump near the diver. I explained that we couldn't pinpoint the exact frame number where the hole was located.

At that point, Bill rushed up to report that Ben had pulled Andy clear and was bringing him up. Andy was unconscious, but alive. I stepped over to the control panel and started the pumps, then wheeled around and hurried back down to the barge in time to hear Ben calling from his phone.

"I'm at the bilge keel now. Take up Andy's slack as fast as you can. I'm letting him go. . . . That's the way; he's all yours, topside."

Andy was brought the remaining thirty-eight

feet to the surface. Rush and I jumped into the water and pulled the seemingly lifeless diver up the ladder. We struggled to get him aboard and lay him out on the deck.

"Oh Christ, look at his right hand," Cary cried.

Andy's hand was a grotesquely swollen, misshapen mass of blue-blackness, the flesh of the fingers swollen to their bursting point. His four fingers melded together so tightly that it was difficult to determine the definition between them. Only the bulbous thumb was discernible as part of a human hand.

We were speechless with shock for a few moments. Then I asked Bill to bring a pair of heavy duty scissors out of the toolbox so we could cut his sleeve away.

"I can't do it," Rush said. "My hands are shakin' so bad, I'm afraid I'll pierce the skin."

"Here, Bill, let me have those scissors. My hand is steadier," Ben volunteered quietly.

Ben's giant hands carefully sliced the rubberized canvas sleeve up the side, exposing the horribly battered arm. As with the hand, the arm was black up to the shoulder, and the flesh expanded to four times its normal size.

"Oh my God," cried Ben, tears rolling down his cheeks. "Look at his arm."

Cary took the scissors from him. "I'll finish cutting him out," he said, his face twisted with emotion.

Andy was carefully and lovingly undressed. As

the last of his suit was stripped from his body, he regained consciousness.

Looking up at us, he murmured through pain-racked lips, "I'm okay, I'm okay."

The doctor arrived at the barge, and Andy was placed on a stretcher and transferred to the naval hospital. Ben insisted on accompanying him and promised to keep us informed of Andy's condition.

Shortly after Andy was removed to the hospital, Cameron returned from sick call.

"Hi, guys," he called cheerily. "The doc says I've got a slipped disc in my spine and it's pressing on a nerve. He's sending me to see a specialist."

He gazed at the downcast and stricken faces of the crew. "Hey, what's happened?"

No one answered. We simply sat, staring out at the harbor or down at the deck of the barge.

"Come on, you guys, tell me what's goin' on. You guys look like you lost your best friend."

"Shut your damn face, Cameron," Bill snarled.

Cameron recoiled at the venom in Bill's voice. He turned to Moon for an explanation.

"It's Andy. He's hurt bad. He caught his arm in one of those damn holes. His arm is swollen ten times its size, and it's black as hell. Odds are, he'll lose it."

"Yeah, you miserable goldbrick. It's 'cause of you and your friggin' off that Andy's in this shape. He took your dive, while you pranced off to play hookey. . . ." Rush's eyes were full of hate.

"How could I know Andy would run into trouble? I wouldn't want anything bad to happen to him. Why is it always my fault?" Cameron turned and walked away, rubbing the tears from his eyes. "Everything I do turns to crap."

Later that afternoon I visited Andy in the hospital. He had been pumped full of morphine, but I could easily understand him. He seemed resigned to the probability that he would lose his arm.

There was a long silence between us. He had been a fine shipmate, and I respected him for his diving ability and also as a man. I wanted desperately to comfort him, but I couldn't find the words. He seemed to understand my discomfort. He asked me to keep the crew from blaming Cameron for the accident. I said I would try.

Andy was drifting in and out of consciousness, so I headed back to the barrack to report on his condition.

Later that evening, Cameron approached Moon and me as we sat on our bunks. He wanted to reiterate his concern for Andy and his feelings of guilt and responsibility. He was bent over in obvious pain from his back ailment, and we knew he wasn't faking it. His physical illness and mental distress made him a pitiful figure. I told him that most of the anger directed at him by Bill was probably due to the frustration we all felt over our helplessness to save Andy's arm.

Moon and I assured him he was not in any way responsible for the accident.

He appreciated our understanding, but he was sure the other guys would not see it that way. He said he was requesting a transfer to the Submarine Training Tank, because he couldn't face diving on the *Oklahoma* again. I tried to change his mind, but he was adamant. He was transferred the following week.

On our last visit to the hospital, Ben and I spoke to Andy's doctor about his condition. Much to our relief, the doctor said Andy would not lose his arm. He said the pain would be intense for a long time, and he would need a great deal of physical therapy to regain limited use of his arm. Andy would be sent to a stateside hospital near his home for further treatment.

The whole team visited Andy before he was transferred. We assured him that he was one of the most valuable members of the team, and that he would be sorely missed.

A Tour for the First Lady

Plans for dry-docking the *Oklahoma* seemed closer to reality. The ship had gained another twelve inches of draft and now stood at thirty-eight feet with only another two feet necessary to meet the docking requirements.

I was climbing into my diving dress when a messenger arrived to notify me that Commander Haynes wanted to see me on the double.

I caught the launch and walked over to his

office and checked in. The yeoman ushered me in immediately. Haynes motioned me to a seat, which was an unusual gesture.

He asked how the repairs were coming along on the *Oklahoma*. I gave him the latest report.

I waited for the next question as he lit a cigarette, folded his hands in front of him, and assumed a serious expression.

"The reason I sent for you is because CINCPAC, Admiral Nimitz, received a confidential dispatch notifying him that the First Lady is arriving in Pearl Harbor tomorrow morning at 1000. Mrs. Roosevelt is visiting as the president's personal envoy. As such she will be getting the royal treatment."

I shifted restlessly in my chair, wondering why I was pulled off the job to be told this news. I had missed out on my dive, which would cost me fifteen or twenty dollars in diving pay. I was not happy.

"Mrs. Roosevelt requested she be taken on a tour of the *Oklahoma*, preferably by an enlisted man. Since you did such an admirable job with the news correspondent a while back, you will accompany Mrs. Roosevelt."

I was startled and agitated by the order. I had spent my life in a family of die-hard Republicans who had no use for FDR, his family, or his policies. Their greatest scorn was reserved for Eleanor, whom they considered the biggest buttinsky in the world. Aside from that, the First Lady had not endeared herself to me after I read her uncomplimentary remarks about sailors before the war began.

I said that we should not subject a woman to the dangerous and filthy conditions belowdecks on the battleship. But Pappy reminded me that no one told Mrs. Roosevelt what she could or could not do. She had been briefed on what she could expect to find on the ship, and it was up to her.

He said Admiral Nimitz's barge would bring her out to the *Oklahoma* at 1115 hours. The salvage officer would greet her and at the proper time introduce me. I would give her a guided tour of the ship, if she desired one, answer all her questions, and get her back to the quarterdeck promptly at 1200 hours. She would leave the ship and return to Admiral Nimitz's quarters for lunch.

Mrs. Roosevelt arrived on the *Oklahoma* right on schedule. She wore a khaki-colored skirt and matching blouse. A cap with a bill covered her gray hair. Her black low-heeled shoes were sensible and right for walking the decks of the *Oklahoma*. She was tall and held herself very erect. Dressed in her Red Cross uniform and cap, she reminded me of a female Charles de Gaulle.

She was quickly surrounded by Admirals Ghormley and Furlong and too many captains to count. I was afraid the poor woman was going to be smothered in gold. After being introduced to her, I described the interior of the ship and explained our efforts to raise the battlewagon. I tried to make my remarks clear and concise by translating navy-ese into layman's terms.

When I asked her if she would like a tour belowdecks, she declined, but indicated a desire to "just poke my head down one of the hatches" to see how the cleanup work was progressing.

After seeing the mess belowdecks, she asked me some very intelligent questions pertaining to the salvage and said she would like to see much more but her schedule would not permit her the time.

She shook my hand and walked down the crew way. As I watched the boat sail away, I realized I had been impressed with her. Mrs. Roosevelt had been a charming and gracious lady, and I felt a little ashamed of myself.

Grandma Juliet had painted quite a different picture of Mrs. Roosevelt and her family when I was growing up. I smiled as I remembered teasing my beloved grandmother about her strident dislike of FDR and Eleanor. Grandma traced her lineage back to John Hancock, and she had inherited many of the rebel traits of old John. She was a self-described "Black Republican," as conservative as her idol, Westbrook Pegler, and just as rabid on the subject of the Roosevelts. She was convinced that FDR would ruin America, and that Eleanor was the biggest buttinsky that ever lived. She didn't even have a kind word for their little dog, Fala. What would she say to me if she knew I had spent half an hour with Mrs. Roosevelt and had enjoyed her visit? I smiled to myself as I walked back to the diving barge.

Death of Cary

By the early part of November, the leaks on the *Oklahoma* were reduced sufficiently so that the dewatering pumps were staying ahead of the ingress of water. The draft was at thirty-six feet, six inches. Only an additional six inches of draft was required to enable her to clear the sill of the dry dock.

Work for all the divers was winding down, so Commander Haynes started sending two divers a month to the diving school in Washington, D.C. Bill and one of the newer divers left on 1 December 1943. Bill could at long last try his luck with the "babes" in the capital.

Finally the day arrived when the *Oklahoma*'s draft reached thirty-six feet and maintained that level for three days. It was determined that it was safe to move her across the channel without danger of sinking. On 28 December 1943, she was positioned into dry dock.

On 1 January 1944, Moon and I were promoted to chief petty officers. On this same date, Ben and another new diver left for Washington, D.C., to join Bill. Ben assured Moon and me that he and Bill would have all the babes corralled for us "slick arm chiefs" when we got back to civilization.

Moon, Cary, and five new divers formed a new

diving team and moved to the *Utah* to help in the righting phase already under way.

Meanwhile, Haynes received a request from the naval shipyard for the loan of a salvage diver with experience in handling dynamite. Since I had gained experience using explosives in Guadalcanal and in Pearl Harbor, Pappy picked me for the assignment.

I checked in with the shipyard's leading diver, Howard Gottchalk, who needed help in developing a method of changing a ship's propeller while it was waterborne.

But he was not ready to start the project for at least another week. Since Moon said he could use some extra help on the *Utah*, I volunteered to help him during the week.

The last diving job necessary before the righting operation could begin was the removal of the five-inch antiaircraft shells. Moon, Cary, and I had all been through the operation on the *Oklahoma* and were familiar with the techniques and hazards involved.

Cary volunteered to make the first dive. As had been the case on the *Oklahoma*, Cary declined the use of shoes and a fully weighted belt, making it easier to climb up and down the long ladder.

Moon sat on the dressing stool partially dressed in diving suit and breastplate, ready in his role as designated standby diver. Another diver manned the telephones while I was helping to dress and tend the divers.

Cary reported that he was having trouble burning through the bulkhead into the ammunition magazine. He continued burning for some time, and reported that he had cut through one frame and was starting on another when his voice was cut off by a large, muffled explosion.

"Cary, you okay?" the telephone talker asked.

"I — I . . . don't know." Cary was dazed; he mumbled something indiscernible.

"Cary, what's happening? Are you hurt?" the talker yelled.

"I'm upside down. I'm floating on the overhead," Cary cried out in panic.

Moon grabbed the phones. "Turn off your air, grab your chin button, and pull yourself upright."

"Which way does my air turn off?" Cary screamed.

Moon and I gaped at each other incredulously. This question from Cary, an experienced diver, profoundly shocked us. My first thought was that he must have hit his head during the explosion and was delirious or disoriented. Moon answered Cary in a calm, steady voice.

"I want you to take hold of your control valve with your left hand and turn it clockwise toward your body."

Cary was moaning unintelligibly during Moon's instructions.

"Stop talking and listen to me," Moon commanded, and repeated his instructions.

"My arms are straight out, and I can't bend

them enough to reach the control valve. I'm upside down. My suit's going to burst. Help me, oh God, help me!" he shrieked.

"Get hold of yourself, Cary. Grab something and pull your feet down." Moon was worried now. I was not surprised by Cary's reaction. Panic must have taken over his senses and rendered him helpless. It had almost happened to me on the *Arizona*.

We finished dressing Moon and helped him over to the diving ladder.

The telephone talker told Cary, "Moon is on his way to help you. Hold your exhaust valve closed with your teeth and it will keep the water out."

"The water . . . pouring . . . in . . ." Cary's anguished voice trailed off, and I could barely hear his final words.

Moon made his way down the ladder, slipping, missing rungs, sliding in his haste to reach the bottom. Within minutes he had reached the inert and lifeless diver.

"His suit is blown up like a balloon," Moon reported as he turned off Cary's air and pulled him down from the overhead. "He must be unconscious; he's just lying in a heap." Moon's breathing was heavy with exertion. "He was upside down and his arms and legs were spread-eagled. There's no way he could reach his control valve."

As we brought him up, Moon made sure his lines were free and guided his body over and around the debris.

Cary's helmet broke the surface and five of us heaved and dragged him up the twenty-eight feet to the diving station.

One of the tenders hurried to Ford Island for a doctor. We stretched Cary's body out, and he was hurriedly undressed. When his suit was removed, gallons of water poured from it. His sightless eyes stared up at us. His face was a death mask, ashen gray, teeth clenched and facial muscles contorted in terror. He had suffered a deep cut on his jaw where the breastplate had struck him during the explosion.

Artificial respiration was administered until the doctor arrived twenty minutes later. No signs of life were ever observed. The doctor pronounced him dead, and the autopsy determined that he died of drowning.

We buried Cary with full military honors at Red Hill Cemetery. All of Cary's friends and Commander Haynes attended the graveside services.

With the sounds of the gun salute and the mournful notes of taps ringing in our ears, many of us wept unashamedly. Cary's death deeply affected all of us. We mourned the first death of a member of our diving team, which had seemed indestructible, working through explosions, lethal gases and cave-ins, but through all adversity had accomplished impossible jobs in pitch darkness. His death also undermined some of my self-confidence and my feelings of indestructibility. It seemed impossible that one of us

could die in the way Cary had. He was a seasoned diver with almost two years of experience.
If this could happen to him, it could happen to
any one of us. I was never quite so self-assured
again.

Propeller Replacement Underwater

After Cary's funeral, I contacted the shipyard's
leading diver again and listened intently as he
explained his plan to change ship propellers while
the ships were waterborne.

If this could be accomplished, it would save
huge amounts of time and money by eliminating
the dry-docking of ships for this purpose.

Damage to ships' propellers was an endemic
problem in Pearl Harbor because of floating
debris dredged up after the 7 December attack.
Especially susceptible were the submarines. It
was essential that a quick means of changing
propellers be developed.

As Howard explained his idea, I became more
and more enthusiastic. His plan was so simple I
was sure it would work.

The shipyard manufactured a large, closed-
end hexagon wrench, fashioned from one-inch-
thick steel plate. They drilled a two-inch hole in
the handle and attached a shackle. Howard
made the dive and attached a wire pendant to
the shackle and led its other end up to a lifting
crane. Then he removed the cone-shaped dunce
cap from the end of the propeller shaft, which in
turn made the hexagon shaft nut accessible. The

wrench was lowered by the crane, and he slipped it over the nut. A strain was taken by the crane until the nut was loosened. Then he backed the nut off by hand a few turns on the threaded, tapered shaft.

Howard placed sticks of dynamite between the forward hub of the propeller and the strut bearing. Then he placed four one-hundred-pound sacks of sand over the dynamite in order to contain the blast and direct its force against the forward hub of the propeller. He wired a dynamite firing cap to the sticks of dynamite, then carried the two firing wires to the surface and connected them to the exploder box. He then climbed aboard, and I detonated the dynamite.

The shock from the explosion jarred the propeller loose from its tight, pressed fit on the shaft, and moved it a few inches down the shaft until it contacted the loosened propeller nut. Howard screwed a lifting eyebolt in a hole in the propeller hub, and the crane took a slight strain on the propeller. Then he backed the propeller nut off the remaining threads by hand and directed the crane's operator to lift the propeller clear of the shaft.

An old WWI destroyer was used for the experiment. We tried varying the number of sticks of dynamite that would jar the propeller loose without damaging the underwater hull of the destroyer. After many trials we determined that four sticks of dynamite were sufficient to do the job. It was also decided that if this charge was safe for a thin-hull destroyer, no damage would occur to thick-hull submarines.

To install a new propeller, the operation was reversed. The diver attached the wrench and the crane drew the new propeller up snugly on the shaft.

Once the efficacy of this plan was established, submarines and destroyers routinely used this method to change damaged propellers.

Moon and I Leave

Moon and I finally received our orders to the diving school. Transportation to the West Coast was provided by the *McKinley*, a troop ship berthed at the Pearl Harbor supply depot. The two of us reported aboard and she got under way for San Francisco on 2 March 1944.

As the ship passed the burned-out hulk of *Arizona*, all hands stood at attention, manned the rail, and rendered her passing honors.

The ship gathered speed as it maneuvered around the northern end of Ford Island. But as it neared the USS *Utah*, on the western side, it slowed to five knots to avoid leaving a wake that could damage the small boats tied to the partially righted ship. By now the *Utah* was righted to ninety degrees, and the entrance hole we cut in 1942 was clearly visible above water.

As the ship crept by the decommissioned hulk of the *Utah*, Moon noticed a small figure in khaki squatting on his haunches peering down into the blackness of the hole in the hull.

"Good God almighty, Ed, do you think that could be ol' Lieutenant Commander Arnold lookin' down in his stateroom for his missing boot?"

I squinted, trying to get a better view. "It sure looks like him, but I can't be sure. Naw, it can't be him, Moon. Even Arnold couldn't be that cheap."

"Oh yeah, who else would have any interest in that hole? It's got to be Arnold."

I had to admit his logic was more intriguing and satisfying than my own.

Just then a strong gust of wind tore at our uniforms. It was followed by a rain squall that battered the ship and headed east, passing over the *Utah*. The torrential rain and violent wind caught the crouching figure unaware and quickly drenched him. Through the dense rain, we watched the dim form start to rise, then the force of the wind bowled him over on the seat of his pants. The squall lessened. The forlorn figure rose to his feet and stood there for a moment still peering down into the stateroom.

"Ben would have given a month's pay to see this, assuming it is the commander," I said. "He'd want to help him find his boot, I'm sure."

"Sure he would," Moon agreed facetiously, "by shovin' his sorry butt down into the hole."

We howled with laughter at the thought. Our tears obscured the bedraggled figure on the *Utah*, but my last vision of who I believe was Lieutenant Commander Arnold would be remembered the rest of my life.

EPILOGUE

USS *Nevada*
After repairs were made by the Pearl Harbor Naval Shipyard, the *Nevada* set sail for Bremerton, Washington, where she was thoroughly overhauled and modernized. She participated in numerous battles, such as Midway, Aleutians, Normandy, Iwo Jima, Okinawa, and operations against the Japanese mainland. At one time written off as totally unsalvageable, the *Nevada* became a formidable enemy of Japan and Germany.

USS *California*
California followed the *Nevada* and was completely overhauled and modernized at Bremerton. She participated in numerous campaigns against Japan, winning seven battle stars. She was credited with helping sink a Japanese battleship of the Fuso class in the Battle of Surigao Strait.

USS *West Virginia*
Also overhauled and modernized at Bremerton, the "Weevie" participated in the battles of Surigao Strait, Leyte, Luzon, Iwo Jima, and Oki-

nawa. She was the first of the old battlewagons to enter Tokyo Bay and anchor off the Japanese capitol, a witness to the formal surrender onboard the USS *Missouri* on 2 September 1945.

USS *Oklahoma*

She was dry-docked and made watertight by the Pearl Harbor Naval Shipyard. No attempt was made to refit her for further active service. She was moored during the remainder of the war at the West Lock Ammunition Depot and used for storage purposes. After the war ended, she was sold for scrap to a salvage firm that attempted to tow her back to the mainland. During her tow, a violent Pacific storm was encountered and the *Oklahoma* again capsized and sank. True to her reputation, she remained a hard-luck ship.

USS *Utah*

After partially righting the ship to approximately the ninety-degree position, it was decided by the Navy Department that the cost of raising the ship was not justified, because she had little or no military value. *Utah* remains on the bottom of the harbor and is used for the training of divers and harbor clearance operations.

USS *Arizona*

All topside structures and projections from the *Arizona*'s hull were cut off by divers. A memorial structure was built over the hull of the ship, which is the final resting place of more than one thousand men. A marble wall in the shrine is inscribed with the names of the men who were lost on the *Arizona* on 7 December 1941.

Arizona is the only sunken ship that remains a commissioned vessel of the U.S. Navy. It honors all those who died during the attack on 7 December 1941. Passing honors are rendered to her as warships sail past.

The memorial was built with funds from private donations, with some governmental assistance. The National Park Service is responsible for its maintenance and upkeep.

The Battle for Guadalcanal

Guadalcanal ranks among the most important victories ever won by the American forces. Even the Japanese high command acknowledged and recognized that whoever won control of the island would win the war. The hell that was Guadalcanal had one redeeming virtue; it proved to the Japanese high command that their forces were not invincible.

American marines, sailors, and soldiers showed that on the ground, at sea, and in the air they could defeat the best units the Japanese military could throw at them.

Japan never recovered the initiative after her defeat in "the 'canal."

The Divers

Most of the original divers who helped raise the battleships were awarded the U.S. Navy and

Marine Corps Medal for heroism. Mullen and I were presented this medal by Adm. Chester Nimitz in the name of the president. We also were awarded navy commendation medals for assisting the aircraft carrier USS *Saratoga* and heavy cruiser USS *Portland* to reach safe harbors.

Myths, Omissions, and Mysteries

When I began to write this book about events I had witnessed and lived through more than fifty years ago, I decided to check my memories against official navy records and the writings of historians. While many of the records and histories agreed with my recollections, there were also differences. I will focus my remarks on those variances.

I started my search for accuracy and truth in the accounts of the salvage of the battleships at Pearl Harbor. Much to my surprise, two historians claimed that women were involved in the salvage of the ships. This simply isn't correct. While many women worked in the shipyard, none worked aboard the sunken ships.

None of the historical accounts reported that personnel were killed in accidents during the salvage operations. Only one book mentioned "a casualty to a civilian," but it didn't describe the accident or state if the casualty was an injury or death. But in the next breath it asserted that the safety record for the salvage operations was miraculous.

While the overall safety record of the salvage

operations was good — considering the magnitude of the work undertaken and the inherent dangers encountered — nevertheless, accidents, injuries, and deaths did occur as I have related them in the pages of this book. These can be verified by checking the logbooks in the National Archives.

The miraculous side of the story is that there weren't more accidents and deaths, given the fact that most safety precautions were developed after we experienced the dangers, not before. For example, everyone knew that hydrogen sulfide gas was lethal in high concentrations, but no one knew it was explosive under those same conditions until the accident occurred on the *Oklahoma*.

Next, I studied the record of the *Seminole* during the time I was aboard her, and I really became confused. Historians claimed the *Seminole*'s sole contribution to the war effort consisted of "channel escort duty in Tongatabu Harbor." Since the reader has already read the true account of the ship's extensive salvage contributions in this book, I won't repeat it here.

But I did want to determine if my memory was faulty, so I sent away for copies of the daily deck logs of the USS *Saratoga* and USS *South Dakota*. I discovered that the names of our salvage team from the *Seminole* were listed as members of the repair crew from the USS *Vestal*.

Seminole was also excluded from her part in rescuing the survivors of the *Meredith* and the

Vireo, and from recovering the barge. Only one historian, Miller, correctly identified the *Seminole* in his book, *The Cactus Air Force*.

After the *McFarland* reached civilization, she and her crew became national heroes as their exploits in "single-handedly" saving their ship became known. Apparently this heroic acclaim was too heady an experience to share with the *Seminole* salvage team. The true and complete account is as I have written it. Without the expert help from the salvage group from the *Seminole*, the *McFarland* would still be sitting in Tulagi Harbor as a station ship.

On the morning of 13 November 1942, when we were trying desperately to prevent the *Portland* from turning in circles, I assumed her circling problem originated from the hole in her stern. But when I made my inspection dive on her and discovered the rudder was jammed at least thirty degrees to starboard, I was sure the jammed rudder was the culprit. The hole in her stern had little or no impact on her swing to starboard. Proof of this came during our voyage to Australia when the ship manuevered and maintained course and speed on her own without outside help.

After clearing the restricted waters of the Solomon Islands, the *Portland* cast off her tow line to the USS *Navajo* on 24 November and traveled the remaining six days to Sidney steering only with her engines and the jury-rigged rudder we had devised.

I think I solved the mystery of why the official *Portland* record and all the historians reported that her rudder was jammed at five degrees instead of the thirty degrees I had reported after my inspection dive. Maybe no one believed me, because the rudder indicator on the bridge showed the rudder jammed at five degrees when she was torpedoed. I think the mistake occurred because no one considered that the bridge rudder indicator was controlled by electric-hydraulic power. When that power was destroyed by the torpedo blast, no change in rudder position would show up on the bridge indicator.

All the histories written about the *Portland*'s voyage to Australia erroneously state that the USS *Navajo* towed her the entire distance. They even created a name for this event: "The Long Tow." If any of these historians had checked the *Portland*'s deck logs dated 24 November 1942, they would have discovered the true facts of the voyage as I have related them in this book.

The most memorable portion of my voyage aboard the USS *Portland* was the camaraderie I experienced with members of the crew, especially those in the shipfitter shop.

I was treated like an old, trusted friend, despite the fact that I barely met them two weeks before. One week of which was spent in the sick bay with malaria.

The shipfitters lavished hundreds of dollars on me so I could enjoy myself in Sydney. I'm sure none of them expected to be repaid.

The greatest kindness of all that they showed me was to make me feel welcome by inviting me to join them on liberty to share in their fun.

Friendships, such as I have described, are a phenomenon that civilians rarely experience. I still retain strong feelings of gratitude and camaraderie for the old crew of the *Portland*.

I received word that on 23 July 1994, a scuba diver, Ewan Stevenson, from New Zealand, located the USS *Seminole* in one hundred feet of water off the island of Guadalcanal.

After fifty three years on the bottom, the *Seminole* is lying on her starboard side and is still fairly intact. The *Seminole* is home to many large fish, which swim in and out of large holes in her hull and superstructure. Ewan reported that the fish are not timid with divers. They often nosed up to his faceplate and looked him right in the eyes.